D1044723

IN
THE
EVIL
DAY

IN THE

EVIL DAY

ForeEdge

VIOLENCE COMES TO ONE SMALL TOWN

RICHARD
ADAMS
CAREY

ForeEdge
An imprint of University Press of New England
www.upne.com
© 2015 Richard Adams Carey
All rights reserved
Manufactured in the United States of America
Designed by Mindy Basinger Hill
Typeset in Minion Pro

For permission to reproduce any of the material in this book,
contact Permissions, University Press of New England,
One Court Street, Suite 250, Lebanon NH 03766; or visit
www.upne.com

Library of Congress Cataloging-in-Publication Data

Carey, Richard Adams.
In the evil day: violence comes to one small town / Richard Adams Carey.
pages cm
ISBN 978-1-61168-715-6 (cloth : alk. paper)—ISBN 978-1-61168-819-1 (ebook)
1. Murder—New Hampshire—Colebrook—Case studies. I. Title.
HV6534.C635C37 2015
364.152'34097421—dc23   2015004775

5   4   3   2   1

For the people
of the town
of Colebrook,
New Hampshire,
and of the
surrounding
North Country

And the family endures,
just as ours had.
The same must
hold true for a town,
I thought.

Russell Banks | *The Sweet Hereafter*

CONTENTS

Photographs follow page 172

PREFACE

THIS IS A WORK OF NONFICTION and is as true and as accurate as I can make it after thirteen years of research and writing.

My sources include 1,500 pages of transcribed personal interviews, 2,600 pages of police reports and documents, and a large archive of contemporary media accounts.

Even at that, questions remain. In many instances, I found myself with conflicting testimony about the course of certain events. In this situation, I chose the version most widely corroborated. In the absence of such corroboration, I chose what I judged to be the most plausible.

The dialogue in this narrative has been reconstructed from contemporary accounts and/or the memories of the participants in each scene. To a certain degree, I have used imaginative license to fill in the gaps in remembered conversations. Such invented dialogue is consistent in every instance with the concerns of the characters present in each scene and with the dramatic contours of each incident.

Imaginative license has also been exercised in describing Carl Drega's thoughts, memories, and state of mind as he climbed out of his Dodge pickup in the parking lot of LaPerle's IGA and as he prepared to destroy his home and flee into Vermont. The rendering of such episodes from Drega's point of view represents my best educated guess, as a storyteller, in the portrayal of moments that must ultimately remain inscrutable.

Otherwise, everything in this narrative is founded in documented fact — at least as best as that may be defined through a haze of blood, grief, love, and time.

ACKNOWLEDGMENTS

THE RESEARCH AND WRITING of any nonfiction book is a team effort, and I was very fortunate in all who joined me in this effort — especially considering the grief that still afflicts so many of those who chose to help, and the tears that it cost them.

First, my thanks to these citizens (or friends) of the North Country who consented to personal interviews: Steve Barba, John Begin, Steve Breton, Steve Brooks, Norm Brown, Earl and Irene Bunnell, Earl Bunnell, Jr., Tom Carlson, Jeff Caulder, Scott Champagne, Norman Cloutier, Dan Couture, Woody Crawford, Phil Ducret, Jan Corliss, Gene Ehlert, Jeff Fair, Paul Fink, Rob Haase, John Harrigan, Penny Henry, Steve Hersom, Dan and Dean Hook, Bud Hulse, Ed Jeffrey, Charlie Jordan, Kevin Jordan, David King, Jim Kneeland, Karen Harrigan Ladd, Beno and Karen Lamontagne, John Lanier, Helen Lord and her daughters Debbie and Linda, Claire Lynch, Dick Marini, Gerry Marcou, Sue Miller, Mark Monahan, Kim Nilsen, Audrey Noyes, Dan Ouimette, Mark Pappas, Kenneth and Isabelle Parkhurst, Marcia Parkhurst, Dave Perry, John Pfeifer, Brad and Jo Presby, Frank Prue, Albert Riff, Jana Riley, Dave Robidas, Terry Rosi, Julie Roy, Wayne Saunders, Bob Soucy, Sam Sprague, Kenn Stransky, Gerry and Margaret Upton, Bert von Dohrmann, Phil Waystack, Howie Weber, Chuck West, John Wimsatt, and Susan Zizza.

Eric Stohl not only consented to several interviews but also generously loaned me a valuable collection of memorabilia. In the New Hampshire attorney general's office, Marie Howard was patient and helpful in providing lengthy public records. Scott Stepanian and Tom Yorke generously supplied direction and references. My colleague Jeff Fair provided an interview, much sound advice, and several crucial introductions. Granvyl G. (Bud) Hulse, Jr., was an invaluable and authoritative source on Colebrook history.

Certain people not only provided multiple interviews but also consented to read drafts of the manuscript and correct errors of fact. These included Earl "Bunny" Bunnell, John Harrigan, Karen Harrigan Ladd, Charlie Jordan, Kevin Jordan, and Susan Zizza. Major Kevin Jordan of New Hampshire Fish & Game arranged access to a crucial collection of documents and reports.

Many of the photographs in this book are here thanks to the generosity of the following individuals and organizations: Charlie Jordan of the *Colebrook Chronicle* and the former *Northern New Hampshire Magazine*; Karen Harrigan Ladd of the Colebrook *News and Sentinel*; Kevin Jordan of New Hampshire Fish & Game; Cathy Grondin and Bruce Pelletier of the *Coös County Democrat*; and Frank Chilinski, president and publisher of the Salmon Press.

My friend Jim Brewer donated his time to provide precious copy editing and early feedback as drafts of the manuscript were produced. At the University Press of New England, copy editor Mary Becker found the glitches both Jim and I had missed.

In the later stages of the project, I received wonderful editorial guidance from members of the faculty of Southern New Hampshire University's MFA in Fiction and Nonfiction program. These included novelists Robert Begiebing, Diane Les Becquets, and Katherine Towler. Also on that faculty, novelist Merle Drown was — after reading the entire manuscript — as wise as he was frank in weaning its author from some, well, less than optimal narrative devices.

Credit for that is owed as well to my editor at the University Press of New England, Richard Pult. Richard first championed my project in that house and then worked patiently with me to make it better. Good suggestions and precious support also came from my agent, Anna Ghosh of the Ghosh Literary Agency.

Support is something that exists as a community dynamic as well, and it's like oxygen to the isolated spirit of a writer. I'm grateful for the oxygen provided by the Holderness School community and its head of school, Phil Peck, and especially for that provided by the Southern New Hampshire

University MFA community and its legion of writers: its students, faculty, and alumni. At Holderness I owe special thanks to librarian Mary Kietzman for help in my research.

In Colebrook, support, trust, and dozens of make-or-break introductions were provided by Earl and Irene Bunnell and by John Harrigan. The Bunnells were particularly gracious in welcoming me into their home during my many visits to Colebrook. They and John Harrigan — in their courage, resilience, and refusal to yield to bitterness — provided inspiration as well.

Finally, I am grateful to my wife, Susan Carey, who for thirteen years has shared me with this other very demanding alliance and has done so with grace, forbearance, good cheer, and plenty of good commonsense advice of her own.

PART
ONE

THE
NOONDAY
OWL

IT'S JUST A SMALL NEW HAMPSHIRE TOWN, 2,500 souls or so, but still — there should have been portents, signs more universal than personal, omens more public than the terror Vickie Bunnell kept almost entirely to herself or state trooper Scott Phillips's hunch that the situation with Carl Drega had entered a darker phase. There should have been a blood moon over Monadnock, or a noonday owl calling from a cornice on Colebrook's Main Street, or unnatural births among North Country dairy herds.

There should have been something like the celestial theater performed over Titus Hill in the early years of the Civil War. "It happened on a dull overcast day, as the farmers of Titus Hill and Columbia cast a weather eye at the clouds and hurried to get the hay in ahead of the oncoming storm," wrote physician and Colebrook historian Dr. Herb Gifford. "Suddenly the clouds parted and there in the sky was a great battle in progress — hundreds of men, horses, and guns in a massive struggle. This phenomenon was reported by at least 21 people scattered from Titus Hill to Columbia, and all claimed to have seen it at the same time."

There was nothing like that in 1997 — only an odd little incident recalled in a one-column story in a corner of the August 13 edition of the *News and Sentinel* newspaper. On Friday the eighth, a man from Columbia, a town of seven hundred just south of Colebrook, had gotten into an argument at a grocery store with a couple driving a van bearing North Carolina plates. The van followed the Columbia man to his home on Bungy Road. Then five shotgun blasts were fired into the house as the van — sporting a "Tennessee Volunteers Militia" bumper sticker — drove back and forth on the road in front. The homeowner returned fire with an unspecified weapon. "Although several state police units responded," wrote reporter Claire Lynch, "the van could not be found."

That Columbia man was not Carl Drega, who would not have called the state police for help in any event, and the incident has no known relationship, direct or otherwise, to the events of Tuesday, August 19, 1997. It was just a sort of noonday owl.

That day John Harrigan woke, as he usually does, at 5:00 a.m. Streaks of light feathered the sky from the direction of Bear Rock and Mudget Mountain, and the last of the stars were making a stand over Canaan, on the far side of the Connecticut River. Except for a couple of pets, he was alone in the rambling farmhouse — which had been built in 1850 and had become Harrigan property when bought and renovated by John's parents, Fred and Esther, sometime in the '60s. John was fifty years old, and his older children, Karen and Mike, were out on their own. Sixteen-year-old Katie still lived at home, but she was in New Mexico, visiting her mother.

The only sound was the creaking of old floorboards, white pine and balsam fir, as he eased himself out of bed, careful of his back, and padded downstairs to the bathroom. His parents had once had the floorboards shimmed in a vain attempt to quiet them. Noisy floorboards were all right with John. He liked being able to hear what was moving around at night.

That morning he heard the toenail-clatter of Kane — a 110-pound Labrador retriever–bear hound mix, a present from Vickie Bunnell — as the dog thundered across the floorboards to greet him. Cody the black cat, his tail spiked in the air, advanced mincing in the great dog's wake. Once John got out of the bathroom, he went to the kitchen and filled their bowls. Then he went into the living room, which looked out on the front yard, on South Hill Road, and on his pastureland beyond the road.

Bisecting that view was a flagpole. Its American flag flew throughout the summer and served as a handy combination of anemometer and weather vane. John looked to the Stars and Stripes with some old verses running through his head:

Wind from the north, venture forth;
Wind from the west, the fishing's best;
Wind from the east, the fishing's least;
Wind from the south, gotta put it in their mouth.

The flag ruffled faintly in a mild northerly, and John smiled. The fish would be hitting. He and Bunny — the fly-fishing father of Vickie Bunnell, the woman he had almost married — had picked a good day.

He let Kane and Cody out and went upstairs to dress while the coffee brewed. He had coffee and an English muffin on the deck he had built outside the bedroom, beneath a sky laced with only a few thin clouds, like cobwebs, high and pale and distant. This is a region where a hard frost can occur each month of the year, and had done so two years before. But not last year, and this year July and — so far — August had been frost-free. The weather was shaping up like yesterday's: sunny and dry, midday temperatures in the 70s, one of those clear, ringing days in the North Country — a day made like a summerhouse for the angels — on which it was impossible to stay inside.

After breakfast John read the first of three newspapers he devoured each day, if he had time. He spread the *New York Times* out on his kitchen counter, out of the breeze, enjoying the pillowy feel of its paper, the sweet mild scent of its ink, and the newspaper industry's best writing, in his opinion. He decided he didn't have time for the *Caledonian-Record*, out of St. Johnsbury in Vermont, the only daily published in this area and another paper he admired. But once he got to the office, he'd get to the *Union Leader*, published down in Manchester but whose stories covered all New Hampshire.

The *New York Times* was a day old. Colebrook was at the nub end of the *Times*'s distribution route in New England, and only a half dozen copies got dropped late in the day at LaPerle's IGA, the big supermarket north of town. John had the manager there put one copy aside for him. So news about the rest of the world arrived late for John, but soon enough. Most of what happened out there wasn't going to change anything in his world anyway. "If a hurricane's coming or war breaks out," he wrote once in one of his newspaper columns, "someone will let me know."

The local news was another thing. Improbably (since journalism wasn't what he had in mind growing up), it had befallen John to be the messenger of all that happened around there in the Upper Connecticut Valley, whether hurricane-scale nor'easters or Bungy Road wars or, more commonly Kiwanis scholarships and Old Home Day celebrations. He did so with the two weekly newspapers he owned — the *Coös County Democrat*, based in Lancaster, thirty-six miles south of Colebrook, and the *News and Sentinel*, out of Colebrook — as well as the print business he owned in Lancaster, the Coös Junction Press, which published both newspapers.

John bought the *Democrat* in 1978, when his father, Fred Harrigan, owned and ran the *Sentinel*, its nearest competitor. Ticklish? Yes, it was. Then John inherited the *Sentinel* after Fred's death in 1991. John used to be editor in chief at both papers but lately had eased away from that. He still wrote editorials for both and also two syndicated columns: "Woods, Water, and Wildlife," which appears in the *New Hampshire Sunday News*, an affiliate of the *Union Leader*; and "The North Country Notebook," which runs throughout the state in other small weeklies like the *Sentinel* and *Democrat*.

The *Democrat* was printed on the other side of the Connecticut, in Vermont, when John bought it. He soon tired of accommodating his print runs to somebody else's schedule, especially since he was as much interested in that publishing end of the business anyway, and in 1980, at an abandoned printing plant in southern New Hampshire, he found a Goss Community web offset press — seventeen tons, thirty-three feet long, four printing units and a folder, a sort of Rube Goldberg machine on steroids. He and a friend jackhammered the rig out of its concrete flooring and rolled it on a dozen steel bars to a loading dock. From there a flatbed truck took it to an empty cement-and-cinder-block structure, the former Whitney Machine Shop, built over the site of the Coös Junction railroad station in Lancaster.

John learned to run the behemoth himself, supervising noisy print runs that stretched deep into the night. It wasn't hard to stay awake. He was piqued as much by what might go wrong — the thing might throw a plate or break a web or, if your attention wandered, take your arm off — as by what came out at the other end when it all ran smoothly. The scale of the stories was different from those in the *New York Times*, sure, but they invested their subjects with at least something of the history-as-it-happens gravitas that the *Times* provided its tycoons and statesmen.

Last week's history would go to press today, and Tuesday was always the craziest day of the week at both the *Democrat* and the *Sentinel*. You try to get all your news copy, photographs, and advertisements squared away by Monday night, but it never fails that there are late-breaking stories and other post-deadline arrivals on Tuesday. So you try to jam that stuff in at the same time you do your typesetting, proofreading, and pasteup work. Each Tuesday was its own sort of problem, but at least you could go home when the mechanicals went out the door to Lancaster. On good days that might be early afternoon, but usually the pre-press work took until 5:00 p.m., sometimes 6:00.

John couldn't help feeling sorry his employees had to be inside in weather like this. Susan Zizza, who took turns each week with Dennis Joos (rhymes with "dose") as editor in chief of the *Sentinel*, believed that regional holidays should be called on days when the weather was this good. John wouldn't mind, really, if only the rest of the North Country took the day off and if everybody behaved while they did so. But that was too much to ask, even up here — some might say especially up here.

John recalled it was Susan's turn this week. He himself would leave early, once he'd taken care of a few things. He had a Kiwanis Club meeting at the Wilderness Restaurant on Main Street at seven this morning. That was a regular event on Tuesdays, and it was time to start planning the fall fundraisers. Vickie Bunnell, a lawyer and one of the club's first female members, would probably be there. So would Vickie's dad, Earl — a.k.a. Bunny, who had served in the U.S. Navy during World War II and then worked by the side of his father, Sliver Bunnell, for twenty years as a barber in a shop just off Main. Bunny and his wife, Irene, knew everyone in town and had been special friends of Fred and Esther Harrigan's. John remembered being taken to the Bunnells' barbershop for haircuts while Vickie and Earl, Jr., played on the sidewalk outside.

John admired the men who came back to the North Country from World War II. They were youngsters who had gone from these shops and mills and hill farms directly into the pages of the *New York Times* and the terrible history being written there. "They had seen the worst that human beings could do, and came out of it determined to accomplish the best they could do," John wrote in another column. "So they wanted three things out of the rest of their lives: raise their kids as well as they could, build strong and safe communities, and have a hell of a good time doing it."

It made for a personality type, he thought, long on zest and conviviality, short on sanctimony or cynicism — a guy like Bunny, for example: a hell of a fisherman, always good company out on the water, and of course someone who nearly became John's father-in-law. John was still single — his marriage to Belinda, his college sweetheart, broke up a few years after Katie was born — and more and more John liked to think that he and Vickie weren't quite done with each other. Bunny might yet become his father-in-law, and Vickie might yet be waking up with him each morning on South Hill. It was something to think about.

In either event, John and the old man would go fishing that day. John planned to finish the *Times*, digest his coffee, make a quick stop at the Sentinel Building, have a little more coffee at the Wilderness while needling his fellow Kiwanians just enough to keep sanctimony at bay, and then be back at the Sentinel by eight. That would be about when Dennis and Susan and the rest of the staff would start showing up, along with Vickie, who ran her law practice out of the office once occupied by Fred Harrigan.

Then John would answer his mail, write the editorial for this week's issue, and help on a consulting basis with the proofing and pasteup of everything else. He figured he'd have done enough of that by 2:00 p.m. and be at the opposite end of a canoe from Bunny soon thereafter. They might go to Fish Pond, which was still full of trout in August, despite being so close to town. He thought Bunny and Irene were going out to their cabin on that pond anyway. But they'd settle that at the Wilderness.

John went out at six, pleased to be in just his shirtsleeves. It would take only a few minutes to drive three and a half miles into town, but first he had to check on the livestock: a dozen sheep and three goats. He needed to make sure none had disappeared in the night, that the fences were sound, that the herd had enough water. Then he had to walk the rest of the grounds as well, just to see that things were in order, that nothing had gone amiss while stuff was moving around in the dark. The sheep and goats were all in the pasture across the road, near enough for him to hear the sheep bleating as he walked down his driveway. The air was cool and clean. It felt like aftershave on his skin. Kane came up behind him and walked like a small pony at his side.

John halted for a moment at the road, which dropped down toward town between guardian trunks of sugar maples, just to drink it all in. This was the best vista for what he describes as his "thirty-five mile view, the point from which I can gaze over the sovereign ground of one state — New Hampshire — and two foreign countries — Canada and Vermont."

The foreign countries unrolled before him, one blending into the other in a dew-laden quilt of cow pastures and second-growth forest. To the southwest, just across the Connecticut River, the forested bulk of Monadnock Mountain was turning a jade green in the early light.

This was going to be a fine day, John thought — not good enough for the news to go on holiday, probably, but good enough to go fishing.

Twenty-six years before John Harrigan woke that morning, one night in the summer of 1971, a small doe was killed on the Columbia stretch of Route 3. A young New Hampshire Fish & Game conservation officer named Eric Stohl got a call at home from his troop dispatcher in Colebrook. "The driver wants the meat," the dispatcher said. "Can you go handle that?"

In New Hampshire, motorists can claim the carcasses of deer or moose they happen to kill so long as they are state residents and they notify Fish & Game. The officer's job is to ascertain no obvious intent to kill on the part of the motorist, record the sex of the animal, and issue a possession/transportation tag. Stohl got into his uniform and drove his cruiser to the intersection of Route 3 — which follows the banks of the Connecticut River and is the main artery through the valley — and Columbia Bridge Road, which angles off Route 3 to cross a covered bridge into Lemington, Vermont.

Stohl arrived a little before 8:00 p.m. at a spot on Route 3 where it rounds a bend and drops down a mild slope. A rampart of rock and brush, the rock scrawled with graffiti, rose sharply from the east side of the road. To the west, just across the New Hampshire Central's railroad tracks, a field of half-grown corn stretched to the river. A late '60s-model Ford station wagon, pale yellow with faux wood siding and New Hampshire plates, was on the shoulder with its emergency lights flashing. A man got out of the driver's seat as Stohl pulled up behind the Ford and turned on his light rack. The man was six feet, a few inches over, lean and wiry through the chest and shoulders. "Good evening," Stohl said.

"Hi there."

In the pulse of the Ford's blinkers, Stohl could see the carcass lying in a heap of fur and splayed legs on the traffic side of the road shoulder and several feet behind the station wagon. The man's face was hard to see in the failing light. Then it was lit up in the headlights of a south-bound truck: a broad forehead, like a billboard, with high eyebrows and deep-set eyes, high cheekbones, the lips hewed thin across a strong, assertive chin. Both eyebrows had a pointed arch, like a couple of cats faced off for a fight. It was a skeptical sort of face, with nothing written on the billboard. Stohl guessed the man was in the neighborhood of forty.

"Looks like you had a little run-in tonight," Stohl said.

The man stared back at Stohl. "Looks like I did."

"We got your call. So you live nearby?"

"Well, there's a house just up the other side of that bend. I called from there. They let me use the phone."

The voice was quiet, with a resonance that made it sound deeper than it really was. Stohl waited a moment for the account of the accident that usually follows unprompted at this point. Finally he said, "Deer jump in front of you, did it?"

The man nodded. "Just like it was waiting for me. Banged up my fender, scared living hell out of my wife."

Stohl saw that there was a passenger in the car. "From which side of the road?"

"This side. The cornfield."

Stohl walked to the front of the station wagon with the driver following. He squatted in front of the grille. "That right fender. Right there," the driver said. "Where the hell did it think it was going? Nothing but rock on the other side."

Stohl could see that this was where the deer had struck, but couldn't see much damage: a ragged crimp, feathered in clumps of fine brown fur, on one side of the headlight frame, the paint still intact. He went back to examine the deer, which might have been sleeping, except that its legs stretched for something they couldn't quite reach and its fixed black eye looked more mineral than animal in the yellow pulse of the blinkers, the blue strobe of the cruiser's light rack. A chorus of crickets, singing in the cornfield, swelled in the wake of a car heading north to Colebrook.

"She's a doe," Stohl said. "Not a big one. Maybe 125 pounds. I'd say she got hit in the head. Could have been a lot worse."

"Could've left us alone too. My wife's still in there beside herself."

"Are you a hunter?" The man shrugged, then nodded. "Looks like you got your deer early this year."

"Well, we'll get something out of this, at least."

"Your wife like venison?"

The man finally volunteered a smile. "Not so much, I guess, but I like the way she cooks it."

Stohl smiled as well. "All right if I see your license, sir?" He didn't mean to make this sound like a traffic stop, but he was struck by how swiftly the man's smile vanished. "Just to confirm you're a state resident."

The man shrugged again, finally, and reached for his wallet. Eric went back to his cruiser to log the incident into his duty journal and fill out the tag. The name on the license was "Carl Drega." He noticed that the street address was in Bow, a little town about the size of Columbia and just south of Concord, in the central part of the state. Drega had gone to sit with his wife. He got out again when Stohl walked back to the deer.

"So you live in Bow," Stohl said.

"That's right."

"I was stationed down there for five years. But we lived on the other side of town from you. What kind of work do you do?"

"Millwright mostly. Or carpenter."

Stohl mentioned the names of men he knew in the building industry around Bow. Drega said he didn't know them, that he often traveled to his jobs.

"Did you grow up there?"

"No — I'm from Connecticut."

"So you're up here on vacation."

"No, Rita's from around here — Groveton. We bought some land on the river in Columbia. Just last year."

Stohl nodded and smiled. "Little getaway place?"

"No, we're gonna move up here for good — someday. Kick back, watch the river go by." He turned to look at the covered bridge, left open to the wind on its north side, and then swept his eyes over the railroad tracks, the stalks of corn, and the crowns of the hardwoods rising from the riverbank. They came to rest, finally, on the woman in the car, who sat in the front seat with her head bowed, her face obscured. "I suppose you could call it a getaway place."

Stohl knelt to fasten the tag to one of the doe's sticklike legs. "This is just in case anybody asks you how you got this."

"Huh — what business would it be of theirs?"

"I'm thinking of another game officer, for example, or a policeman."

"Oh — I get you."

Stohl straightened. A sedan came fast around the bend, braking to a near skid at the sight of Stohl's cruiser. Then its taillights dwindled slowly toward Groveton as the crickets kept fiddling in the corn.

"Thanks," Drega said. "I appreciate your coming out here so fast."

"Glad to do it. You need help lifting this into the wagon?"

"That's all right. I can manage."

"Okay, then — enjoy your steaks."

Stohl sat in his cruiser and finished filling out his duty journal, ready to help in case there was trouble handling the doe. But Drega stayed with his wife in the car for as long as it took Stohl to finish his journal. At last Stohl turned off his light rack, swung his cruiser into Columbia Bridge Road, backed onto Route 3, and headed home. The couple from Bow remained in the Ford, its blinkers still flashing and getting brighter in the dark, the doe stiffening in a stunned heap on the pavement beneath its bumper.

By 1997 Eric Stohl was the lieutenant in charge of Fish & Game's Region 1 district, which is to say, the North Country — that portion of New Hampshire, about a third of the state but containing less than 5 percent of its population, above the White Mountains. He was a member of Colebrook's Congregational church, a fishing companion of Bunny Bunnell, and would become a representative in the state legislature — Coös County District 1, the same seat once occupied by his grandfather.

His career in law enforcement, however, had introduced him to some people quite different from those he and his wife, Lois, knew at the Congregational church, and at some point he began sleeping with a loaded handgun, a Smith & Wesson .38 Chief Special, near his bed. This calls to mind something Vickie Bunnell — from her own experience in law enforcement — once told her father: "If you knew who lived in some of these places in the back woods, you wouldn't sleep at night."

The Stohls lived in the Bungy Loop — meaning Bungy Road and its offshoots, that backwoods web of dirt roads off Routes 3 and 26, a lattice straddling the Colebrook and Columbia town lines, angling past Fish Pond and the little cabin Sliver Bunnell built in the summer before Pearl Harbor. Vickie lived on the Loop as well, in a house she rented from a family that spent most of each year in Bermuda. That house was on the slope of Blue Mountain, about a quarter mile from the Stohls as the crow flies, or else a five-minute drive down Bungy and up Stoddard Road.

And one night in February 1997, on her way home from work, Vickie knocked on the Stohls' front door. Then, calmly, she asked Eric if she might borrow his Smith & Wesson for just a bit.

In fact Stohl had offered to loan her the weapon before. He knew she had a gun in her house, a 20-gauge double-barreled Parker shotgun that she used for hunting grouse with her English setter, Tallak. But circumstances had become such — Stohl thought — that she needed something she could conceal on her person and use in tight quarters. At first Vickie dismissed the whole idea. Then something happened to change her mind, and she ordered a handgun through Ducret's Sporting Goods in Colebrook, almost next door to the newspaper building where she worked. But that piece hadn't arrived yet, and now something else had happened. Vickie wouldn't say what — only that she'd sleep better if she had a gun under her pillow that night.

Stohl fetched the .38, but then he had to show her how to use it. For a moment she just stared at the revolver as it lay on the kitchen table: a balled-up fist of stainless steel, its heft cut cunningly with chambers and slots and levers, with a pretty walnut grip that looked warm to the touch. Vickie had grown up with the rifles and shotguns that her father kept for hunting, and had learned from Sliver and Bunny how to use them. But this was different. This was something stamped with that uncanny beauty miniatures possess, and built for no other purpose than to kill or maim another person at close range.

Stohl wasn't sure what sort of gun Vickie had ordered. He thought it might have been a .25, something people in law enforcement call a woman's gun — lighter and even easier to hide, a good belly gun that could in fact kill you, but only after a while. This Chief Special was more expeditiously lethal.

He broke out the cylinder and sent its five blunt-nosed bullets clattering across the table. He showed Vickie how she could fire by cocking the hammer with her thumb or else allowing the trigger to pull the hammer back. She did some dry firing and got used to pulling the trigger. It took only moderate pressure for the hammer to move, to rise and snap down with a crisp metallic snick.

Stohl advised her not to shoot with her arm extended, but with her elbows tucked into her ribs, both hands around the grip. Even in plain sight, even in Vickie's small hands, the gun seemed nearly to disappear, to nest as easily in her palm as a set of brass knuckles. Stohl noted approvingly that there was no wiggle to its barrel, no shake to her hands.

"And once you start shooting, you should keep shooting until the cylinder is empty," he added. "Five shots are generally enough to take care of the situation. If they're not, well — you won't have time to reload."

Finally she slipped the .38, reloaded, into her purse. Then Stohl suggested she wait there while he went alone to check her house. Vickie said no, that wasn't necessary, but finally she was persuaded that it was. "Anybody can find out where you live," Stohl said.

Lois served some tea and sat with Vickie at the kitchen table. Lois wondered what you talk about with a woman who goes home from work every day with just her dog to an isolated rental, who contemplates shooting another person in self-defense, has just acquired the means to do so, and thinks she might be spending her five rounds that very night. Lois guessed you don't say anything about that, and they talked about her day at work. In fact her day at work was part of the problem, but Vickie could linger with an old friend and talk around it, her hands easy on the teacup, the .38 in her purse, and Eric prowling about her house. She smiled and chatted, summoning a laugh now and then, as if she had come to borrow an egg.

But she couldn't stay long — being Vickie, and least of all because some-one told her to. Meanwhile Stohl, packing his service revolver in a holster at his waist, had found the driveway untracked. He parked and went around the house, a two-story Cape, where the glancing beam of his flashlight showed that the snow lay undisturbed. He made a wider circle, extending into the woods, slogging his way through the drifts, and then a wider one beyond that. He was just returning to the house when he saw a pair of headlights knife down the driveway. "Who the hell is this?" he wondered. He wasn't surprised, really, to see Vickie's Jeep pull up next to his truck. "I thought I told you to stay put," he said.

Vickie patted her purse. "Thought maybe I should rescue you if you were pinned down."

And since he was there anyway, Vickie wondered if Stohl might go with her into the house. They went through the porch and into the living room. Stohl poked about in the other rooms. Nothing seemed amiss, and Tallak was calm. He told her again, as he had several times that night, to call him any time she needed help.

"Sure. Thank you, Eric — really." Then she gave him a hug at the door of his pickup.

He pulled out of the driveway mildly astonished. Vickie wasn't usually a hugger — as friendly as a day in spring, but not a hugger. As he turned onto Bungy Road's smooth white macadam of snow and sand and ice, not far from Marshall Hill, Stohl remembered that Marshall Hill Road used to be notorious in mud season, rougher than a cob each spring. But the summer before last, the town of Columbia widened the road, paved it, and put in culverts. That was just after Vickie had completed the second of her two terms as a Columbia selectman, from 1988 to 1995, and at the last town meeting Vickie rose as a private citizen to complain that the highway department had wasted money on that project. Then she made a motion to cut the department's budget in half.

The moderator wondered if anyone else wished to comment. "I would have to disagree with my learned colleague," Stohl offered. He explained that in his view the department had done an excellent job on a road that needed improvement, and he saw no reason to reduce its budget.

The question was put to a vote. "All those in favor of the motion, please stand." Stohl was nonplussed when Lois, in the seat next to his, rose to stand with Vickie. He was more so when the votes were tallied in Vickie's favor.

Stohl granted himself a rueful smile. Bottom line, Vickie just didn't want anything like civilization — or its conveniences or its improvements — back there in the woods where she lived. And most anyone who drove up Marshall Hill had four-wheel drive anyway. She was right — the hot-top wasn't needed, and now the road was ridge-backed all winter with frost heaves.

But these woods could feel a little too wild when it was just you, and you were afraid. Stohl remembered how small Vickie had looked in his rearview mirror as she and Tallak had watched him pull away. He still had no idea what had happened that day, but he could guess it involved his old friend — a phrase Stohl used with all due irony — Carl Drega. And he knew Vickie wouldn't forgive him if he mentioned this to Bunny or Irene, or her brother, Earl, or any of her friends. "You and the state police know what's going on," she said. "That's enough."

He didn't hear from Vickie again that night, and he checked to make sure she showed up at the office the next morning. When the handgun she had ordered arrived a week or two later, Vickie returned the .38 to Eric with all five rounds.

One of the odd circumstances of the events of August 19, 1997 — among many — was the fact that the nineteenth was a Tuesday, press day at the *News and Sentinel*. Since then the usual milepost anniversaries have been marked: the first, the fifth, the tenth, and so on, more so by outside media than people in Colebrook, who choose to observe the date in their own way. But the first authentic anniversary occurred only when the days of the week allied with the moon as they had in 1997, and the nineteenth fell once again on a Tuesday.

It was 2008, and on the Monday evening before, a thunderhead settled over Monadnock. Travelers coming up through Franconia Notch and along Route 3 saw heat lightning to the north. It came in sheets of light that burst soundlessly from the mountain and the clouds, as though the sky were an empty warehouse whose banks of fluorescent lights were being flicked on and off. Later, threads of fire dropped in spooky silence to the earth. At eight o'clock the thunderhead burst in volleys of wind, rain, and artillery fire. It was the soundtrack, perhaps, of that display over Titus Hill.

Up on South Hill, John Harrigan began to reach for his phone. He and Vickie had shared a love of thunderstorms, and John got in the habit of calling her when one arrived. They would bet dinner on whether the storm would go up the Mohawk Valley and over to the Bungy Loop where she was or else veer northeast over South Hill. That night he felt no more than the impulse and then, once more, gave it up. He called out to his wife, Nancee, to make sure that the windows were closed as the storm rolled over the hill. A few minutes later the lights went dark in Colebrook and in towns across the river.

Bunny and Eric Stohl were out fishing at Perley-Terrill Pond, off Indian Stream Road, north of Colebrook. They had enjoyed a meal of venison burgers cooked over a gas grill, had caught seven brook trout, and were paddling back to shore when the storm broke. Bunny sat in the truck, enjoying one of the privileges of age (eighty-two) as Stohl hurried to disassemble the fly rods in the drenching rain. Then Eric came dripping into the cab, and they waited for a lull in the rain to go out and load the canoe. The one-lane dirt road was turning to mud beneath them as they left the pond, as Stohl swerved to avoid a spruce that had blown down partly across the road. They got back to Bunny's house in Canaan, on the Vermont side of the river, just as the lights flickered back on at eight thirty.

Irene brewed tea and told Stohl that the angels had been bowling in heaven. "That's what we'd tell the two kids whenever there was thunder," she said. The angels bowled a while longer as Bunny cleaned the fish and Irene served the tea. Bunny sat down and added a dollop of whiskey — "a little oh-be-joyful," he said — to Stohl's cup and his own.

In the morning Irene was up early, as she always was, and so was Bunny, who usually slept in. Another privilege of age, accruing only to longtime Kiwanis Club members, was the freedom to attend club meetings, or not, as they chose. Bunny had had trouble sleeping and had not so chosen in some time. But the Moose Festival, an annual three-day event mounted in Colebrook and several neighboring communities, was scheduled for next weekend. The Kiwanians had some fund-raisers planned on behalf of their scholarships and other philanthropies — a barbecued chicken dinner, a bluegrass concert, a few raffles — and Bunny's sense of duty brought him stiff and blinking into the morning light, which drenched his bean stalks and tomato plants and flower gardens outside, then poured in a freshet through the living room's picture window.

Monadnock rose nearly out of the Bunnells' backyard. The Connecticut River was in front, on the other side of Route 102. Bunny and Irene had come to live in Vermont more by happenstance than design: Irene was pregnant with Vickie in 1952, and houses were cheaper on that side of the river. They found it to be a good place to raise kids, and Bunny served on the Canaan school board for a while. "But we only sleep here," Bunny always said to those who asked. "We've lived our whole lives in New Hampshire."

Nonetheless, Bunny was treated like an illegal alien on his way into the Wilderness Restaurant at 7:00 a.m. "Haven't seen you in a while," one man said on the sidewalk outside. "So they let you across the bridge, did they?"

Assuming the role assigned to him, Bunny said, "I'm just here as part of my missionary pact."

Another man observed that the border must be open this morning. "They do a body cavity search?"

"Yes, and now they're sorrier than I am," said Bunny.

The Wilderness was an old-fashioned meat-and-potatoes place, and the meeting took place in a narrow room off its dining section, a space that also served as a bar. A row of six circular tables stretched like a dotted line between, on one side, the pool table, the marble-top bar and its stools, and the mirrors and beer spigots and squadrons of liquor bottles and, on the other, the two American flags, the four blue-and-gold Kiwanis banners tacked to the wall, and the rectangular folding table at which sat the club's officers. Some thirty people, mostly men middle-aged or older, in baseball caps and jeans or chinos, milled about and settled in.

John Harrigan was among those seated at the table beneath the Bud Light clock. Bunny made his way to a middle table and was ribbed from all directions about his state of origin these past fifty-six years, his Vermont-style left-leaning politics, his recent spotty attendance. Bunny gave as good as he got. The man seated next to him shook his head. "Not many compliments available here," he said.

There were no compliments even for Brad Brooks, given an award last spring (Bunny providing the certificate and handshake) as the club's Lay Person of the Year. That day it was the task of this trim, bespectacled man — a retired car dealer and utility company executive — to lead the singing that followed the opening prayer and the Pledge of Allegiance. After the pledge, a few dozen dog-eared songbooks were passed around. Still standing, the membership joined a cappella in melodically approximate versions of "We Are Kiwanis" and "America the Beautiful." After the second song, Brad glanced around the room. "Did everybody get a book?" he asked.

"I propose a fine," shouted a man at the table next to Bunny's.

"What for?" asked club president Judy Houghton, a social worker, from behind a microphone at the officers' table. One chair at this table was empty, had been routinely left so for the past eleven years.

"Brad asked too late about the books. Obviously he should have asked before we started singing. What's the point now?"

"All in favor?" said Judy. "Opposed?" The ayes overwhelmed the nays by volume, narrowly. "The ayes carry. Fine imposed." A man with a piggy bank materialized almost instantly beside Brooks, who sheepishly dug into his pants pocket for a quarter and never found out if everyone had a book.

Other twenty-five-cent fines followed, all proposed from the ranks: for talking during the Key Club report by a student from the high school; for being late getting raffle tickets ready for the Fourth of July events; for not addressing officers by their proper titles. One officer, Vice President John Falconer, was fined "for being John Falconer." The ayes carried.

Some members volunteered to contribute the larger deposits known as "Happy Dollars." One man stood to say that his niece had married a fine young gentleman last weekend, and stuffed a dollar bill into the bank. Judy Houghton chipped in, saying that she had now gone seven years without cigarettes.

John Harrigan, dollar in hand, rose to say that he had some good news as well. "My first grandson, John Peter Harrigan," he said, "has finally reached the age where he actually looks like a person instead of a Frank Perdue oven-stuffer chicken. Now I'm just trying not to have him called Johnny, which you all know is a hospital gown."

"As opposed to John," cried a voice from another table, "which is a toilet."

Amid the laughter, Bunny tried to recall if Vickie had a Happy Dollar to contribute on this day eleven years ago. In fact he remembered nothing of that Kiwanis meeting, though he knew that Vickie did have a favorable event to report. Later that day in 1997, after lunch, Bunny went into Colebrook again to get the mail, but only after picking a bouquet of flowers from his garden — day lilies, petunias, hollyhock, and blue delphiniums. Then he drove across the river and up Bridge Street to Vickie's office in the News and Sentinel Building.

Dennis Joos and Susan Zizza and the rest of the newspaper staff were there, all working hard, but not John Harrigan, who had been called unexpectedly to the *Democrat* down in Lancaster. Bunny stopped at the front desk and left a message with Jana Riley (advertising) for John to call him, though Bunny couldn't say now in respect to what.

Then he carried his flowers past the desk of Chandra Coviello (advertising design) and into the office once occupied by Fred Harrigan, the office to which Bunny had delivered mail every day while he worked at the post office, after Sliver had died and the barbershop had closed. Vickie, with her tousled hair, brown with red highlights, and her snapping brown eyes, sat at her desk. Tallak asleep on the couch. Those eyes lit up when she saw her father and the bouquet, which had been put into one of Irene's vases. "No special reason," he told her. "Just passing through."

He set the vase on her desk and went back out, stopping at the door, near the coat rack from which hung her judge's robe. "She was happier than a clam in a mud bank," Bunny remembered. "All her clients were taken care of, and she was going to close the office at the end of the week. Then she was off to the Mediterranean for a one-week cruise with Warren and Ann Brown. They had a sailboat there."

The Browns, known locally as the Browns of Bermuda, were the people from whom Vickie rented her house and were more friends and admirers than landlords. They had decided to extend their cruise from one to six weeks, and Vickie had just heard that she was welcome for the whole time. But she was saving that news as a surprise for her parents. Bunny would learn that she had intended to tell them just before she left the next week. Even the one-week version of her vacation, though, would have sufficed for a Happy Dollar at the Kiwanis Club.

Bunny reminded her about dinner later at the cabin on Fish Pond, and then he saw a day lily with a crooked stalk leaning clear on one side of the bouquet. "Look at that one," he said to Vickie. "It's peeking around the corner at you."

Vickie laughed and peeked back at it as her father disappeared around the corner and into the balance of his life.

2

"THE SWEET SMELL OF NEWSPRINT"

WHILE JOHN HARRIGAN WAS CHECKING his livestock that morning in 1997, Julie Roy was at the cash register of J.R.'s Minimart in Pittsburg, population about nine hundred, some twenty miles north of Colebrook and the last town before the Canadian border. Julie and her husband combined management and labor at this convenience store and deli. They offered glossy magazines and locally tied fishing flies, Reese's Peanut Butter Cups and homemade muffins, Snapple soft drinks and quarts of strong coffee. They sold to the hunters and fishermen from away in the summer, to the snowmobilers in the winter, but survived on the loyalty of their Pittsburg regulars.

One such was a state trooper who lived in Pittsburg. Les Lord — some called him Les, others used his boyhood nickname, Lucky — came in at 6:30 a.m., as was his custom when he was on duty at 7:00. If he was late, he'd call Troop F down in Twin Mountain to clock in while still paying for his coffee and doughnut. But he wasn't late that day, and it only seemed like the laugh arrived before he did, that rumbling chortle that always rolled ahead of him like a tidal swell. For Julie and the regulars — that morning it was Sonny, Howard, Ray, and Dennis — that laugh was another kind of caffeine, a different version of the lights coming on. At the counter Lord spooned sugar into his coffee, put on his chipmunk grin, and traded gossip and repartee with the boys.

Most of that day's commentary had to do with age, Viagra, senility, and the privilege of growing old — "which beats the alternative," observed Lord.

At forty-five, he was eighteen months from the date he had set for retiring from the state police, and Julie knew he wasn't just counting the days — he was tallying up the hours, marking off the minutes.

Lord was out the door at 6:40. "Hey, Lucky," someone called after him. "How about a ride in that shiny new cruiser they gave you?"

"Any day now," Lord promised. "We just need a little more evidence."

Lord nearly collided with his wife, Beverly, at the door. Bev laughed, shook her head, ordered coffee and a Danish. Julie remembered her own supply of coffee at home was getting low. She wondered if her friend Kim Richards might be going shopping at LaPerle's IGA. If so, she'd see if Kim wanted company once she got out of the Minimart at noon. She rang up a pack of gum and a *Union Leader* for another customer as Lord waved good-bye to Bev and eased that shiny new cruiser into the southbound traffic on Route 3.

John Harrigan wasn't born with an antipathy to journalism. Rather it had been taught to him by his parents.

"They both had an affinity for the written and spoken word, and the *News and Sentinel* became their orphan child," he said of Fred and Esther. "They were devoted to that paper. It permeated their whole lives, and I got to hate the whole thing. So once it became apparent that I wasn't well suited for living in town, they sent me to live up at Rudy's hunting and fishing camps when I was twelve or thirteen, except for when Rudy and Joan shut down in the winter. There were no hard feelings."

Rudy Shatney would become a second father to John, but by way of the first, John's roots stretched back to a farm near Franconia Notch, where his grandfather Carl Harrigan had grown up, and then Lisbon, a town halfway between the Notch and the Connecticut River. Carl worked there forty-seven years as a gandy dancer — that is, a laborer — and a track section foreman on the Boston and Maine Railroad. In those days seven steam-powered trains a day ran through Lisbon, with three of them continuing up to Colebrook.

Carl's son Fred grew up with an affinity for words and a photographic memory as well. Fred went to Harvard on a scholarship, graduated magna cum laude in 1942, and enlisted in the navy in the hope of becoming a pilot. Instead he spent the war four stories underground in Washington, D.C., where he labored with other powerful minds at penetrating Japanese and German military codes.

Esther was from Littleton, a bigger town northeast of Lisbon. She and Fred met at a high school dance before the war, and she had gone on to Bates College. They were married in 1944, and a year later Fred entered Georgetown University Law School on the G.I. Bill. John said it was one of "life's little accidents" that the Harrigans ended up in Colebrook after law school. Fred was offered a job at a law firm in the southern New Hampshire city of Nashua, but Fred and Esther wanted to raise their children in a place more like Lisbon. A friend suggested Colebrook. "Where the hell is that?" Fred asked.

"It's up near Canada," he was told. "It's peaceful. All they do is swap wives and husbands, try cow cases and timber overcuts — and the only attorney in town is retiring."

Once, around the turn of the century, Colebrook had been, per capita, the wealthiest town in New Hampshire. Millions of board feet of lumber went down the Connecticut each spring, and its farms produced a hundred thousand bushels of potatoes each year. At the south end of town stood a bustling luxury hotel, the Monadnock House, and a second would have been built had it not been for an 1893 storm that destroyed its frame. By the 1940s, however, the log drives had ceased, the soil was exhausted, the Monadnock House had become a Catholic school, and the paper industry was moving south, where pine trees reached pulpwood size in only twenty years. Colebrook had indeed become peaceful and a good deal like the out-of-the-way town Fred had grown up in.

The four Harrigan kids — Susan, John, and Peter, all born between 1945 and 1948, and finally Mary Jay in 1960 — were raised in a sort of time warp. They lived on Park Street, on the eastern edge of town, where some of the houses still had iceboxes. John remembers watching Roland Jondro snag chunks of ice from the back of his refrigerated truck with tongs and then lug the heavy, gleaming blocks against his leather apron through neighbor Belle Frizzell's front door.

Many farmers still rode buggies into town, either one- or two-horse rigs, and Main Street was littered with what were called horse puckies. John worked for a while at a grocery store on Colby Street in his early teens, and he remembers Ray Potter — who was blind, it was said, from injuries sustained in the Spanish-American War — being driven into town on a one-horse rig by a pipe-smoking companion known only as "his woman." The woman would come into the grocery store and hand someone a list of items. Someone else would go about the store putting up a couple boxes of groceries, and then John would load the boxes onto the buggy.

"Then Ray, who always spoke," John wrote in one of his columns, "and his woman, who always did not, would cluck, one or both at once, and the horse would take them back up to Main Street and the short distance up Parsons Street to the Colebrook Restaurant, at that time a dive most kids were told to avoid on penalty of a good hiding, and they'd park the horse, often with a feed bag over its muzzle to keep it happy, and go in to sample the liquid wares, and when they were helped out and loaded into the rig, often in the wee hours, they'd collapse together on the seat in a sort of propping-each-other-up embrace, sound asleep, and with the bartender's gentle slap on the rear, the horse would take them home."

John also remembers the wandering strangers his father brought home to dinner. "Many times I was the first one to get to the telephone, which was a wall affair with a crank. Mabel the operator would get a call from wherever Dad was, and — as she'd always say — 'patch him through.' 'Essie?' I'd hear, my father mistaking my high-pitched prepubescent squeak for my mother's voice. And then, 'Tell your mother I'm bringing home one more for supper.'"

This might be a man hitchhiking home from the Groveton mill, or a soldier thumbing home on leave, or a college student off to anywhere. An extra place would be made, and the conversation set in motion. Politics and journalism were favored topics. Two were forbidden: town gossip, which Fred abhorred, and any discussion of class — working versus professional, blue-collar versus white — distinctions deemed specious by this learned son of a gandy dancer.

Meanwhile the Harrigans were considered bohemians by many of their neighbors, a suspicion confirmed whenever Esther — who believed children should be outside entertaining themselves, whatever the weather — would throw the kids out to play in the rain, sometimes with rain gear, sometimes not. John never had to be thrown out, though, and he didn't like being inside during the school day either. Colebrook Academy overlooked the

Mohawk River, and the constant sparkle and gurgle of that running water was torture to John.

He and some friends commonly sneaked away early to a hairpin turn in the river called Big Bend. There they roasted hot dogs and cast squirming knots of worms into the river for brown and brook trout. About every fifth cast struck trout. Otherwise they caught big, silvery suckers, which they tore off their hooks and punted into the bushes like footballs. "Species bias," John said. "Suckers are good to eat in the spring, before they get worms."

At some point in the '50s, Fred Harrigan — John said — "poked his nose into the *News and Sentinel*" office in what would have to be counted another of life's little accidents. The newspaper had been born in 1870 as the *Northern Sentinel*, printed off a flatbed letterpress in a room over what is now Howard's Restaurant and as an organ of the Democratic Party, dedicated to "the overthrow of Radical power and corruption," wrote founder James Peavey. The *Sentinel* offered a combination of national news as the Democrats saw it and local color as Peavey saw it. But Peavey sold the paper after two hardscrabble years, and its next owner — Albert Barker, a lawyer — wrote in his first editorial, "For ourselves we seek neither fame nor popularity, and the experience of our predecessor extinguishes even the hope of riches."

In fact, for all its history Colebrook's weekly newspaper was a hand-to-mouth affair, run and staffed by people who learned their journalism on the job. In 1913 Alma Cummings, who became owner, editor, and publisher when her husband died, complained about how often she had to resort to bartering with her subscribers: "We have taken wood, potatoes, corn, eggs, butter, onions, turnips, pumpkins, beets, cucumbers, peppers, cabbage, squash, chickens, stone, lumber, labor, sand, calico, sauerkraut, second-hand clothing. Coon-skins, tape measures, pickles, sour milk, doughnuts, Dutch cheese, apples, clotheslines, old guns, cart wheels, grindstones, bicycles, bee's honey, nails, barbed wire, fence posts, oats, grass seed, and articles too numerous to mention, on subscription in our 22 years of editorship, and now a man writes to us to know if we would send him the paper for six months for a large owl. There are few things a country editor would refuse on subscription, and if we come across any person who is out of owl, and is in need of one, will surely accommodate this man by selling paper for owl."

In the '50s the newspaper was more commonly paid in cash than owls for its subscriptions and advertising space, but not a lot, and it was printed in space now occupied by the lounge side of the Wilderness Restaurant, where the Kiwanis Club meets. Meanwhile Fred had found himself not entirely absorbed by his divorce settlements and cow cases. On the day he "poked his nose in" at the *Sentinel* office, he got hired as a part-time editorial and features contributor. In 1956 he began writing a personal column, something like a modern blog, called "Meandering Comment," which would run in the *Sentinel* for the next thirty-five years. In 1960 Harrigan bought the *News and Sentinel* and began scaling back his law practice. So in the same year that Fred and Esther's belated fourth child arrived, Mary Jay, they also acquired their fifth, this "orphan child" of a newspaper, a sort of cowbird chick whose outsized appetites for money and attention would in some ways squeeze out the other nestlings in the family.

John became a newsboy, selling newspapers on and around Main Street out of a sack slung over his shoulder. He remembers editor Merle Wright standing on the operator's platform of an old Whitlock flatbed press, "his nimble fingers feeding in the sheets while his feet worked the control pedals." On production days, "the place was a flurry of female fingers as elderly women speedily folded and collated the finished sheets, and out the door I went with my sack full of papers."

Early one winter morning in 1961, John woke on Park Street to the telephone ringing off the hook. He raced down the backstairs to answer and heard Izzie Haynes, whose husband was a fireman, shout through the earpiece, "The Sentinel's afire!" He woke his father. They raced on foot through the icy darkness to find the south end of Main Street aglow with the flames. "In the following days," he wrote about that time, "I helped a rigging crew drag out and load up fire-blackened printing equipment for repair and restoration, and began the long task of sorting the tens of thousands of pieces of type and spacers that had been spilled from the cases during the fire-fighting effort. For weeks I did little with my spare time but sort type."

For that and other reasons, John liked newspaper work no more than he liked being inside all day at school. Fred's firstborn son was running wild, the black sheep among his siblings, and maybe the twenty-seven-inch lake trout he caught one day through the ice at Big Diamond Pond was, in a certain way, sacramental. "My mother already had supper prepared, but quickly wrapped the main course (meatloaf, again) and put it aside," John wrote in a column. "'Gimme that fish,' she said, and snatched it away to rinse in the sink.

"The fish, of course, was already cleaned. I never brought fish home without cleaning them first, usually at the water's edge. She made a little bowl of thick sauce of lemon and butter, brushed it on the fish, and set it aside. She made up a quick batch of stuffing, which some people call dressing, and packed it into the lake trout's body cavity, and administered various spices, and then sewed the belly-flaps together. One more slathering of lemony butter and roll through the flour, and the fish was ready for the oven.

"We all sat down to the sight of a big fish steaming from a big platter in the middle of the table. We had never seen such a thing. Since I had brought home supper, I carved. The big flakes of fish rolled right off the bone. To this day it remains the best fish I've ever tasted. I barely remember the carrots and rice."

That fish was among the articles in a declaration of independence that took John away from the house on Park Street — and the *Sentinel*, which had moved to its present brick-and-cinder-block structure on Bridge Street after the fire — and off to Rudy and Joan Shatney's sporting camps as soon as mud season came.

In 1988 Carl Drega wrote a letter to Fred Harrigan that was published in the *News and Sentinel*: "I have owned land in Columbia, NH, since 1970. Over the years I have experienced many problems with the Board of Selectmen and the Planning Board regarding their application of the law of New Hampshire and local ordinances. Specifically their selective enforcement of the law. Back in 1972 I was actually sued because I had erected a building and used tar paper siding instead of approved siding materials. Judgment was rendered against me and I satisfied the judgment."

Drega continued, noting other buildings in Columbia with tarpaper siding. To his way of thinking, judgment had been rendered against his building, a barn, because he was from away, was a "flatlander," and because his wife, Rita — who was from the North Country — was part Native American, and so similarly despised and discriminated against. The letter does not touch on the circumstance that immediately conspired to compound its author's anger with grief.

Carl Charles Drega was born in New Haven, Connecticut, in 1935, according to his birth certificate, though he himself, for whatever reason — perhaps to be thought closer in age to Rita — claimed 1930 as his birth year, altering the date on his own copy of the certificate.

He was the youngest of the seven children of Joseph and Anna Drega, Polish immigrants and Catholic, Joseph being a house painter. Carl Drega quit school after the tenth grade and earned membership in the United Brotherhood of Millwrights and Machinery Erectors, as well as the United Brotherhood of Carpenters and Joiners. He got short-contract jobs out of union halls in Boston and Manchester, New Hampshire, working at sites all over New England and elsewhere in the country — Ohio, Texas, Alabama, Wisconsin, and several other states. Between jobs he lived on unemployment benefits.

No matter how distant his job sites, Drega went in a pickup with a camper on the back, sleeping on-site in the truck to save money. At work he was a loner, eating lunch by himself, cultivating few friends, and acquiring a reputation for a quick temper in response to perceived slights or injustices. But his bosses liked him — Drega neither drank nor used drugs; was neat, honest, hardworking, highly skilled, and always ready to work double shifts. He had no trouble passing background checks to work several stints at the Vermont Yankee Nuclear Plant in the 1990s.

Those job-site virtues — and sometimes the temper — were twisted up in a streak of perfectionism that was never off the clock. Jerry Upton, Drega's best friend, lives in a Vermont home full of handsome furniture that he built for his second wife, Margaret. Upton is a highly skilled carpenter, but once, while driving a tractor around a corner of the barn that Drega built at his place in Columbia, he accidentally hooked a board and pulled it loose. He stopped the tractor and asked Drega for a hammer to nail it back. "'Nope,' he told me," Upton said. "I couldn't be trusted. He wanted it done just so, just exactly — and I mean exactly — the way he wanted it."

Drega moved to Manchester, New Hampshire, from Massachusetts in 1965. That was where he met Rita Belliveau, who came from Groveton, just north of Lancaster, and who was fifteen years older than he was. Rita worked as a waitress in a Manchester restaurant Drega favored. It was his first marriage, her third. In 1969 the couple bought a two-acre lot in Bow and lived in rooms Drega built over a metal-sided garage. They lived quietly there, though once a complaint was filed against Drega for trapping a neighbor's dog in a wire snare — but after the dog had broken into a pen and killed some of the pheasants Drega kept. The dog came back and was snared that second time.

Physically, Drega was something of a protean figure. In newspaper accounts he was described as large and hulking, but the measurements ascribed to him — even in police records — varied widely (like his age), from 5'10" to 6'4", from 165 pounds to 230. Margaret Upton remembers him as tall and slender, 6'2", 180 pounds or so, "and very good-looking." Some others, people who met Drega only briefly, remember him as being of average height and frail-looking. But he was powerful enough to astonish Upton and others — when they were helping to line his riverfront with riprap — with the boulders he could lift.

He was also that sort of prickly, wary soul who could become a close and loyal friend. The Dregas were social with neighbors in Bow, George and Bernice Prusia, and in 1991 — after George Prusia had broken his ankle — Drega kept the Prusias' driveway plowed all winter. Jerry Upton, who for many years ran a sawmill in Bow and also did excavating work, met Drega through a mutual friend after Rita had died. Their friendship began when Upton's father suggested he take a plate of food to a man who was all by himself on Thanksgiving. Upton was surprised to find the widower moved nearly to tears by the gesture.

The property that Carl and Rita bought in Columbia in 1970 — a six-acre lot on the east bank of the Connecticut, land that had once supported a gravel pit — was intended eventually as the site of a retirement home. Its driveway off Route 3 led to a ridgetop and then down past the gravel pit to a two-bedroom stick-built cabin on a grassy swale near the river. Drega added a greenhouse and solarium to the cabin and then began work on a monumental three-story barn, built partly into the ridge, with three carports and a palladium window at its peak. Later Upton came up from Bow to help with that work, getting paid whatever Drega could afford and staying several days at a time. Upton remembers his friend using thin, triangular dowels of wood as forms in blocking CARL DREGA into the wet concrete on a wing wall outside the structure. When the concrete dried, it looked as though the words had been engraved there.

Upton and Drega did other jobs around the property together or else rode the back roads looking for bargains in vehicles or heavy equipment. During one rainy ride they took far afield to look at a tractor, the windshield wipers went out on the orange 1974 Dodge D100 pickup gifted to Drega by his brother Frank. So Drega tied the wipers to string threaded through both the driver- and passenger-side windows, and they continued on, laughing, each taking turns with a yank to the string.

Sometimes they put Drega's canoe into the Connecticut and rode downstream to his cabin, with Upton fishing for trout, Drega often content to paddle. They resolved some day to canoe the length of the Allagash River in Maine, and talked about that often.

Upton was hardly aware of the judgment rendered against his friend in 1972 or the rage incubating in the shadow it cast. Drega didn't speak of it.

John Harrigan never developed into a likely candidate for college — unlike Susan, who went to Connecticut College and then Yale, or Peter, who went to Harvard — but Fred and Esther insisted. "In high school I was going out with this beautiful blonde, and my folks were afraid I was going to get tied down into an early marriage," John said. "So they sent me as far away as they could."

Which was out to New Mexico State University. John took a plane to Dallas–Fort Worth and then a bus to Las Cruces. "I got out, and there were tumbleweeds blowing across the ground, and I thought to myself, 'What the hell am I doing here?' That fall in the dormitory I found a scorpion in my slipper. I stayed long enough to determine that college wasn't for me, that I was wasting my parents' money. I went home in February and told my folks I was all done with that."

So he packed a lunch pail — like his grandfather Carl had — and took a job at the Ethan Allen furniture factory in Beecher Falls, Vermont. There he ran a slot-and-bore machine making bedposts ready to receive rails. When he had saved enough money, he sent for a beautiful brunette he had met at New Mexico State, Belinda Ramirez, the daughter of a security guard at Los Alamos.

Belinda may have wondered what the hell she was doing in a place like New Hampshire's North Country, once she came across the border from Montreal after John picked her up at the airport. But she found a job as a receptionist for Doc Gifford, the local historian who was also the family doctor for the Harrigans and — along with his wife, Dr. Marjorie Parsons, a.k.a. Parsie — most everybody else in the Colebrook area. In 1957 it had been Doc Gifford who pointed out *Sputnik* to John as the satellite whirled over Main Street one night. Ten years after *Sputnik* — to Fred and Esther's dismay, and to John's contrarian tied-down-early satisfaction — John and Belinda were married.

Then the young couple abandoned the North Country. In 1968 they moved to Milford, in southern New Hampshire. At the Lorden Lumber Company, John was apprenticed to a master in the art of grading lumber and making 30 percent more money than at the furniture factory. But one day John got sick of always being outside in the mill yard and shivering through the winter. On his day off, he went from door to door down Main Street in the neighboring city of Nashua, where his father had nearly set up shop, looking for someplace where he could work inside.

The office of the *Nashua Telegraph*, a daily newspaper, was the last place into which he poked his nose. No, he didn't have a college degree. No, he couldn't type. No, he didn't have experience working at a newspaper beyond selling one on a street corner. "But I can do any job you give me better than anybody else."

It was only the bluster, what John calls his "French-Irish arrogance," that got the attention of *Telegraph* editor Mike Shalhoup. "He stuck a well-worn twin-lens Rolleiflex into my hands and growled, 'Go find me a picture for the front page,'" John wrote in a column. "I had utterly no idea what to do except drive around looking for something unusual. The Nashua-Hudson bridge was being replaced, the old one recently closed off as the new one received finishing touches. I spotted a stray cat on the empty bridge, jumped out, composed the shot, and made two exposures — the old rule of two negatives, never just one. And there it was, that very afternoon, page one."

Shalhoup's stray-cat new hire soon learned how to find a lot of photos, and develop them. John began working the police, fire, and courtroom beats and, at last, writing a humor column that was a little edgy for a conservative paper like the *Telegraph*. In 1971 the *New Hampshire Sunday News*, which was associated with Manchester's *Union Leader* daily but had its own editorial staff, called to offer John a position.

"That was a kick-ass job," he said. "I did news, photography, feature-writing, covering the whole state, but most of all I got to cover the outdoors. And no one else was doing outdoors writing at the time — there was a tremendous hunger for it in the marketplace. It's T V without the script and the set. Nature provides the storyline."

John contrived to do what he wanted, mostly, by being sure to arrive at each Wednesday editorial meeting with a list of his own ideas for articles. It was a way to get paid for hiking the Appalachian Trail, or going out on logging jobs, or tagging along on border surveys. By then he and Belinda were living in Nashua, but even around there he found places where he could fish and hunt for birds on his own time. "I was young and stupid. It was all an adventure, all a party. People told us that these were the happiest years of our lives, and sad to say, it's true. You're not staring death in the face, you're not visiting friends with ravaging ailments. It's all an open road."

Meanwhile Fred Harrigan's *News and Sentinel* had attained the dubious distinction of being the only newspaper in New Hampshire still printed in-house on an ancient web press — specifically, a 1929 Duplex Model A, already an outmoded machine when it arrived to replace the Whitlock flatbed press in the late 1960s. Nonetheless, it was a sensation in Colebrook.

"The Duplex was a gigantic, black, cast-iron monstrosity, with big solid-brass oil cups and a huge fly-wheel driven by an equally huge electric motor ensconced in a pit below," John wrote in a local history of the paper. "The whole affair was engaged by a hand-clutch, which sort of reminded me of the hand-clutch on Lyman Forbes's huge old John Deere tractor. When the big clutch was eased forward, the Duplex clanged and clattered into life, its massive motor drawing so much current that the lights in the whole building dimmed. People came from all over to watch that press, standing agog as gears and pistons and carriages flew back and forth and paper streamed off the three-quarter-ton roll and through the maze of machinery to appear as the finished product. Entire generations of schoolchildren were spellbound."

By 1976, however, the *Sentinel*'s Duplex was one of only two such machines still in operating condition, and Fred had decided — reluctantly — that it was time to retire both that and his old Linotype machines and to start sending negatives of his pasted-up pages to a modern offset printer, where those page photos could be burned onto an aluminum drum and then run more cheaply off that drum. He asked his stray-cat older son — who somehow, in one of life's little accidents, had become a newspaperman — to come home to help with that conversion. And John did so, reluctantly quitting that kick-ass job at the *Sunday News*.

"It bears noting here that I had no technological experience concerning newspapers," John would write later. "So it was that when I walked into the *Sentinel* in 1976, having had no experience at my parents' paper and having known only the reporting end of things, I was totally unprepared to take over the production of a weekly newspaper. As I stood there in the front office contemplating the near-museum pieces that were rattling and cranking and grinding on a busy Monday morning, and the sheer pandemonium of it all, I was tempted to get back into the truck and head for Manchester."

Of course "near-museum" applied literally to the Duplex. "Chief pressman Calvin Crawford and I drew the sad duty of making the Duplex's final press run," John wrote. "Across the web, where the slitted sheets of printed paper came down across the former to be folded and cut, we scrawled '30,' the age-old printing lingo for 'The end.' For several years my Dad and I tried to get someone, anyone, even the Smithsonian, to take the old press. . . . In the end, unwanted and too expensive to move, it went to the scrap heap."

John kept thinking about heading back to Manchester, but finally it was the poignant wonder of the old machines he was helping to discard, and also this crash course in the production side of the news, that kept him at the *Sentinel*. Otherwise, he wrote, without the Linotype machines and other odd gizmos there, and particularly that Duplex, he would never have known the direct gratification of "the sweet smell of newsprint, ink, and success at seeing that week's issue coming out of the business end of the press and into the hands of waiting readers."

The conversion took two years, but one aspect of it didn't go as far as John wanted. "As far as we are concerned," Fred had written in his first editorial as publisher in 1960, "local misfortunes, such as court convictions and family scandals, will simply not be in our columns, unless criminal offenses of real seriousness are involved. Instead, we will try to represent the North Country as the rugged, happy-go-lucky area it is, and anything which is good for the region is good for us and vice versa."

John had no more interest in gossip than his father had, but he believed the paper needed a stiffer dose of hard news in its happy-go-lucky mix if it was to speak to the real nature of North Country life — and if it was to pay its way.

The Harrigans hired Bud Hulse to carry the page negatives of each issue to an offset printer in Vermont, wait while it was being printed, and then drop off bundles at distribution points on the way back to Colebrook. Hulse was a retired CIA officer who had come to Colebrook to be the vicar of St. Stephen's Episcopal Church and who had also succeeded Doc Gifford as the town's unofficial historian.

Meanwhile John and his father were at loggerheads about changing the *Sentinel's* content. John got to thinking about working in the Pacific Northwest, in the big woods out there, and set about coaxing job offers from newspapers in Washington, Oregon, and Idaho. At the same time Fred heard that the next-nearest weekly and the *Sentinel's* chief competitor, the *Coös County Democrat* in Lancaster, was up for sale. He decided to buy that and install John as its editor.

But John refused. "If I was going to run the newspaper, I wanted to be able to run it my way," he said. "In other words, I'd have to own it. Dad didn't like that idea at all. It made for quite a tussle between us."

Fellow journalist Charlie Jordan would serve for three years as editor of the *News and Sentinel*, succeeding Dennis Joos, but he was a freelance magazine writer in those days. One afternoon in January 1978, Charlie came into the Sentinel Building to pick up a copy of a photograph John had made for him. John was taking a telephone call in the building's corner office. After a moment John came out of that office, Charlie remembers, with his face lit up like a birthday candle. "Charlie," he said, "I just bought myself a newspaper."

3
DEATH
OR
HIGH
WATER

JANA RILEY, in a black skirt and short-sleeved sweater, arrived at the News and Sentinel on August 19 at 7:30 a.m.

She parked in the municipal lot behind the building, then walked by the back entrances of Ducret's Sporting Goods and an apartment house, both of which lined the eastern side of the lot. To her right, a granite Civil War soldier — standing high atop a pedestal rising from the grass of Monument Park, his musket at rest — stared down the river where the log drives used to go. On the other side of the park, and the far side of Bridge Street, the belfried white clapboard building that housed both town hall and the police department was streaked in shadow.

Jana went in through the back of the Sentinel Building, fiddling skillfully enough with the balky handle on its wooden screen door that it yielded quickly. A breeze whispered through the tops of the spruce trees that lined the back of the park, and in the early chill, the olive skin of her forearms was stippled in goose bumps.

She went without stopping through the newsroom, past the empty desks of coeditor Susan Zizza, typesetter Vivian Towle, reporter Claire Lynch, and finally Dennis Joos, the other editor. Opposite these, on her left, loomed the pasteup board, which walled the newsroom off from the pressroom, where lurked the machinery used in the *Sentinel*'s side business — printing small runs of business cards, envelopes, certificates, and the like. The pasteup board was already hung in Scrabble-like columns with yesterday's work, early proofs of the advertisements and back-page contents of the August 20 issue.

A short corridor running past the door to Vickie Bunnell's office also accommodated the desk of Chandra Coviello, the young woman who did advertising design. Jana's desk was up front, behind the vinyl-topped counter that met whoever came in through the front door and turned right. A left turn would take the caller into the office of Susie Sambito, Vickie Bunnell's secretary.

Jana saw that the door to John Harrigan's corner office was open, and she guessed that the owner had already come and gone. Had she been there an hour earlier, she would have seen John park on Bridge Street in the big 1988 Lincoln Town Car that once belonged to his father. He spent twenty minutes catching up on his messages, until Bunny drove up Bridge and flashed his lights outside. John hopped into Bunny's car, and they rode around the corner to their Kiwanis meeting at the Wilderness Restaurant. The Lincoln was still parked in front.

Jana's job was to sell advertising space — and while she was at it, to answer the phone, attend to the front door, and help Chandra as needed with ad design. "Wired" is how she describes herself, and production days like Monday and Tuesday accommodated themselves well to her levels of nervous energy. On Tuesdays she got a jump on selling next week's space and joined the rest of the staff in proofreading ads and news copy for the next day's issue.

Jana flicked on the lights, unlocked the front door, powered up her first-generation Macintosh computer, and opened the locked file cabinet next to her desk. She took out a zippered pouch of cash, sifted the bills into the cash register on the front counter, and pushed its drawer shut. She went back to the newsroom to start the coffeemaker, which rested on a counter behind the pasteup board, and returned to the front office to switch on the copier.

The east side of the building — bookkeeper Gil Short's office space and photographer Leith Jones's darkroom area — was entirely still. Jana went there to check the police scanner, which rested on a windowsill facing the abandoned gas station on the corner of Bridge and Main. She wanted to make sure that the device was on, as it usually was.

The scanner was quiet that morning — no fires anywhere, no police activity — and Jana settled in to her email. The gurgle of the coffeemaker, the faint hum of the copier and the fluorescent lights, and the whisper of an occasional car down Bridge barely displaced the silence.

People in the Bunnell family, for generations, had tried to leave Colebrook — and had always come back. Among them was Sliver Bunnell, Vickie's grandfather, whose first career as an assistant to an ill-tempered cook in a logging camp came to an end when he broke a five-pound sack of sugar over the cook's head. Sliver went west to Saskatchewan, where he and some friends meant to follow the wheat harvest. "Then he looked at how big one of those wheat fields was, and he poked his nose into a barbershop instead," Bunny said. "I suppose that's where he learned how to do it."

Sliver ran his barbershop in Colebrook for sixty-one years, until Beatlemania and the winnowing of barbershops in the '70s. Back in 1913, one of Sliver's clients was Harry K. Thaw, the sadistic playboy husband of the showgirl Evelyn Nesbit and the murderer of Nesbit's former lover, the architect Stanford White — an incident trumpeted as the twentieth's first crime of the century. Thaw subsequently escaped from an upstate New York hospital for the criminally insane and was captured by Colebrook police. Then Thaw was put up comfortably at the Monadnock House hotel for several weeks while New York and New Hampshire wrangled about his extradition. He had become to the national media something of a romantic outlaw hero, and his strolls about town, accompanied by a deputy, soaked up column space in what was then the Colebrook *Sentinel*, while Sliver kept him cleanshaven and trimmed. Eventually Thaw was returned to New York, deemed sane, and set free — until he horsewhipped a teenage boy in 1924 and was recommitted.

But cutting hair was just Sliver's day job. Otherwise he was famous throughout the North Country as an outdoorsman, guide, and sled dog racer. He hunted deer, grouse, and rabbits; escorted convoys of flatlanders into the woods; won races throughout the Northeast with a fleet team of, yes, Irish setters; and contrived to go fly fishing every day of his life until he died in 1972. He and his wife, Henrietta — a waitress and the piano player for silent movies at the local cinema — lived in an apartment on Main

Street but spent much of their time at the cabin on Fish Pond, where Sliver offered boats to rent.

Bunny served in the Pacific during World War II, aboard a U.S. Navy cargo ship. In 1946 he came home to resume his courtship of Irene Roberts and begin on-the-job training with Sliver, a proud man who asked his son how long his government-funded apprentice program extended. "Six months?" Sliver cried. "You'll be lucky if you know how to comb hair in six months."

Bunny well remembers the first customer he shaved, a man with craggy cheeks, a prominent Adam's apple, and a rough beard. "Dad said he had to go out, and he didn't come back," Bunny says. "I kept lathering and lathering, and finally I had no choice but to get started. I nearly got into the chair with the poor devil before I was done. But he was easier to shave than some of those loggers who came out of the woods in spring with their beards full of tobacco juice. Sometimes I nearly had to throw up."

Bunny and Irene married in 1948. By then Irene's mother, Marge, and her second husband were running a drive-in restaurant and trailer park in Gary, Indiana, and Bunny and Irene went out there several times during slow winters at the barbershop in the '50s. They might have stayed — they hoped to earn salaries in Marge's husband's businesses while Marge took care of Vickie and Earl, but Marge never followed through on promises to do that. "She was too busy learning how to bowl and enjoying herself," Irene said. Eventually the family settled year-round and permanently into this native soil.

Which is where Sliver and Bunny took both kids hunting and fishing. Vickie preferred fishing, Earl, Jr., the former, though Earl — three years younger and as good an all-around athlete as Sliver — could cast a fly so perfectly that Vickie despaired of ever living long enough to equal it. Earl never even thought about leaving the North Country, but Bunny and Irene knew that Vickie would go. They remember the winter of 1958, when they were out in Gary and Marge took the family to a steak house in Chicago. Vickie loved the skyscrapers and city streets, the restaurant, and her thick cut of steak. "Grammy," the six-year-old girl beamed to Marge, "I think I was born for this."

Vickie built a good résumé for herself at Canaan Memorial High School.

She performed in school plays, sang in the chorus, played clarinet in the band, served as scorekeeper at the basketball games, made the National Honor Society, was elected president of her class. After the school day, she did clerical work in Fred Harrigan's law office at the News and Sentinel.

Earl was content to go to work after starring in three sports at Canaan High — good enough in basketball to earn the nickname "Pearly," after NBA star Earl "The Pearl" Washington — but Vickie had to go to college. She applied to Plymouth State, just an hour of so south of Franconia Notch down I-93, in a town where she had some relatives and could earn money babysitting. Meanwhile Sliver had passed the land he owned around Fish Pond — thirty-five acres — down to Bunny, who sold all but a three-and-a-half-acre lot around the cabin to pay Vickie's tuition.

Vickie returned after her freshman year in 1970 to intern at the *News and Sentinel*, but the next summer she went to live with Marge in Indiana and work as a bartender in the restaurant. Bunny drove to Gary to pick her up at the end of the season and was told to look for her out at the local airport. He got there in time to see a small plane floating down to a runway. "That's Vickie right there," someone said. Bunny learned that Marge had paid for flying lessons for Vickie, and by then she was only a few hours short of soloing.

She majored in history at Plymouth State and spent another summer as a groundskeeper and gravedigger at the Colebrook Village Cemetery. She came out of school determined not to go into nursing or teaching — in other words, not to follow the professions that might keep an educated woman in the North Country. "On the day she graduated," Bunny said, "she saw an ad on a bulletin board for a paralegal program at a school in Pennsylvania — one that guaranteed a job in Pennsylvania when you were through. Well, we could have cried the day we left her there that summer of '74. It looked like we were leaving her someplace in Africa."

That guarantee was a hollow one, but Vickie made do. She got a job as a secretary at a Boston law firm and then worked her way up to paralegal status. Finally she went to law school — not in Boston, but out West, at the University of Puget Sound in Seattle. Bunny and Irene flew out to see her graduate in 1978, and the grand meal Vickie once had with Grammy in Chicago was honored several times over in the Northwest. "She took us out to Chinese restaurants where we were the only non-Chinese," Bunny recalled. "We had breakfast at Snoquomish Falls, where you need reservations six weeks in advance. Fancy restaurants in Vancouver — we lived it up."

Vickie liked the Northwest just fine, with its hiking trails and bike paths, not to mention its fine restaurants, and once she had passed the Washington bar, she got a job in the legal department of a Seattle bank. Then she found work that better suited her interests in Washington's public defender's office. When asked about setting up a practice in Colebrook, she cited the very cases that in their small-town banality had appealed to Fred Harrigan: "Cow cases, timber overcuts, and bar fights — no, I don't want to spend my life doing that stuff."

In fact she was happy enough in the Northwest that, when attorney Phil Waystack called from Colebrook in 1980, there was no reason to think she would even consider his invitation. Waystack had come from Boston — which made him the most egregious sort of flatlander — and had opened a practice in Colebrook in 1975. It was slow-going at first while he haunted the local district courts, passing out his card to anyone willing to take it. In 1977 the Superior Court in Lancaster appointed him to defend a murder case, and he earned an acquittal. He started getting plenty of work after that, but he got nervous in 1980 when he was appointed to a second murder case.

A woman named Rotha Purrington had confessed to killing her husband, but the man had been a wife beater, and Waystack saw there was a case to be made for self-defense. The attorney general's office was prosecuting Purrington with a team of two lawyers; Waystack didn't like being outnumbered, and he was busy enough then that he generally needed help anyway. Then he remembered hearing about Vickie — a female attorney, good, who was from this area but currently on the West Coast.

"The woman is charged with second-degree murder," he told Vickie over the telephone. "She's already spilled her guts to the police. I need some help, and I'd really like to have a woman on the team for this kind of case."

The next question, had he known Vickie, would have surprised Waystack. "What about after?" she asked.

"Well, I'm sure I could use you on a permanent basis if things work out."

But Vickie was guarded about that with her parents. "I'm coming home to help with this murder case," she told them. "But not for good — five months, maximum."

Waystack was taken aback when, on the first day of the trial, Vickie stopped to pick some lilacs from a bush outside the courthouse in Lancaster. "Lilacs are the New Hampshire state flower," she told him, as if that were explanation enough.

"But you can't bring those into a courtroom," Waystack said.

Vickie did so anyway, laying a spray of blossoms at the side of the defendant. The judge called for the counsels for the prosecution and defense to introduce themselves, and then he asked Waystack, "What are those flowers?"

"Your honor, those are lilacs." Then, after a pause, "Which happen to be the state flower of New Hampshire."

"Please remove them from the courtroom."

The lilacs were excused, but the team of Waystack and Bunnell won an acquittal, and Waystack asked Vickie to stay on.

"I have no idea why she changed her mind, because she liked Seattle so much," Bunny said. "But I don't know — she ended up doing so much pro bono work with Phil, maybe she figured she could do more good here."

Certainly, in hindsight, there was that, but maybe there was this too — that she wanted to go hunting and fishing out the back door again. Maybe she decided that what she was really born for was just that.

During a warm, rainy night in June that year, John Harrigan was in Lancaster at the Coös Junction Press, printing that week's run of the *Coös County Democrat* in the capacity of chief pressman. He went outside on a break just as Vickie happened to be driving by on her way to the Lancaster courthouse. He had heard she was back from the Northwest, but hadn't seen her yet.

He waved and Vickie stopped. She said she liked the work she was doing with Phil and that she was starting to look around for her own place to live. "She was so vibrant and energetic that I wondered if she really meant it about staying around here," John recalled. "And she was a woman. I thought, 'What's there for a woman to do in the North Country?'"

So he asked her that. "What about after work? Don't you get bored around here with nothing to do?"

Vickie's eyes widened, enough so that John might have seen in them sun-streaked shadows of all the wild ponds, streams, and fields that Sliver and Bunny had showed her, that Rudy Shatney had showed John.

"Nothing to do?" she scoffed.

If there were a Tarot card bearing the image of Carl Drega, it would look like this: a man in sunglasses and a claw hammer in his hand, astride the peak of a barn. The sky is that of Titus Hill, lit with St. Elmo's fire or else the mortar bursts of contending armies.

In 1991 Jerry Upton went through a tough divorce, but he was buoyed through it all by the sympathy and encouragement of his best friend. And it was Drega who helped cut the last of the lumber at Upton's sawmill in Bow. Then Upton closed that business and moved to Hardwick, Vermont, where he soon got hired to build a barn. He in turn hired three other builders, one of whom was Drega. They worked sixteen-hour days, making their own trusses by hand, with Drega applying shims to make sure all the trusses were exactly — exactly! — the same height.

Upton has the snapshots he took of that project. The barn is a Noah's ark of a building, forty-by-sixty, with an aluminum roof, batten-board siding, and a strip of Plexiglas windows around its circumference under the eaves. Half of it was for heavy-machinery storage, the other half a workshop. Upton is squeamish about heights, but Drega was fearless, and many of the photos are backside views of a lean and rangy man in blue jeans, T-shirt, and a carpenter's belt on a high narrow catwalk, or at the top of a tall ladder, or striding boldly across the roof. Some are of a figure just barely visible, ghostlike, as he bends to his work in the gathering dusk.

That was twenty years after the day in 1971that Drega had taken Rita — remembered by Eric Stohl as "a very nice lady, very quiet" — to Elliot Hospital in Manchester with back pain. The cause was found to be cervical cancer, already in an advanced stage. Months later Drega went into the hospital to visit Rita, and she noticed a slip of paper stuffed into his shirt pocket. "What's that?" Rita asked. It was the receipt for his payment on her life insurance, and it stabbed the carpenter to the quick that Rita should have seen that paper as her life was slipping away. And he punished himself for it. "I felt like the dickens," he confessed to Upton. "It's never stopped bothering me."

Drega was already well into his own barn building then, and it's odd that a man so practiced in construction and its protocols should have neglected to file for a building permit. No matter — Kenneth Parkhurst, a tough-minded Korean War vet and chair of the Columbia Board of Selectmen in 1971, told Drega he could apply after the fact and proceed with his work so long as the papers were in order. Drega grumbled but filled out an application and brought it to Parkhurst's home. There Parkhurst asked him to fill in the blank on what the barn would have by way of permanent siding. "Just write down what you're intending to do there, just so we have it on file," he said.

It was a small thing — seemingly. Perhaps by then these two tough-minded, strong-willed men had already gotten off on the wrong foot together. Perhaps Drega had already noticed that some structures in Columbia — grandfathered in, maybe, under old zoning regulations — didn't have permanent siding. Perhaps this was a matter of new political conviction for a man who had previously abided by zoning regulations in Bow. Be that as it may: "His attitude was that no hick town was going to tell him what to do with his property," Parkhurst later told a reporter from the *Union Leader*.

The blank was left that way. In June 1971, Columbia selectmen denied Drega's application for a building permit. They invited him to reapply within a week or else be charged a fine of ten dollars per day.

Drega refused either to reapply or to pay the fine, and a year later the town sued. "I was the one who saw to that," said Parkhurst. "We had no choice. Either you enforce the laws you've got, or you don't need laws in the first place." Drega did not appear in court, however, answering that Rita was too ill to be left alone. She was — in fact she died on the night of the hearing, June 9, at the age of fifty-two.

Parkhurst has no doubt this coincidence was fateful. "Drega blamed the town for her death, claiming the whole thing was too much stress for her," he told the *Union Leader*. "He was a thorn in our sides ever since."

In time Drega's six-hundred-dollar fine — negotiated down from a much larger amount — was paid by his brother Frank, a machine operator in southern Connecticut. In time — "in his own good time," Parkhurst said — the barn was covered by handsome board-and-batten siding.

But Drega was never able to let the incident go. The complaint he sent to the *News and Sentinel* was written sixteen years after the fact — a letter whose spelling and phrasing had been gussied up by someone else. Drega's own prose style was, shall we say, rough-hewn. But the argument was his, and the bitterness.

For twenty-five years Drega was a familiar figure at Rita Belliveau Drega's grave in the Northumberland Cemetery, on the banks of the Connecticut. At home, whether in Bow or in the North Country, he nursed that grievance against the Town of Columbia — and then others that followed in its wake — in the way a spider nurses its egg.

"The brain within its groove," wrote Emily Dickinson, another solitary resident of a small New England town, "Runs evenly and true ;"

> But let a splinter swerve,
> 'T were easier for you
> To put the water back
> When floods have slit the hills,
> And scooped a turnpike for themselves,
> And blotted out the mills !

John Harrigan was six years older than Vickie. He remembered her from boyhood visits to Sliver and Bunny's barbershop, and he caught other glimpses of her during the years of friendship between Fred and Esther and the Bunnells. He lost track of her when she went to college and then the Northwest. He took sudden notice, though, that summer she was home from Plymouth State and working as a gravedigger for old Roland Martin, the sexton for the town cemetery.

John passed by the cemetery gates one day, saw activity within, and turned in to say hi to Vickie. She and Roland and another man were halfway into a fresh grave. John remembers Vickie — wearing duck boots, khaki shorts, and a dirty T-shirt — rooting in the earth with her pointed shovel like a badger. The girl paused and grinned up at him. John took that gritty smile home with him and kept it.

About a decade later, in the summer of 1980, it was Vickie who spied John taking a break outside the Coös Junction Press building in Lancaster and who stopped to say hi. At that time the Coös Junction Press was only a few weeks old. John had just bought that used Goss Community web offset press and moved the huge machine to Lancaster. With the Goss, John was already printing the *Coös County Democrat* — which he had purchased two years before — and picking up some local business. Eventually he would print weekly runs of his father's *News and Sentinel* as well.

At first Fred Harrigan was furious to have been outmaneuvered in buying the *Democrat*, to find himself still in competition with that operation, and to have his own son at the bottom of it all. At the same time he had to admire John's gumption. Nor were the two papers really such direct competitors. Their base territories overlapped only in Stratford, and only on the biggest stories did their coverage stray farther than that. In time father and son resumed their Thursday tennis matches — which had been suspended — and they made it a point not to talk business. It helped when John offered his father a sweetheart deal in getting the *Sentinel* printed in Lancaster. But on the one occasion when enough of the *Sentinel*'s machinery was broken-down for Fred's staff to have to come down to the *Democrat* to use that newsroom in beating their deadline, John took care to hide his own staff's stories on the pasteup boards under layers of cardboard.

In 1980 John — besides doing much of his own presswork at the printing business — was also writing the *Democrat*'s editorials, doing most of its darkroom work, and on Wednesdays even delivering the papers before dawn to various newsstands after working until midnight to print them. He was rarely home, which was one reason his marriage was on the skids. That next summer John bought a motor home and made himself stop working long enough for a four-week trip out West with Belinda and their three kids. Before that trip, though, while taking the motor home into Vermont for a test drive, John passed the Bunnells' house in Canaan and saw Vickie in the front yard. He stopped and gave her a tour of the vehicle. He couldn't help wishing that he was about to leave for somewhere far away with her.

The vacation was a success, but not, ultimately, the marriage. Tangled up with John's gumption, for better or for worse, is a doggedness that makes it hard for him to veer from the path he's set on. Gene Ehlert — a reporter at the *Democrat* when John bought the paper, and later its managing editor — remembers a winter night on which John came to his house for dinner and brought his daughter Katie, who was still a baby. It had snowed all evening, and Gene asked John to wait a moment before leaving so he could shovel his step and then a path to John's vehicle. John told Gene not to bother, growling that he could handle a little snow — and he promptly flipped head over heels with the baby in his arms.

John stood, cussed, brushed himself off. He went back to the porch to make sure Katie was okay as Gene advanced with the snow shovel. John waved him off, sallied forth again, and just as quickly went arse-over-keister again. Without a glance backward, John regained his feet, cradled the uncomplaining child, and disappeared, without further mishap, into the dark.

So it went at home, with that same sort of compact with fate. By the spring of 1981, John and Belinda were sleeping in separate bedrooms at their house in Lancaster. By the summer, John had moved out. One day in July, with the divorce already in motion, Belinda abruptly left for Montreal, and from there to New Mexico, with Karen, Michael, and Katie. "That nearly killed me," John said. The divorce was followed by a long battle for custody of the children. All three came back in their teenage years to live most of each year with their father, but for a time John's only glimpses of them were from a distance in New Mexico schoolyards.

After the divorce, John worked harder and longer, if that was possible, but also began dating. He took care to avoid women in the Lancaster area so as not to feed the gossip mill. One candidate who met that criterion was Vickie, who by then had begun renting Warren and Ann Brown's house on Bungy Loop. Their first date was a picnic-toting snowshoe trip through wild and untracked forest south of that house. It was April. There was still a lot of snow in the high country, but the streams had broken up and were running high.

They came to a stream that John could usually hop across. It might have been a different matter for Vickie, even in summer. Bunny said that the reason she had been the scorekeeper at Canaan's basketball games, rather than a player like her brother, was that she couldn't jump a lick. In any event, this stream was too fast and too wide for anybody to jump. They made forays upstream and down, but found no rocks or logs on which to step across. The stream, though, was fringed on both sides by stands of supple white birch, and John remembered a trick he had learned from Rudy Shatney. He told Vickie what he had in mind. Her eyes widened, and then she held her mittens out flat with the palms down, as though fastening herself to the ground. "You go first," she said.

John wasn't so sure about this himself, but characteristically, just to be dogged about it, he tossed his snowshoes and backpack over to the other side. Then he picked out a birch that leaned over the stream, whose crown inclined toward that of another birch on the opposite side. He shinnied up the trunk of the near tree and climbed high enough for his weight to swing its branches within reach of its opposite. Then he pitched himself like a monkey into that other birch and shinnied down safely on the far side.

Vickie regarded this result with a mix of wonder and despair. John said she could see how easy it was and beckoned for her to throw him her own shoes and pack. Once she was marooned on that side without any gear, her own sort of gumption began to stir. She started up the birch with her heart in her throat but with no thought of backing off. Meanwhile John couldn't help considering what a wrong-footed start this would be if she fell into the stream and broke her neck. But Vickie scaled the birch, hung on like death as it started to move, and gave herself up to whatever might come next, death or high water, in letting go. When her feet came down next to John's, their fall was accompanied by what he described as a "primal scream."

Years later, in relating this episode from the pulpit of Colebrook's Congregational church, John would begin, "When I first walked with this great woman . . ."

They began each year as soon as the season opened in mud time. Then they went as often as they could and always used flies, never bait, casting them so they just skimmed the water's surface before settling or else floated quietly just beneath like larvae. In the spring they worked the shorelines as the trout followed the smelt into shallow water, as the bass were clearing off their nests there. Later in the year, in the dog days of summer, they might try another trick John had learned from Rudy Shatney, something Rudy called dredging. John would attach a heavier fly — a Black Ghost maybe — to a sinking line and then strip that fly along the bottom through trout lingering in the cool water there.

They almost always went by canoe. Vickie paddled like John did, not from a seat but from her knees, down low in the water so your leverage is increased and your paddle gets more purchase. John would steer with the stern paddle Bunny had given him once he and Vickie had started going out together. One reason they liked the canoe was its quiet, the odds it offered of hearing a partridge drumming in the underbrush, of floating up unawares behind a moose feeding on pondweed. Once in a while they fished the Connecticut River, stopping to build a fire on a shady sandbar, roasting hot dogs or sweet sausage on forked willow switches — but like Bunny, they preferred the lakes and ponds.

In the fall they went bird hunting. That season opened October 1 each year, while the fishing closed October 15. They loved that first half of the month for the opportunity to do both, though they never hunted the first weekend of the season, when the woods were full of flatlanders who scared more grouse than they shot. After that they hunted the untracked fields near Vickie's house, around Bungy Loop and along Nash Stream and up Blue Mountain. They'd get out for a few hours on weekday afternoons or else make a whole day of it on Sunday, packing 20-gauge shotguns and lunch in their fanny packs.

One weekday they got out earlier than usual, around noon. They wandered into an old apple orchard, picked some wild apples, and also bagged four grouse. They returned to Vickie's in time for supper, and John plucked and cleaned the birds. He made a bread stuffing with onion and garlic and thyme, sweetened with the apples they had picked. The stuffing went into the birds with chunks of butter and a dusting of poultry seasoning. They baked the grouse in tin foil and ate all four with steamed broccoli and long-stemmed rice.

Vickie was a fine cook — and every bit the gourmand she had promised to be when Grammy took her to that steak house in Chicago — but John could do great things with wild game. And this was a meal like the one made with the lake trout he had brought home from Big Diamond Pond as a boy — an occasion where everything was so perfect that it stitched body and soul together. John thought about some of the hundred-dollar meals he had been served in Manhattan restaurants during rare visits there. Then he calculated the cost of this meal — "Hardly a farthing," he said — threw in the companionship he had, and pronounced another blessing.

John's other companions during the '80s were an assorted collection of outdoorsmen that included game wardens, loggers, college professors, guides, students, wildlife biologists, mill hands, and schoolteachers, most of them local, but not all. Together they made up a sort of round table — they referred to themselves most frequently, and not unreasonably, as the Gang of Uglies — into which Vickie was inaugurated as the sole vested representative of her gender. The attribute of ugliness was honorary in her case.

There were two biologists in that gang. John Lanier worked for state Fish & Game and found himself beguiled by the group's come-what-may ethos. "A lot of the trips I did with those other guys — and Vickie — were just totally spontaneous," he said. "Somebody would say, 'Hey, wouldn't it be a good idea if we . . . ' and then everybody would just drop everything and go. We'd end up in three different vehicles scattered all over the landscape, all on the spur of the moment. That lifestyle was a little foreign to me, actually, but it was a lot of fun."

The other biologist, Jeff Fair, was from Sandwich, a town just south of the notches, but he often came up to the North Country to do contract work on loons, and so became the group's Loon Ranger. "I had heard so much about Vickie, and when I met her I expected her, I suppose, to be gorgeous," Fair said. "But her face always wore this very interested and observant sort of look, and there was always a presence to her. Anytime you were around her you were aware of her, intrigued by her. She looked you square in the eye and knew enough about anything to be able to talk with anybody in the group. After a couple of months, well, there I was — always glad to lay eyes on her and persuaded that she was beautiful. I guess I fell partly in love with her."

Vickie's patience was tested on the one hand by John's moods, on the other hand by the random groups of Uglies who would barrel into her office during the workday to steal her for a trip, or play a round of cribbage, or else arrive unannounced at her house for dinner. But this was all part of that freewheeling merry-go-round she rode with John. People came and went, and while they were around they were sometimes drunk and pointedly tactless, trading barbs in that gruff, bass-ackward manner in which men appreciate each other. Once Lanier collapsed while deer hunting in upstate New York with John and several Uglies. He was carried out of the woods and to a hospital, entirely conscious, by men who argued theatrically who would get his gun and boots once he was dead. One doctor opined, "That probably made him mad enough to stick around." Vickie could give as good as she got in that rough-and-tumble society and made John's fractious friends feel like they had been expected all the time.

When they traveled, it was usually by rail and almost always north, where the country got wilder and the night skies darker. Lanier and his wife went once with John and Vickie—and Charlie Jordan and his wife, Donna—on a trip to Halifax by rail. It took three days, round-trip, which was fine in the second story of a glass-topped passenger car, sharing drinks and watching the Maritime countryside roll by as the travelers played cribbage.

A snapshot from the Jordans' photo album—one taken by a camera balanced on top of a fence post in Halifax—includes two couples: Charlie and Donna, Vickie and John. The Jordans stand smiling to the left, ramrod straight and adjacent. John looks to the camera and stands with one hand thrust into a hip pocket, the other arm around Vickie's shoulder. Vickie, in jeans and a turtleneck and a white blouse, has hold of John's right hand and has turned her smile to his face. One couple is happily married; the other plainly in love.

Sometimes John left Vickie home and departed with anywhere from four to a dozen Uglies on all-male fishing junkets to Labrador, a thousand miles north of Colebrook. They'd leave at dawn, cross the St. Lawrence at Quebec, drive up the north shore of the St. Lawrence, stay the night at Sept Isles, and then board the Quebec North Shore & Labrador train the next morning. They continued 350 miles by rail until they were dumped—"And I mean 'dumped,'" said John—at the end-of-the-line village of Menihek. From there they dispersed into fishing camps along 35 miles of pristine lakes and rivers.

But it wasn't easy for John to leave his girl home. Jeff Fair remembered one such trip in the mid-'80s when John had to get off the train at every stop in an attempt to find a telephone soon enough to call Vickie. "Lanier and I took note, but we kept quiet about it," Fair said. "Another guy, though, was giving John all sorts of shit—'Hey, John, we're slowing down. You better go call Vickie. I'm telling you, she might get away.'"

The Uglies didn't really think she would. On the way home, during a stretch in which John lay asleep, they debated in fractious whispers what kind of canoe they might buy as a gift once John and Vickie got married.

DECENT,
SANE,
AND
SIMPLE

WHEN DENNIS JOOS AND SUSAN ZIZZA began trading the *News and Sentinel*'s editor-in-chief job between them like a medicine ball — for one issue Dennis was in charge, for the next Susan — John Harrigan made a sign to help the rest of the staff keep track. A replica of the notice that rests on the cluttered desk of the rumpled, cynical, and feathered journalist/antihero of the "Shoe" comic strip, the sign said, "The editor is in." On the morning of August 19, the sign sat on Susan's desk.

And Susan was as surprised as John had once been to find herself, in her mid-forties, the editor of a newspaper. She had grown up in Lexington, Massachusetts, but her family roots went as deep into Colebrook history as the Bunnells'. In 1997 the old Getty gas station on the corner of Bridge and Main stood for sale and abandoned — its pumps removed, its light stanchions bare, its pavement cracking. That spot of ruin in the heart of downtown was emblematic of the economic malaise that wracked the North Country once the paper mills started closing. Later, in 2008, the Great Recession settled in like February frost. But in the '50s, Susan's grandfather had run that station, and Susan kept a photo of her and her brother gazing from behind its plate-glass window in those easier days.

As a girl, she had spent part of each summer on her grandparents' Piper Hill farm in Stewartstown, and her husband, Mark, her high school sweetheart, fell in love with the North Country on his first visit. The Zizzas moved to Colebrook in 1977, and Mark set up as a locksmith in a town, alas, where people generally don't lock their doors. Nor do they go out of their way to engage in commerce with flatlanders.

Mark went looking for odd jobs while Susan minded David, the first of their two boys. Things started to look up when Esther Harrigan hired Mark to paint and wallpaper the farmhouse the Harrigans bought on South Hill. Then Doc Gifford gave him some work, and more jobs followed. Eventually locksmithing jobs started to come in.

When David's little brother, Alex, was old enough to start school, Susan — whose high cheekbones, short auburn hair, and dusky eyes provided a fine showcase for any beauty product — started selling Avon cosmetics door to door. One day she knocked on the door of Esther Harrigan, who said that she already had a regular Avon Lady, but wouldn't she come in for some coffee?

They talked about books they had read and plays they had seen. A while later Esther called to say that the *Sentinel* needed a typesetter. Did Susan know how to type? Yes. Did she get good grades in English at school? Straight As. Was she interested? Well, thank you, no, she was actually doing pretty well with Avon. Esther offered to pay her just to give it a try. Susan began working two days a week in 1986. Then she started doing pasteup and layout. Soon she was writing stories and taking photos, moving up — and getting sucked in — just as Fred and Esther had, and even their stray-cat son.

John promoted Susan to assistant editor in 1995, and a year later Dennis suggested they begin power sharing. She fantasized sometimes about working at a big-city daily or a television station, but here she was only a few minutes' walk from where Alex still attended school. In fact, when David and Alex were little, they would come in during the afternoon to color pictures or do homework at the big table in the newsroom. Fred and Esther didn't mind (the boys made themselves useful by walking Sir George Colebrooke, the Harrigans' wire-haired terrier, named after the East India Company magnate who had lent the town its name), nor did John. Susan's friends on the staff made them feel welcome, especially Dennis. He and David Zizza shared certain passions: Superman comics, Calvin & Hobbes cartoons, Michael Jordan and the Chicago Bulls, baseball cards, most anything else to do with sports.

And Susan liked having the more experienced Dennis by her side on these pressure-cooker Tuesdays, when everything had to fall into place or else be shimmed to look that way — not just the news and sports stories by Dennis or reporter Claire Lynch and the photos by Leith Jones, but the press releases, ad copy, letters to the editor, obituaries, marriage and birth announcements, and also all the "Locals" columns, these arriving by mail, through the front door, or over the telephone from correspondents in Pittsburg, North Stratford, Columbia, Errol, Stewartstown, Lemington, Canaan, and several other towns on both sides of the river.

The "Locals" stretched back to the *Sentinel's* founding, and their volume each week was a point of pride with the newspaper. For example: "On Sunday, August 10, Bud Hulse was a dinner guest of Mike and Joeng Divney"; or "Vernice Rice of Groveton and Lela Fields were Friday callers on Maxie Bordeau at the Coös County Nursing Hospital in Stewartstown"; or "Delight Thibeault saw a movie, 'George of the Jungle,' in Newport with Sarah Fontaine and Kristine Levesque"; and so on for many column inches.

Arguably this was gossip, despised by John even more than Fred, partly because John had so frequently been a subject of it himself over the years. But scandal remained foreign to these columns, which ensured an absence of color, perhaps, but didn't diminish the dignity they attached to the smallest gestures of social life in the North Country. The only problem was that the authors of these pieces were paid by the column inch, which lent itself to, well, prolixity. Susan's first job with these was to cut the columns down to material John was willing to pay for.

Later John would want feedback on and editing of his publisher's column for this issue. He was back from his Kiwanis meeting and working on that piece behind a closed door. In the meantime Susan was scrolling through this issue's first four pages on her monitor. The headline story on the front page, by Dennis, was about the sudden resignation of the town manager. Then there was Dennis's story on the rediscovery — in a Lancaster Historical Society outbuilding, by Charlie and Donna Jordan — of the original sign marking where the 45th parallel transited Clarksville, and the sign's reinstallation by the Jordans.

A couple of short Claire Lynch pieces filled out the front page, stories that Fred Harrigan might have ignored: two boys had run away from Camp

E-Toh-Anee, which hosted troubled teenagers and was known locally as Camp Runaway; and there was an incident of petty vandalism, some lit matches shoved down a mail slot, at the Colebrook post office. The previous week's Lynch story on that weird exchange of gunfire on Bungy Road might possibly have been deemed by Fred serious enough to cover, or possibly dismissed for its lack of happy-go-lucky. That would have been a tough call for Fred, but not for John.

Photographer Leith Jones also did some writing, and on the inside pages Leith had a story and photos on last Friday's Old Home Day in Pittsburg and then a preview of the North Country's biggest moneymaker, the Moose Festival. Now in its sixth year, this event — with its sidewalk sales, craft fairs, hot-air balloon rides, scenic train trips, moose stew cook-off, raffles, and Kiwanis chicken barbecue — was a bigger affair than Christmas for the money it brought in for area merchants, to say nothing of its value to Kiwanis and other charities. Claire would cover that with Leith, and Susan — back to being a reporter then — might do a story on it herself, if Dennis thought it was a good idea.

Susan scrolled to the back pages and remembered that she needed to check with Dennis on the status of the obituaries. Doc Gifford had died in March, while his wife, Parsie, had died in 1994. A memorial service for both physicians, the Reverend Bud Hulse presiding, was scheduled for Saturday at the Colebrook Village Cemetery. Susan wanted to be sure that Dennis or somebody had written a notice about the event and to see if Dennis needed help in pasting up the obits.

Around 9:00 a.m. Susie Sambito, Vickie Bunnell's secretary, arrived, and Vickie herself came in the back door a few minutes later, Tallak trailing behind her. Susie and Vickie had been putting in long days, tying up the loose ends in Vickie's practice before she headed for Greece the next week. But Vickie wasn't so pressed that she couldn't linger at the pasteup board, as she always did on a Tuesday morning, to get an early peek at the week's news and chat about her own plans for the day.

In fact Vickie had gotten far enough ahead to take some time off this afternoon. She said she'd be scooting out to meet an old friend (who might be more than just a friend now, Susan thought) for a ride in his private plane. Then she'd have dinner with her parents and also her brother, Earl, and his wife, Pam, at the cabin on Fish Pond. Okay, Susan thought — there was an item for the "Locals" section.

Vickie was wearing a white blouse and a cool ankle-length cotton skirt with a flower print — similar to the dress she wore in a photograph that hung in the front office. The photo was of the *Sentinel* staff as it was in August 1970. Vickie worked as an intern at the newspaper that summer, and she stood in the front row next to Esther, who wore a long skirt and a ruffled blouse and who draped a maternal hand over the girl's shoulder. Fred's lean and mustachioed face peeked from the back row. They were all ranged in front of the building's white brick facade. Vickie's girlish smile was the same she wore today as she talked and laughed with Dennis.

It seemed odd to Susan that Vickie was the only one in that photo still in the building, but then she reminded herself that it had been taken a long time ago — twenty-seven years this month. Fred and Esther weren't the only ones who had since died and had their obituaries pasted up in the newsroom.

Vickie exchanged greetings with Claire, who had been scratching Tallak's ears, and tore herself away. She vanished into her office with the sound of the dog's toenails clicking after her.

The first case that Fred Harrigan wangled for himself in Colebrook, immediately after the war, had been a divorce proceeding. He kept on practicing law, and then serving as a probate and district court judge, even after he and Esther had bought the newspaper. When they moved into the building next to the gas station, he hung a brass plaque outside its front door: "Frederick J. Harrigan, Attorney at Law." "Sometimes he sat on the same cases he reported on," John said. "He'd conduct an arraignment, and then write about it in the *Sentinel*. It was a different kind of time then. You could wear a lot of different hats and nobody would really question you about it."

Meanwhile Vickie's first job with Phil Waystack — after the Rotha Purrington trial — was a cow case, an incident in which a Vermont farmer refused to return a borrowed cow to his neighbor. From there it was on to divorces and bar fights, and also tax law, real estate deeds, title searches, and wills. Still, the Purrington trial proved a harbinger of a different kind of time — an era in the North Country when things previously just whispered about began to show up in court. Vickie carved a niche for herself in skillfully handling such matters: sexual abuse, spouse abuse, victims' rights, child custody, and adoption.

She stayed with Waystack for five years and then hung her own shingle outside an office in a building on Main Street. "We were getting a lot of cases, and I wanted someone who could work six days a week," Waystack said. "But Vickie wanted to cut back to three days, actually, so she could canoe and hike and snowshoe with John the rest of the time. So we parted company, but as friends, and we always referred cases to each other."

As her own boss, Vickie was free not only to set her own schedule but also to negotiate payment according to her clients' circumstances, which were often distressed, and to do as much pro bono work as she felt she could afford. She began to learn French so she could speak in either language with clients of French descent, became a pioneer female member of the town's Kiwanis Club, and made herself available as well to other local boards and committees. Figure in the time off she devoted to John, and she was making barely enough money to stay in business.

Meanwhile John wasn't getting rich, was still working long hours, but at least he had people to help pick up the slack when needed. He hired Dennis Joos to be the court reporter for the *Coös County Democrat*—until Fred stole Dennis away to the run the *News and Sentinel*. And John hired Charlie Jordan at the *Democrat* as well. When John decided he wanted to cut back a little in the mid-'8os—and spend time with Vickie—he proposed that Charlie take turns with him as editor in chief at the *Democrat*, just as Susan and Dennis would later at the *Sentinel*.

Vickie never broached the subject of marriage with John. It was just something that everybody expected would happen—not only the Uglies, but every vested member of the town gossip mill. As the months passed by, however, and the years mounted, John reached the end of each day thinking he still hadn't quite recovered from the wounds of his divorce from Belinda, that things with Vickie were good enough as they were. "I was just stupid," he said later. "The clock was ticking."

The relationship didn't end so much as it simply lost heat and expired. "It wasn't Vickie's fault things didn't work out," John Lanier observed. In time, in the eyes of their friends, the two went from being joined at the hip to being as on-again/off-again as a woodstove in May and then — around 1990 — to being simply off.

Yet they never fought, nor were ever less than good friends. Maybe that was a mistake on Vickie's part, if she really wanted to reel in this fish, but though she was plucky, it wasn't in her nature to be hard that way. They still took long, rambling truck rides together on the cusp of each season, just to see what was settling in or breaking loose along the back roads. They still called each other to bet the price of dinner on the track of a thunderstorm as it came up the valley. John still went over to the house on Bungy Loop now and then to play cards, share a meal, sit by the fire. The difference was that he no longer stayed the night. The only time Vickie ever mentioned marriage was during one of those visits. "If you ever did marry," she asked him, "would it be to someone like me?"

In 1991, after Fred died, John gave Vickie his father's collection of law books and a sweetheart deal on office space in the newspaper building. Vickie moved into Fred's old office, where Tallak took up residence on Fred's old leather couch. At John's insistence, however, his father's brass plaque remained mounted outside the front door. Vickie had a plaque done in exactly the same manner and hung it beneath Fred's: "Vickie M. Bunnell, Attorney at Law."

Reporter Claire Lynch is of that cast of mind that sees the permeability of past, present, and future; sees time's straddling of that borderland between the waking world and its semblances in dreams. That was one of the reasons — on the morning of August 19 — that she was possessed by gloom, pricked by foreboding.

Well, it was Tuesday, and even someone as skeptical as John Harrigan had noticed that big stories break on Tuesday, on press day, on the one day of the week when big stories were least easily accommodated. Claire had heard it too many times already — John's voice ringing through the building, crackling with exasperation, as though he were still editor, and it was his job, not Dennis's or Susan's, to shoehorn it in: "We can't have this today!"

If not big stories, then acts of God. She remembered a Tuesday when the Connecticut was flooding and stretches of Route 3 to Lancaster were under water. Nonetheless, at the end of the day the page negatives had to get down to the Coös Junction Press. She and John lashed a canoe to the top of his pickup. Then they took Harvey Brook Road through Columbia. The brook was over its banks as well, and in places the water rose high on the fenders. But they splashed through without having to abandon the truck, and the *Sentinel* got printed.

Tuesday was also the day that Claire visited the town, courthouse, and police department offices across the street — though actually she always enjoyed that. At 9:00 a.m., she was just going over her list of those she hoped to talk to there when Vickie Bunnell came in through the back door of the building. Tallak sniffed politely at Susan and Dennis, then came clicking over to Claire's desk, her head bent and her tail gently moving. Claire took both floppy ears in her hands and scratched, drinking in the sweet-and-sour scent that always cloaked the English setter's face, something like overripe cranberries, she thought.

A few minutes later, Claire was cheered — if only slightly — to see a pair of state police cruisers parked on the other side of Bridge Street. One, 608, belonged to Scott Phillips, and that new Crown Victoria, 719, had to be Les Lord's. Its paint and chrome were lustrous, almost fiery, in the morning light.

The scanner had been quiet all morning, but Claire wanted to check for any word on the runaway campers. And these state troopers just happened to be her two favorite sources. Scott was thirty-two, about her own age, and action-hero handsome. He was also frank and honest with her, willing to say what was going on between the lines in the official version of a police story, trusting her enough to speak off the record when necessary. Les couldn't resist a good story, and he was a fine source too, though sometimes his accounts could be a little too good — and just too funny — to be true.

Inside the town police station, though, neither Scott nor Les had news on the runaways, or anything else. They sat at adjoining desks on the downstairs floor. Scott was working on a report, but he laid his pen aside to ask a few questions himself. He made some teasing references to someone else in law enforcement who, like Claire, had just become single again. Scott wanted to confirm eyewitness reports that the man had been flirting with her. He said, "I think there's something going on between you two."

Claire laughed for what felt like the first time in weeks. "No, no — there's nothing going on."

Les was eating at the other desk. He looked doubtfully at her with two oatmeal cookies in one hand and an open can of orange soda in the other. "Hey, you," Claire said. "Don't you have a heart condition?"

She was glad of a chance to change the subject, to preempt anything Les might add, but now she was mad at him as well. She remembered a photo that Charlie Jordan took, one that had been used in a series of ads for the Upper Connecticut Valley Hospital in Colebrook. The ads featured people whose lives had been saved by the proximity of that hospital — for example, Les, who was rushed there a few years ago with a heart attack. In the ad, Les stood grinning behind the open door of his old cruiser and above the quote that served as the ad's banner: "Today I'm well, enjoying my family and my job."

"Is that what your doctor told you to eat?" she demanded.

"Well, he did say this stuff would kill me," Les said. "But he didn't say when."

Claire mentioned Bev and their boys, Shawn and Corey, and how lucky Les was to have a family, and they to have a father. Mostly because she liked him so much, she found herself getting angry enough to annoy Les, which wasn't easy to do. Suddenly the discussion was over. "Claire," Les said, "you know I'm going to eat what I want to eat."

Claire shivered slightly and fell silent. She blamed herself — something bubbling over from that gloom, from what she had learned too suddenly of late about the noonday darkness on the other side of this sky, the cruel mortal speed of each minute and hour. She also had a feeling that Scott and Les were sitting on something they didn't want to talk about yet.

Claire went outside with her notebook empty and her emotions straining again at the leash she tried to keep them on. Within the past several months a series of catastrophes had hit her and her immediate family like drumbeats — the death of her grandmother, and then of her father, and then a close friend's suicide, and then the failure of her marriage. Last night she had dreamed, again, about her father.

She walked by Scott's cruiser, wondering what might happen next, whether it might just be an inconvenient story at work or another harrowing of the spirit. That was when she remembered a dream recently told to her by Dennis, who shared her suspicions about loops in time and different levels of reality. Dennis dreamed that he was sitting in the back seat of Scott's cruiser, this very vehicle, while Susan Zizza was in the front seat, weeping and complaining of a killing headache. He tried to comfort her, Dennis said, but she couldn't hear him — and he couldn't help.

Dennis Joos thought that one problem with the television signal booster Beno Lamontagne had for sale at Lazerworks, the little electronics store across from the Sentinel Building on Bridge Street, was its price — at fifty-nine dollars, not so affordable really. The other problem was his certainty that neither Helen nor Scott Nearing would approve.

He thought about it that Tuesday morning as he stood in Lazerworks's music section and flipped through racks of CDs. He was on a ten-minute break from the newspaper. The booster dangled in its plastic packaging on a rack in another part of the store. Beno waited patiently at the cash register, and Dennis didn't want to betray how much he was struggling with this.

He was frankly ashamed he had a TV and a rooftop aerial antenna for it — or even an electric bill. Dennis had come to the North County (and his wife, Polly, had come back to it) to be spared electric bills, among other things. He had grown up in Exeter, in southern New Hampshire, in a household rather like the Harrigans': educated, middle-class, professional. He wanted a simpler and gentler sort of life than the one he saw around him, and after college (the University of Colorado, political science) he joined the Order of Friars Minor, the Franciscans, vowing obedience, chastity, and poverty. He served a year as a postulant and then, starting in 1961, six years as a novice at a seminary in Callicoon, New York.

One of his classmates at the St. Joseph Seraphic Seminary was a man who — many years later — would post a blog under the name of Geezer Ed: "The ramblings of a gay geezer who is still trying to figure it all out." Dennis earned young Geezer Ed's lifelong gratitude during lunch one day at the seminary, a day when another novice was attacking Ed with homophobic slurs. "Dennis was sitting opposite me and heard every nasty word," Ed posted. "He turned to the boy (whose name I have forgotten) and told him very nicely to shut up. This was the last time I remember the boy hassling me."

In 1967, though, near the end of his novitiate, Dennis was excused from the order. "He was heartbroken," Geezer Ed wrote of the night Dennis learned this. "He cried so hard I was worried for him, but I had no idea what to say." Nor does Ed say why Dennis was expelled, but Claire Lynch believed the problem was obedience — or more precisely, irreverence. "I think he was thrown out for too many practical jokes," she said.

Instead Dennis became a VISTA volunteer, posted to Houston, Texas. He also began studying the back-to-the-land books of Helen and Scott Nearing, thrilling to the first sentence of *Living the Good Life: How to Live Sanely and Simply in a Troubled World*: "Many a modern worker, dependent on wage or salary, lodged in city flat or closely built-up suburb and held to the daily grind by family demands or other complicating circumstances, has watched for a chance to escape the cramping limitations of his surroundings, to take his life into his own hands and live it in the country, in a decent, simple, kindly way."

It was a kindly speech-and-hearing therapist who gave Dennis that chance. By 1971 he was back in New Hampshire and working as an attendant at the Laconia State School, a home for mentally disabled children and adults near where Vickie Bunnell was attending college. Polly Prince was born in Laconia but had grown up in Stewartstown and was anxious to return to the North Country, where land was plentiful and cheap enough to enact the Nearings' model of the good life: a homemade stone house, homemade furniture, an ample garden, a small orchard, a maple sugar bush, and as little contact as possible with the consumer economy and the daily grind.

In 1972 Dennis and Polly pooled their savings and bought a twenty-acre lot off South Hill Road, not far from where John Harrigan lived, but higher on the hill and across the town line. The next spring they made a pilgrimage to meet the Nearings at their stone house in Maine, quit their jobs in Laconia, moved into a 23-by-8-foot trailer on their Stewartstown property, and began building their home.

"The summer of '73 was a glorious time for us," Dennis wrote in a March 1988 article published in the *Mother Earth News*. "We were delighted to be working for ourselves. We used to joke about being unemployed, unmarried, uninsured, and pregnant, but it was the first time either of us had felt such an intense sense of freedom."

The recklessness of it all was part of the glory: "Many of our relatives thought we were absolutely insane, and perhaps we were. Polly had a malignant tumor in her hip when she was a teenager, and the doctors zapped it with a megadose of cobalt radiation. Yet here she was mixing concrete by hand in a wheelbarrow."

They married in June, and their son, Aaron, was born in the fall. In deer season Dennis posted a sign on the property that he never took down: "Please don't hunt here — I don't want to get shot." They had finished the shell of the house before Aaron's birth, and then spent their first winter in the trailer.

By the mid-'80s, Dennis wrote, they were still unhappy with an electrical system they ran at intervals off their car battery, but otherwise "we have reached a point of equilibrium. Aaron is in the seventh grade in a two-room school, Polly works three days a week as a speech therapist, and I work three days as a printer. We can survive on two part-time jobs because we have no mortgage, no electric bills, no car payments, and we make the most of our large, well-weeded garden."

Dennis had started out doing some freelance writing for cash, mostly for the *Civic*, a free weekly newspaper run by Merle Wright, the onetime *News and Sentinel* editor who had hired Fred Harrigan on the day the lawyer poked his nose in. When Wright died in a plane crash in 1977, Dennis was cajoled into part-time work at the printing business Wright had started, at that point run by his widow.

And Dennis was still writing then, doing some freelance reporting on his off-days for the *Coös County Democrat*. Then slowly, inexorably, he got sucked into journalism on a full-time basis: the courthouse beat for the *Democrat* after John Harrigan bought it, then a stint running the *Sentinel* after being hired away by Fred Harrigan, and then a friendly reunion with John when he inherited the newspaper. At home Dennis and Polly had acquired a telephone and a pickup truck; Dennis had built a stone-sided woodshed, a small indoor pool in which Polly could exercise her damaged hip, and a windmill for recharging a bank of 12-volt batteries.

Dennis wrote with an affection for the North Country and its people that pleased Fred Harrigan — and also John. In a profile of Doc Gifford, Dennis took note of the device Doc and Parsie employed to encourage the virtue of patience in people waiting outside their offices: a human skeleton in one chair with a book in its bony fingers and an expired cigarette clamped between its teeth. Dennis also noted that Doc took part in the sometimes saucy musicals mounted as fund-raisers for the American Legion Child Welfare Fund. In one such, an angel was required to descend from the heavens by means of cables and pulleys. One night in his office, after hours, Doc wanted to make sure that his harness worked properly. He took off his shirt, strapped the apparatus to his arms, and heard a knock at the door. He said come in to someone he presumed to be another member of the cast — actually it was a new patient from out of town. "She entered to find the doctor bare-chested with angel wings sprouting from his arms," wrote Dennis. "Some doctors just know how to break the ice with a patient."

Dennis admired Doc's and Parsie's irreverence, their refusal to put on airs. As field boss of the *Sentinel*, he was like that himself. He organized his time according to the Betty Boop calendar over his desk, kept a photo on his wall of his adult self sitting on Santa's lap, came to work in impertinent T-shirts — "Is it recess yet?" — or sometimes fake noses or cowboy hats. With John Harrigan's consent, he sometimes planted bogus stories in the *Sentinel*, such as several about a hermit living in a snow pile in the parking lot behind the building.

But there was nothing flip about the crash course in journalism Dennis taught to Susan Zizza, Claire Lynch, and the newspaper's correspondents in outlying towns — all on-the-job learners, as he had been. There was always more than one point of view, he said, and you had to represent them all. Get the facts and then keep digging — there were liable to be more. Look for the odd angle, the unexpected approach, the catchy lead. If it sounded like writing, you'd have to rewrite it until it sounded like conversation. Tell the truth, but never forget how dangerous and terrible the truth could be.

The truth could be bad enough for Fred Harrigan to want only part of it. John took on more, but at the cost of moodiness and intensity. Dennis's mellow, beatific temperament offered a good counterweight to John's, and his was a mildness stiffened by principles of tolerance and nonviolence that, St. Francis–like, encompassed the breadth of creation. At the *Sentinel*, Dennis was famous for his refusal to countenance even the squashing of a spider. Call him, he insisted, and he'd carry the offending arachnid outside.

Beno Lamontagne was as tough as any of his French Canadian forebears, but he was deathly allergic to bee stings, and Beno was grateful to Dennis for one day removing a bee — alive, by hand, without a sting — that had gotten into Lazerworks and driven the owner under the counter.

As a newspaperman, though, Dennis was challenged and affronted every day by the troubled world's cruelty — a cruelty that couldn't be just silenced, as it had once been during lunch at the seminary. Instead a reporter had to shout it abroad. Dennis never advised Susan or anyone else to allow a source to read or edit a story before it was published — that would be contrary to journalistic ethics. But he did it himself on several occasions: the hair stylist whose thirty-five-year-old daughter had committed suicide or the electric company lineman whose fourteen-year-old daughter had been raped. He allowed them to excise anything they found painful or lurid in his stories.

Dennis warned Claire, when she was hired two years ago, that the newspaper business could make her cynical, to be careful about that. Over the years, behind the wacky T-shirts, Dennis could feel his own mind darkening, his optimism leaching away, along with that old sense of freedom and equilibrium. Sometimes, to his regret, other staffers at the *Sentinel* saw that darkness. John had a name for it: Dennis's Look of Gloom.

Dennis knew what brought it on: the various ways in which people failed to be kind and the tough news stories that resulted; this whole midlife-and-getting-older thing, now that he was fifty-one; and the realization that — despite the promises he had made to the Nearings — he had more or less become a modern worker and had joined the daily grind, "dependent on wage or salary." The money had allowed the stone house to become much more comfortable — especially after he and Polly had consented to be wired into the New Hampshire Electric Co-Operative's grid. Then they bought a TV, that electronic wormhole into the consumer economy, and an aerial that pulled in only a couple of snowy channels. Beno promised that this booster could clarify those channels and pull in a couple more.

One of Dennis's good sources on the crime beat was Howie Weber, a veteran detective in the state police. A few weeks ago they'd been talking about how they both wished they could slow down and appreciate life a little more. Dennis was shocked, really, to find himself in that sort of conversation with a strung-out cop, but it made him feel less alone.

Then, right after that conversation, a surprising job offer came in over the transom: editor in chief for *American Dowser*, a little quarterly magazine with offices across the river in Danville, Vermont. Still a job, still a daily grind, but involving stories about people and water and an inexplicable sympathy between the two, instead of suicide, rape, murder. He could do much of his work at home and have more time for the novel he was writing, *The Curse of the House of Wingate*, a comic — you might say irreverent — tale set in the fictional Coös County town of Sussex. That, and Dennis would have more time with Polly, whose radiated hip had become more painful in recent years.

It was on behalf of simplifying, of freeing himself of a few complicating circumstances, that Dennis had suggested he and Susan take turns as editor in chief. That had helped — he had more fun during the weeks he was just a reporter. But it hadn't helped enough. He still caught himself wearing the Look of Gloom now and then, and now it was also brought on by the prospect of quitting at the *Sentinel*, where he had so many good friends to help ease the grind. Poor Claire was wearing her own Look of Gloom this morning — for good reason, he knew — and finally Dennis decided he needed to get out of the building for a few minutes.

At Lazerworks, Dennis abandoned the CDs and limped back to the rack where the booster hung. Last week he had tumbled off his roof — slippery pieces of slate scrounged from Colebrook Academy's last roof renovation in '74 — and hurt his back. The acupuncture wasn't helping yet, and if he didn't buy this booster, at least he wouldn't have to get up on the roof again. He looked at the device, with its protruding coaxial cable fittings, and thought it looked more like a piece of plumbing. "Beno," he said, "I still can't believe this costs so much."

"Welcome to the North Country," said Beno. "It's brought to you here, at no small expense, from far away."

At the end of that *Mother Earth News* article, Dennis — looking ahead to 2000 — asked, "Will we still be here in thirteen years?" He admitted he and Polly dreamed about warmer, sunnier places whenever it snowed in October or May. But he decided moving was unlikely. "Our souls, you see, are sunk into this place."

That tumble off his roof had gotten him thinking about what might happen to Polly if he weren't around to help. The next day he had made out his will, or what passed for such — just a handwritten note he composed in front of Polly. The will stipulated that his body be cremated and its ashes scattered — privately, by immediate family — on that homesteaded plot of land. There would be no gravestone, no public observance. Decent, sane, and simple.

Dennis sighed and hung the booster back on its hook, saying to Beno, "Well, I guess I'll think about it some more."

Audrey Noyes remembered the last time she saw Vickie and was glad at least that Vickie was happy.

Once Audrey had, briefly, been an employee of John Harrigan. In the '70s, besides running an antique business with her husband and substitute teaching in the local schools, Audrey was an obituary writer and the Colebrook "Locals" correspondent for the *Coös County Democrat*. She was among several on that staff dismayed by the sale of the newspaper and among those who ended up quitting in 1978.

"I liked John, but he had a sense of humor I didn't understand," Audrey said. She was afraid — probably with some justification — that he would slip something offbeat into one of the obituaries she wrote. If Audrey's humor didn't have quite the same ironic slant as John's, it was no less capacious, and over the years, as neighbors in Colebrook, the two became good friends.

Meanwhile, Vickie — during her years at Plymouth State College — became interested in antiques, and she often came to Audrey's shop to learn about them. There Audrey told her something that she often told her students in school: "Not all the action's down in New York City, you know." Mix the beauty of the North Country with a little business acumen, and the wide world would come to you. For evidence she had the guest register signed by visitors to her antique shop: signatures by, among others, General William Westmoreland, commander of U.S. forces in Vietnam; basketball player Meadowlark Lemon of the Harlem Globetrotters; and Jimmy Greenspoon, the keyboard player for Three Dog Night.

Her pet peeve with the school system was that not enough attention was paid, she believed, to local history. So she took time to help with that whenever she substituted. For example, take Monadnock, she told her students — one of a string of towering ancient volcanoes running from Vermont to Quebec, shaved down to its present three thousand feet by a glacier that was a mile thick. The abandoned gold mine on its east flank had been worked fruitlessly by Edward Norton, a man whose mania for gold made him a hermit, chained to that tunnel, until his death in 1922. The mountain was made chiefly of quartz and syenite, and not enough gold to make mining worthwhile.

To Audrey, the mountain's value was more spiritual — in the shelter it provided the town, in the sense of substance it lent to its community. She retired from teaching in 1988 and was Colebrook Academy's commencement speaker that year. "Some of you will leave after today for other parts of the world, and others will not," she said on that occasion. "The one thing shared by you all is that you grew up in the shadow of Monadnock, and no matter where you are, and no matter what happens to you, remember that Monadnock's arms are around you."

Those arms played some role, Audrey thought, in bringing Vickie home again. But then it was mostly John who made her stay. And the last time Audrey saw Vickie was on the evening of August 15, 1997. That was the birthday of Bunny's cousin Ellsworth Bunnell, a small, rotund man whose whole being had a twinkle to it, a self-taught pianist who had founded a swing-style dance band that once toured up and down the East Coast. Then he came back to Monadnock to become a local institution as a musician, composer, writer, historian, and general organizer of revels — such as the American Legion musicals, whose scores he often wrote himself. At Fred Harrigan's funeral, he had played, at John's request, a poignant rendition of "Harrigan, That's Me."

This time the town organized the revel. Ellsworth was turning eighty, and a party was arranged at the Balsams, located in neighboring Dixville Notch and one of the North Country's last luxury hotels. John's friend Paul Nugent ran a transportation company in Colebrook, and one of the more remarked on events of the evening was Paul's arrival in top hat and tails at the wheel of one of his limousines. In the backseat was an unexpected pairing — John Harrigan and Vickie Bunnell. As soon as they stepped out together, a rumor ran across the dance floor that this long-dormant volcano was about to throw off smoke again.

Later, outside the Balsams' Panorama Country Club and beneath the hotel's fairy-castle spires and turrets, with Monadnock bearing witness to the west, Vickie sat alone on a terrace with Audrey. Vickie was in her mother-earth colors: a light beige top and a tan silk skirt, set off by a pink brooch that would appear later in an oil portrait. They talked. Audrey came to understand that Vickie would love to be involved again with John, but she had a feeling he still wasn't ready to marry.

Nonetheless, she was happy. "All her relatives and friends were there, and they were happy for her," Audrey said. "And she was happy because she was with John, back in his arms, dancing."

5
THE REST
IS BLANK

MAYBE THIS WAS A PORTENT of the events of 1997, even if it happened in 1835: the arrest of a Canadian citizen by Sheriff Richard Blanchard for debts incurred in the store of one Luther Parker. Canadian authorities responded by arresting both Blanchard and Parker. This soon led to what was technically an armed invasion of Canada by the smaller of the two nations on its southern border, the Indian Stream Republic.

The citizens of this tiny nation had banded together in their common distrust of government authority. Because of where they lived, they had good reason. The Treaty of Paris — which in 1783 had divided the nascent United States from Canada — had set that boundary in this part of the North Country as "the northwestern-most head of the Connecticut River." But the devil was in the details, since as many as three different streams — Hall's, Indian, or Perry — could be construed as the headwater, resulting in three hundred square miles of territory claimed by both nations.

This area commenced just north of Colebrook, and as settlers there began to build a local industry in potash fertilizer, they found themselves liable for taxes and import duties to both the United States and Canada. Tensions came to a head in 1831 when two young men were conscripted into the Canadian military. The next year some sixty families declared their independence from both nations and established the Indian Stream Republic — ruled by an executive council, a general assembly, and an independent judiciary and featuring (according to legend) an enormous overturned potash kettle that served as the Republic's jail. Both New Hampshire and Lower Canada made political efforts to assert jurisdiction, but these were rebuffed, and internally the Indian Streamers governed themselves peacefully.

But the arrests of Blanchard and Parker — the latter was president of the Republic's executive council — provoked war, at least in a manner of speaking. An armed Indian Stream posse freed the prisoners just north of the Canadian border. Then the posse went on to Hereford to wage a street brawl and arrest the Canadian magistrate who had ordered the detentions. This official was carried back to Indian Stream but then quickly released. After several more skirmishes and amid rumors of an attack from Canada, New Hampshire governor William Badger dispatched a company of state militia into the Republic. They entered unopposed, and that spring the Republic passed resolutions ceding sovereignty to New Hampshire.

In 1842 the Webster-Ashburton Treaty recognized what had come to pass and defined the border as it exists today. British negotiator Lord Ashburton, opposite Daniel Webster, was of the opinion that the land had no economic value anyway — though within five decades Colebrook and Pittsburg would be flush with the bonanzas of their spring log drives, their flourishing potato and sheep farms, their luxury hotel–driven tourist industry.

The last log drive down the Connecticut was in 1915. Soon almost all the hotels went dark, and many of the tired farms were reclaimed by forest. But the border was still there, as was a local smuggling industry that antedated the Treaty of Paris and had facilitated the Underground Railroad, which ran through Colebrook and Pittsburg. During Prohibition, Colebrook was not only a conduit for liquor from Canada, but — thanks to its several stills — a productive source of domestic spirits. "Of course there was no such thing as 'aged liquor,'" wrote Doc Gifford in his history of Colebrook. "As soon as it cooled, it was bottled and shipped to Boston or the Balsams. If there was ever a question about the quality of a batch, it was tried on Hollis Sweatt, and if he survived, it went on the market."

Outdoorsmen like Rudy Shatney would later find where some of the fast cars used by rumrunners sat bullet-pocked and rusting up in the woods. "It was an era of excitement, as the trucks from Canada rumbled through town with the 'real stuff,' the police in hot pursuit," Gifford continued. "On one occasion, a load was 'ditched' in front of the Legion Restaurant and the bootleggers dashed through the dining room between startled diners and out through the kitchen with the law at their heels. Some of our citizens say that with the repeal of the 18th Amendment some of the 'zing' went out of the town, but those who are still in the know say, 'If 'tain't one thing it's another.'"

Whatever the thing, then and now, it owed — still owes — some part of its zing to the acts of secession and armed resistance that produced first the American republic and then the Indian Stream, not to mention that basic distrust of human nature that lurks deep in the country's Protestant roots. It followed from this that authority was to be particularly distrusted, held to constant scrutiny, and, if necessary, defied.

Among the New England states, New Hampshire was the fiercest in this suspicion and the most distinctive in its laissez-faire government and low tax burdens, the table thump of its "Live Free or Die" state slogan, the don't-tread-on-me chin thrust of the Old Man of the Mountain, the famous rock formation that overlooked Franconia Notch until 2003. Philosophically, Bunny and Irene Bunnell were quite comfortable in Vermont, but John Harrigan spoke for many of his neighbors when, looking at that state's more activist government and, only half in jest, he pronounced Vermont a foreign land.

In 2001 Jason Sorens — then a doctoral student at Yale, now a Dartmouth lecturer — founded the Free State Project. Mounted on behalf of "those of us who believe government in the U.S. is far too involved in our daily lives and far too removed from the control and influence of ordinary people," this was an initiative to gather enough libertarians from across the nation into one state and then to influence the politics of that state enough to reclaim such control. Two years later, after considering a number of states to target, the FSP chose New Hampshire. Sorens and his leadership liked not only the state's historically libertarian culture but also its religious diversity — that is, there were no dominant voting blocks of more authoritarian-minded Roman Catholics or evangelical Protestants. This helped to sustain a high level of social tolerance throughout the state, a tendency to let other people think or do what they liked.

They liked something else as well. Sorens cited the geography of New Hampshire — its small towns sprinkled among hills, mountains, and valleys — in helping to preserve its town meeting model of local government.

"The town meeting system allowed citizens to keep their government officials close enough to 'grab them by the scruff of their necks,' if they overstepped their power," Sorens wrote. "Essentially what developed was a kind of 'communal libertarianism' different from the individualism of the West, where one could simply escape the company of others."

The North Country, though, is that one portion of the state big enough and unpopulated enough where one indeed can "simply escape." Colebrook and other towns not only cultivate their own hermits, cranks, eccentrics, and obsessives — such as gold miner Edward Norton — but attract them from elsewhere as well. Arguably Dennis and Polly Joos arrived with a little bit of a kink that way. All such are generally left alone so long as complaints aren't lodged. And that culture of tolerance keeps the complaints to a minimum. It makes for a world where the "communal libertarianism" of southern New Hampshire is hybridized to a landscape where Clint Eastwood–style Strangers roam the hills. Sometimes the most suspicious of these clump together into twitchy-fingered militias.

This makes for its own sort of zing. There is much more territory than the various law enforcement agencies — state police, municipal police, Fish & Game, the Border Patrol — can effectively patrol, in the event of complaints or laws being broken: sixty miles of interstate, three thousand miles of state and local highways. The state police and Fish & Game are run from Concord, which can seem as distant as Washington, D.C., if you put a mountain range in the way. The Border Patrol — well, that would be Washington. The local police are supported by towns that have little or no tax base, or much inclination to tax anyway. These municipal forces are chronically understaffed, underpaid, undertrained, underequipped.

Mediating between the populace and those who enforce the laws are the people you see at town meetings — not politicians who come out only for news conferences, photo ops, or campaign rallies, but rather the grocers, schoolteachers, contractors, lawyers, shop owners, and so on, who volunteer — or get roped into — serving as selectmen: in other words, citizens who are at once the government officials *and* the ordinary people whom Sorens sets opposite each other. They know getting "grabbed by the scruff of the neck" comes with the territory, so to speak, especially given that the right of defiance is enshrined in Article 10 of the state constitution: "The doctrine of nonresistance against arbitrary power, and oppression, is absurd, slavish, and destructive of the good and happiness of mankind."

But somebody has to exercise power in defense of mankind's good and happiness — on out to that disputed border between just and arbitrary, between order and oppression. Somebody has to do it. And on which side of that line did the Eighteenth Amendment fall, anyway? Who deserved to be put under the potash kettle for that one? Well, that was Washington, though first a lobby of zealous Protestants, who were sure they knew what was best for us all.

What about a building permit for a barn?

John Harrigan sometimes had trouble describing just how out-there this part of the world was. He said that telling people Colebrook was ten miles from Canada "just doesn't cut it, so I try to put it into better perspective. The nearest traffic light from our doorstep is 57 miles. So are the nearest Burger King, Pizza Hut, and Walmart. This kind of information can bring startled looks in some quarters, and a sigh of envy in a hunting camp shared with people from away."

Outside the hunting camps, the merchants and municipalities are pretty much left to their own devices — those of an engaged citizenry — in respect to good and happiness, order or oppression. Strangers roam the hills. In certain respects, the Indian Stream Republic lives on.

Eighteen years passed between the tarpaper dispute in 1972 (accompanied by the death of Rita Drega) and the Columbia town hall incident in 1990.

The latter happened on a Tuesday night in April, after a winter in which starving deer had come to the roadsides to chew the new shoots off the spruce and tamaracks, and midway through Vickie Bunnell's first term as a Columbia selectman. When Vickie saw Carl Drega begin to rifle through the town's file cabinets that night, she decided it would be best if it were she — as the only woman present — who intervened.

Early that evening Drega had appeared a few minutes after the start of a regular selectmen's meeting, called to order by Kenneth Parkhurst. Bill Higgins was there as the third selectman, and also there, for a time, was the town's part-time treasurer. As board secretary, Vickie was writing a series of checks to be taken away by the treasurer. Drega parked his Dodge pickup in front of the small clapboard building on Route 3, stood gravely before the board, and said he wanted a copy of the minutes from the selectmen's February meeting.

"Okay — but we just started this meeting, and I haven't gotten into that file and pulled the minute books out yet, Carl," Vickie said. "And the copier's not warmed up. While we've got the treasurer here, we want to get some checks written. Can I get those minutes for you later and mail them to you? Would that be all right?"

Drega, glaring at Parkhurst, required a promise that he'd have the minutes within a week. Then he left. The years had only strengthened Carl Drega's conviction that zoning ordinances, and property tax assessments as well, were being unevenly applied in Columbia, that there was paperwork to prove this in the public record — if only he could find it, if only the guardians of that paperwork would provide it to him, as was their duty. Not wishing to leave this latest request to chance, Vickie finished her checks, excused the treasurer, and then made Parkhurst and Higgins wait while she located the February minutes, copied them, and put them in an envelope addressed to Drega.

Two hours later, Drega reappeared without explanation. Vickie handed him the minutes, and he read them as Parkhurst wrapped up the board's last bit of business and adjourned the meeting. "Okay, now I need some other minutes," Drega said.

"The meeting's over, Carl," Parkhurst said. "It's been a long day. We're going home."

Drega took a deep breath. "Well, I don't suppose you need to be in a formal meeting to provide a citizen with a public document, to respond to a legal request."

"No, the town clerk can help you too. She's here Monday and Wednesday, three to five — "

"Your wife."

"That's right, and by now you know Isabelle's hours better than we do, Carl, all the trouble you've given her."

Vickie held up her hand. "What other minutes, Carl?"

"That meeting from two years ago." Drega pulled a slip of paper out of his pocket and squinted at it. "February 3, 1988."

"Here we go," Higgins said.

"Carl," Vickie said. "You know I can't find minutes from two years ago at the drop of a hat. That was before my time, and I don't even know what kind of notebook they're in. I'll be happy to pull those minutes for you, once I find them, but I really can't do it right now. I can come back, though. We can set up a time."

"No, Vickie, that's not your job," Parkhurst said. "Isabelle can help the nice gentleman tomorrow afternoon."

At that, the die was cast. The chairman wanted Drega to come back for those minutes — and Drega wanted to grab Parkhurst by the scruff of the neck. When Drega dove into the file cabinets himself, initiating his own search through the length and breadth of the town's records, it was Vickie who threw herself like a terrier between him and the files. Had it been Parkhurst or even Higgins, there would have been fisticuffs — or worse. And when Drega went to another cabinet, Vickie interceded again, slamming the drawers shut and demanding he leave. When Drega refused, she called the Colebrook police.

Drega took a seat and was still seated when a Colebrook patrolman and two state troopers arrived ten minutes later. "I spoke with the woman that identified herself as BUNNELL," wrote Trooper Kathleen Grealy in her report. "She stated that they had just completed a meeting of the town selectmen, and wanted to leave the building, but the individual seated at the table would not leave. I confronted the man sitting at the table by telling him he would have to leave the property. He stated he would not leave until he received minutes from a town meeting that took place several years ago."

Grealy asked the selectmen if it was possible for Drega to obtain those minutes. "BUNNELL told me that they had already explained the situation to the individual, and had told him that he would have to make an appointment with the selectmen to discuss his request. Knowing that the individual was aware of his options, I again asked him to leave the premises. He again refused. I advised him that he was under arrest for Criminal Trespassing. DREGA was taken into custody and transported to Colebrook Police Department."

He was released that night, under his own recognizance, on three hundred dollars' bail. On his bail bond form, above his signature, he wrote: "I DO NOT UNDER STAND."

The other responding trooper was Les Lord. Drega refused Lord's offer of a ride back to town hall, where Drega's pickup was parked. Instead he walked the entire distance from Colebrook to Columbia, six miles, with the stars like bone chips overhead and the April rush of the Connecticut loud in his ears.

The trespass charges were later dropped. "It's not worth the trouble," Vickie told Parkhurst. "We got him out of there. Let's forget about it and move on."

Carl Drega's disputes came to involve others beside the Columbia town government. Eric Stohl remembers his sole visit to Drega's cabin by the river. In January 1991, Stohl parked his cruiser at the head of the driveway off Route 3. He hiked up to the bluff where the old gravel pit was and from there took a narrow footpath, between deep banks of snow, down to the barn and cabin. Inside the cabin, the lights were on and loud country-and-Western music was playing.

Stohl knocked on the door several times, received no answer. He tested the door and found it unlocked. He opened it slightly — "Carl?" Finally he opened the door and stepped inside the foyer — "Carl, are you here?"

Inside Stohl saw a space that was less a living area than a tidy workshop: a single chair, unfinished plywood floors, a table saw, a saw bench, a pair of sewing machines, some wooden benches. Drega's living quarters, in fact, were in the basement. Light on this floor came in only from the west, from the ice-bound river, since the windows facing east were boarded with plywood. Leaning against a wall near the door were a 12-gauge shotgun and a high-caliber bolt-action rifle. "Carl!"

Stohl nearly spun out of his boots when Drega spoke up behind him, "Where the hell are you going?"

Stohl took a breath to compose himself, explained that he had knocked and heard music. Drega received this without comment. "So what do you want to show me?" Stohl asked.

Drega turned and motioned him to follow. They went down another footpath to the river and then over the ice to a hole Drega had chopped. The hole had started to freeze over at the bottom, and both men bent to clear it. At its bottom a rock was visible beneath clear running water. Drega gestured to a post on the corner of his cabin. "I'd like you to come and measure the distance between this rock and that post."

They measured the distance — eighty feet. Drega produced from his hip pocket a rough overhead sketch of his cabin and the riverbank, with several rows of stone fringing the latter. He also had a handwritten document with a blank line at the bottom for a signature. "My permit lets me put riprap down here out to eighty feet, as far as this rock," Drega said, pointing to a rock on the sketch. "I'd like you to sign this statement, verifying that you saw this rock, and it's eighty feet, and the riprap stops here."

By then it had been five or six years since Stohl — floating down the river in spring as he released schools of young hatchery-raised trout into its waters — had come around a bend and noticed a new rampart of stone extending from the shoreline of the Drega property into the river. Stohl saw that the stones jutted out far enough to alter the course of the current and accelerate the rate of erosion on the opposite bank, which was Bernard Routhier's farmland.

Stohl had grown up on this river and loved how wild and pristine it remained here. He didn't think that the state Department of Environmental Services in Concord would approve someone dropping that much fill into the river, but when he checked, he found that DES had in fact granted Drega a permit to replace land washed away from his property during the breakup of an ice jam in 1981. Drega had put the stones in with help from Dan Ouimette, a local contractor, and Gerry Upton. Stohl advised Concord that this amount of fill far exceeded mere land replacement, and there the matter rested until 1990, when Drega filed an application to lay down more riprap. This was necessary, the application read, to make the bank completely stable.

As required, a public notice was circulated about the application, and Stohl was joined by Routhier and a Fish & Game biologist in raising objections to it. Stohl also provided Concord with aerial photographs of that bend of the river before and after the presence of the fill. Drega maintained that he had abided by what was specified in his permit, and his countermove was the affidavit that he wanted Stohl to sign that January day.

Stohl read the document and said, "I can see a rock there, Carl, but I don't know if it's the rock in your drawing, or if your fill goes out farther than this or not. There's no telling this time of year. I can't sign this."

They argued. They argued until they got cold feet and went back to the cabin. Stohl felt like he was trying to talk one of those rocks in the river into moving. And eventually, as Drega became more strident, the hair started to lift on the back of his neck. At last — mostly just to get out of there — Stohl signed a statement allowing that he had seen a stone eighty feet from a shoreline landmark, nothing more.

Theirs was not a friendly parting. Stohl walked that path through the snow back up the hill wondering if Drega had left it so narrow to prevent him from dodging, left or right, should Drega want to train the deer rifle on him. He allowed himself a long, easy breath once he cleared the crest of the bluff.

DES would go back and forth on the permit, first ordering Drega to remove all the riprap — a much more difficult procedure than installing it — then reinstating his permit ("Once Carl had gone down to Concord to pound his fist on their table," said Stohl), and finally revoking it again.

In 1994 Drega filed suit in the Colebrook District Court against Stohl, charging that the officer was carrying out a personal vendetta in "giving unsworn falsification to the N.H. Wetlands Board." Acting as his own attorney, Drega disputed Fish & Game's jurisdiction and swore to the rectitude of his work, but — when prompted by Judge Paul Desjardins — had no evidence or testimony about Stohl exceeding his duties or acting out of malice. Desjardins quickly dismissed the suit.

Drega was furious, but he had to remain at the courthouse that day for another proceeding. He had withheld half of Dan Ouimette's fee for work on the riprap and for some trenches Ouimette had dug, since he was dissatisfied with the work done by Ouimette's crew. Now the contractor was suing Drega for the balance. Drega would again act as his own counsel and lose that suit.

By the summer of 1997, the riprap — and a little more of it, in fact — was still in the river.

"Hey, Norman, want to meet Mr. Drega?" Vickie Bunnell said one afternoon in May 1993. She had appeared unexpectedly at the garage of Columbia excavator Norman Cloutier, now a fellow selectman. By then Kenneth Parkhurst was no longer on the board, and Vickie was into her second term. "Could be today's your lucky day."

"What's going on?" Cloutier asked. He didn't say so, but he had met Drega once before, back when Drega was casting around for help on his riprap project. Drega had hired Dan Ouimette instead, which was a good thing, Cloutier decided, given how that went for Dan, whom he knew to be a skilled excavator.

"I got a call at my office from Louis Jolin, the tax assessor," she said. "The poor guy's scared out of his wits, and I would be too. He's also on foot."

Vickie told Cloutier the story. Jolin, a careful and amiable man in his mid-sixties from Berlin — a man who had been doing tax assessments for Columbia for several years — was visiting all the properties in town, and the town had mailed notice of this to homeowners. That day Drega's place was on the docket. Jolin had parked his Jeep Cherokee at the top of the bluff overlooking the cabin, the great barn, the several outbuildings, the neat lawn with its stony beachhead, and had taken the footpath down to the buildings. He found Drega working outside and tried — mostly in vain — to engage him in conversation. Finally Jolin shrugged his shoulders and set about measuring a storage wing, with neat board-and-batten siding, that Drega had recently added to the barn. One side of the addition was against the hillside and choked by brush, so Jolin went inside the barn to take that measurement.

When he came out, he found Drega angry that he had entered the building without permission. "I would've asked, but he didn't seem in the mood for small talk," Jolin had told Vickie. "And he was standing right there. He could've stopped me." Then Drega demanded to see Jolin's clipboard and to know exactly what the addition was going to cost him in taxes. He claimed to have been taxed the previous year for a fireplace he didn't have.

At last Jolin fled up the hill to his vehicle. When he started the Jeep, he saw Drega planted at his rear bumper like a hitching post, preventing him from backing up. "If you won't move out of the way, sir," Jolin said, "I'll have to go get help."

"Help?" Drega tugged thoughtfully at the chinstrap beard he had recently grown. "You got any help in mind?"

"I'm here for the selectmen today. I know Ms. Bunnell is in her office. She's a lawyer."

"A lawyer, huh?" Drega gave a low whistle. "You're not just trying to scare me, are you?"

Jolin shook his head. "I just mean she could help you with some of your questions."

Drega seemed to nod slowly. "I bet she could. I bet she won't. But that's okay — you go tell Vickie Bunnell to get her fucking ass down here."

With that, Jolin abandoned the Jeep, sprinted for the driveway gate, and called Vickie from the T&T Mobile Home Park on the opposite side of Route 3. "So I'm going to pick Mr. Jolin up at that park, and then help him get his car," Vickie explained to Cloutier. "It could be ticklish. Want to come along?"

Cloutier had acquired a customer in the meantime, and he ended up following a few minutes behind. Vickie parked in the trailer park and walked with an apprehensive Jolin back through Drega's gate and up to the bluff. "He's gruff and occasionally nasty," Vickie told him. "But his bark is worse than his bite."

There was no sign of Drega around the Jeep, but they found railroad ties placed as chocks behind its rear tires. As Vickie bent to remove one tie and as Jolin unlocked the driver-side door, a gunshot rang out behind them.

"Drega fired a shot and hollered something about what did we think we were doing," Vickie wrote in her report of the incident. "By that time he had come up behind the Jeep, clutching a rifle with a pistol on his hip, faced me and demanded that I get my 'fucking hands off [his] property.'"

Jolin wrote, "I looked up to see Mr. Draga [*sic*] approaching towards us with a rifle leveled towards her and I and a pistol in a holster. Ms. Bunnell attempted to reason with him and let me drive my vehicle off his property. He then brought up some past town business using some abusive language."

After a dose of that, Drega clapped the stock of his rifle, a .30-06, and dared Vickie to touch the second tie. That was when Cloutier came up the rise, seeing what he thought at first was Drega out hunting varmints. He soon understood otherwise, but stood with Vickie and Jolin while Drega renewed his demands for Jolin's paperwork. When Cloutier joined in the argument, he "was ordered off the property [by Drega, who was] holding his rifle in crossward position and very close to Mr. Cloutier," wrote Jolin.

All three turned to retrace their steps. "Well, we'll just have to go up another avenue," Vickie said, once they were out of earshot from Drega. She sounded calm, but later her friend David King — the lawyer who had taken her place in the Waystack practice — would say that she left the property no less terrified than Jolin.

Half an hour later three state troopers walked up Drega's driveway in a row across its breadth. Their cruisers were at the driveway's locked gate, and they saw that a tractor had been parked behind Jolin's Jeep. They walked in a row so that if they were fired upon, Detective Howie Weber could return fire while Troopers Scott Stepanian and Tom Yorke took cover. They wore no body armor and carried only sidearms.

"Procedures were a little different back then," Weber said later. "You didn't necessarily call in a SWAT team the first thing whenever a situation like this arose."

At the top of the bluff the driveway angled right, took a wide sweeping turn toward the river, and was bordered on either side by a low wall as it neared the barn. They saw the owner on his knees laying rock into an unfinished portion of the wall. The troopers halted and called out to him. "He heard us, but he didn't look up," Weber said. "He just kept building that wall."

The troopers advanced and called a second time. This time Drega looked up, laid a stone aside, rose, and walked slowly into the barn. He still wore a pistol on his hip, and he came out of the barn with the .30-06, now equipped with a scope and sling. The troopers stopped about a hundred feet away. Scott Stepanian knew Drega a little bit, had been leading an investigation of some firearms burglarized from Drega's cabin. Weber let the even-keeled Stepanian do the talking.

It was mostly a one-sided conversation. A sphinxlike Drega offered no response to a request to lay his weapons on the ground. Eventually Stepanian wondered if he might at least sling the rifle on his back. Drega simply stood with the rifle pointed off into the brush but capable of being raised much faster than a trooper could draw a pistol. Stepanian kept talking, and Drega asked why he had once gotten arrested for trespass at the town hall, a public building, while a trespasser on his land gets police protection. After fifteen minutes, long enough for each trooper to sweat through his shirt, Drega lowered his rifle and — per Stepanian's latest suggestion — went to stow his weapons in the cabin.

Drega came out and submitted to a patdown by Stepanian while being read his Miranda rights. "In those days we didn't always handcuff suspects," Weber said. "So we may not have. I think we felt we had secured his cooperation."

Drega went in Stepanian's cruiser to the Colebrook Police Department, where he was charged with reckless conduct and remanded to the county jail. In a 1995 handwritten statement to the Coös County Superior Court, Drega would write in his all-capital script, which conveyed the effect of shouting: "I WAS ARRESTED FOR RECKLESS CONDUCT ON MAY 19-93 THERE WAS NO BAIL, IN COLDBROOK DISTRICT COURT I ENTER MY PLEA OF INNOCENT THE NEXT THING I KNOW THERE IS 1,500 CASH BAIL PUT ON TO ME. THAT WAS NOT A BAIL HEARING, I DID NOT HAVE 1,500 CASH ON ME (JUDGE?) MILLER HE SAID THAT HE IS GOING TO BE SURE THAT I WILL BE IN COURT. I OWE PROPERTY IN COLUMBIA FOR 25 YEARS, I OWE PROPERTY IN BOW, I AM A UNION TRADESMAN IN GOOD STANDING FOR 30 YEARS MILLER PUTS IT THAT I AM A WALKER! I REQUEST THE STATE POLICE TO TAKE ME TO MY RESIDENCE IN COLUMBIA I MAY HAVE 1,500 THERE NO F — K WAY WRIGHT TO THE COUNTY FARM."

From the jail Drega, who kept most of his money in cash hidden at his cabin, called Gerry Upton in Vermont, asking him to wire the bail money. "I'll pay you right back."

Upton said he had once wired money to his son in California, and the transfer had cost him eighty dollars. "So I'll just bring it up, Carl. I'll drive up there now."

"No, hell — that's all right. I'll just stay here. See how the food is."

"No, thanks. I'm on my way. Margaret'll come."

A staff member at the jail would later tell the *Maine Sunday Telegram* that he heard Drega shouting in his cell while waiting for Upton: "He kept yelling, 'Live free or die — bullshit! Or, 'Live free or die. Hah!' Then he'd go off into a spin [criticizing] tax collectors."

Late that night, Drega made the Uptons wait outside his cabin. "Margaret never went into Carl's house for as long as we knew him," Upton said. "He didn't think his housekeeping was clean enough for her." Drega appeared in a few minutes with fifteen hundred-dollar bills.

In the aftermath, Drega denied that he had ever pointed his rifle at anybody. Vickie and Jolin both swore that he did. In New Hampshire, reckless conduct was just a misdemeanor, but nonetheless Drega paid several thousand dollars to retain one of the state's prominent criminal defense lawyers. Then it never came to trial. All parties agreed that the charge would be dismissed after twelve months of good behavior; also that Drega would have access to town records during that time and be able to attend selectmen's meetings on notifying a town official in advance and if accompanied by a law officer. Drega abided by those terms, and at last the case was dismissed.

A year later, in August 1995, Drega filed another civil suit in the Coös County Superior Court, this one against Vickie Bunnell, Louis Jolin, and the Town of Columbia. Drega's writ of summons alleged that "SELECTPERSON VICK BUNNELL VIOLATED THE RIGHT TO KNOW LAW RSA 91:4-5-6. FORGED TOWN RECORDS RSA 641:2 CRIMINAL TRESPASS RSA 635:2. GAVE FALES SWORN STATEMENT RSA 641:2 SELECTIVE INFORCEMENT OF TOWN ZONING." Similarly, Jolin was accused of violating the right-to-know law, of committing both criminal trespass and unauthorized entry, and of giving false testimony.

Drega once again represented himself, appearing in a mechanic's jump-suit and aviator's sunglasses. The hearing got off to a fractious start when Drega refused to rise for the entrance of Judge Harold W. Perkins and then scuffled with Sheriff John Morton, who tried to help him rise. Drega delivered a seventy-four-page statement to the court, this containing his complaints about the bail process attached to his arrest and much else besides. In fact it was an encyclopedic review of all his grievances back to 1972, beginning with the barn siding and Rita's death, now including the dismissal of his suit against Dan Ouimette.

During the hearing, Drega meandered through these affronts and again failed to present evidence to support his testimony. Perkins had to warn him several times about swearing. The defendants' attorneys — Phil Waystack and David King — urged that the suit be dismissed, and Perkins obliged.

After the hearing, which took place at the Lancaster courthouse, Waystack saw Drega standing on the steps outside. Waystack asked Morton to come help "if this guy starts kicking my ass," and then walked up to the plaintiff.

"Mr. Drega, I was very sorry to read about the death of your wife," he said. "Those were very unfortunate circumstances. But you know, Vickie Bunnell was just a kid in high school when that happened. She's not anyone you should be angry with about that."

Drega bowed his head, turned away, and removed his sunglasses. When he turned back, Waystack saw that his pinched brown eyes and sunburned face were clouded with emotion. "No one ever said that to me before," he said. "About my wife, I mean."

For whatever reason, Drega had never mentioned his polygraph test to Perkins. Before the hearing, he had gone to Concord and had personally arranged to take such a test on the issue of whether he had pointed his rifle at anybody on the day he drove Jolin off his property.

Maybe it came down to what the definition of "point" might be. Examiner George E. Tetrault told the *New Hampshire Sunday News* that he concluded Drega was being truthful. "He was one of the most interesting people I've met in my 24 years in the business," Tetrault said. "I've done thousands of tests, but I've never had a person who could see right through you. He had an intensity I've never seen before."

Carl Drega carried on a busy correspondence with state government officials, one that increased in frequency and intensity during the mid-'90s. At some point, Drega began adding the title "A Sovereign Citizen" to his signature on letters.

Item: In September 1994, Drega mailed the seventy-four-page summation of his complaints — the same document he would later submit to Judge Perkins in August 1995 — to New Hampshire attorney general Jeffrey R. Howard. "All I want to accomplish," wrote Drega, as his cover letter was later rendered in the *Union Leader*, "is to get town officials in Columbia to treat everyone equally, not to play favorites, whether it be when they assess property taxes or enforce town ordinances." He later set down in his own records that he never got a reply from Howard.

Item: On February 7, 1995, the New Hampshire Supreme Court informed Drega that it would not consider his appeal of Judge Desjardin's ruling against him in the suit filed by Dan Ouimette. A week later Drega wrote to U.S. State Attorney Paul M. Gagnon, complaining that he had yet to receive the transcript of the Ouimette proceedings, for which he had paid $326 in August. Drega set down that he never heard back from Gagnon.

Item: On March 15, 1995, Drega wrote Governor Steve Merrill and the state executive council, complaining about the appointment of Vickie Bunnell as a special judge to the Colebrook District Court. Drega enclosed his seventy-four-page catalogue of grievances. As reported by the *Union Leader*, Drega's cover letter about Vickie "alleged she had denied him public records, selectively enforced the zoning ordinance against him, trespassed on his property, and lied in an attempt to get him jailed."

Item: On May 3, 1995, David S. Peck, executive secretary of the Supreme Court's Judicial Conduct Committee, wrote Drega to inform him that the committee had dismissed the complaint he had filed against Judge Desjardins. In a note on that letter Drega wrote, "I TAKE IT THAT THE JUDICIAL COMMITTEE DO NOT FEEL THAT I AM INTITLED TO A TRANSCRIPT THAT HAS BEN PAID FOR OVER 9 MOS."

Item: On July 11, 1995, Nina C. Gardner, executive director of the state judicial council, wrote Drega to suggest that he resubmit his transcript request to the Colebrook District Court and to request a refund for his original request.

Item: On July 17, 1995, Drega wrote again to Merrill and the executive council, demanding why they had not responded to the packet he had sent in March or interceded on his transcript request. "WHO BETTER THAN THE GOVERNOR + COUNCIL + DESJARDIN TO DENY A MAN WHAT HE HAS PAID FOR," Drega wrote.

Item: On July 31, 1995, Tina L. Nadeau, legal counsel to the governor, wrote Drega to say that the governor and council must "remain independent and separate from the judicial branch" and could not intervene in any case before the court. She suggested he hire a lawyer. Drega responded, "THE GOVERNOR IS TO SEE THAT ALL THE STATE'S LAWS BE INFORCE, THAT IS WHY HE IS CALL HIS EXCELLENCY."

Item: On August 9, 1995, Phil Waystack, acting as legal counsel for the Town of Columbia, wrote Drega to say that the transcript he wanted had never been typed, since the Supreme Court had declined to review the case. He added that the Colebrook District Court had sent him a refund check in March, "but apparently you have not negotiated it." He also suggested that Drega return the refund check and renew his request for the transcript, and it would then be typed and made available. On November 3, David S. Peck wrote Drega with the same advice.

Item: On November 13, 1995, Drega renewed that request in a letter to Jan Corliss, clerk of the Colebrook District Court. Three months later, on February 8, 1996, Corliss wrote to inform Drega that the transcript was ready and could be picked up on any Thursday or Friday. Drega wrote on that letter, "I RECEIVE THE TRANSCRIPT ON APRIL 4, 96. IT TOOK ONLY ONE YEAR + HALF TO RECEIVE THIS TRANSCRIPT."

Item: On May 13, 1995, New Hampshire representative William H. Zeliff wrote that he had forwarded Drega's packet of grievances to the attorney general's office. "I feel confident," said Zeliff, "that Attorney General Jeffrey Howard and his staff will be able to help you."

Item: Also on May 13, Drega's packet was delivered to the Berlin office of Senator Bob Smith. Drega's notes indicate that he never received a reply.

Item: On May 14, 1995, New Hampshire representative Charles F. Bass acknowledged receipt of Drega's information. Bass replied that he had no jurisdiction in such matters and had forwarded the material to the attorney general's office.

Item: On May 17, 1995, Joel Maiola, Senator Judd Gregg's chief of staff, wrote that Drega's dispute with Columbia was a matter "to be decided in the courts." He returned Drega's material and advised him to "seek the advice of an attorney."

Item: On September 18, 1996, Executive Councilor Raymond S. Burton wrote regarding the packet he had received three months earlier. "It appears to me that your avenue for relief and justice is through the judicial branch," Burton said, suggesting he telephone Chief Justice David Brock. This completed the circle that began with the rejection by Brock and the Supreme Court of Drega's appeal of the Ouimette ruling.

Item: On January 13, 1997, Drega nonetheless called Brock's office. "AS OF 2/2/97 I HAVE YET TO RECEIVE A REPLY," Drega noted.

John Begin (rhymes with "region") was still in his twenties in April 1996. A native of Manchester in southern New Hampshire, husky and good-natured, he was fresh out of the Police Academy and posted for just a month to the North Country, where Scott Phillips served as his field training officer.

"You have to deal with people differently up here," Phillips had told him. "Whenever you talk to someone, make sure you're talking *to* them, not over them. And if you go into someone's house, take off your hat. Walk in there like you're just anybody else. If you walk around in that uniform puffing up your chest, things won't go well up here."

Begin had done traffic stops with Phillips, as well as Les Lord, and had seen firsthand how well things could go. Officer and driver would greet each other on a first-name basis, complain about the weather, inquire after the family. Then the violation would be mentioned, the warning issued, or a ticket written. All parties would take it in stride and get on with the day. With these guys, even arrests were usually handled without rancor. The exception that proved the rule would have been Carl Drega's arrest.

On April 4, Begin and Phillips were filling out reports at the Colebrook Police Department when District Court clerk Jan Corliss phoned from upstairs. She said Mr. Drega had come in asking for paperwork that she didn't have and had become abusive — she was still shaking. She also had heard from the courthouse in Lancaster that Drega had been down there to obtain the home addresses and tax assessment records of Judge Desjardins, Judge Perkins, and the just-appointed judge Vickie Bunnell; attorneys Phil Waystack and David King; Fish & Game officer Eric Stohl; and Troopers Stepanian, Yorke, and Phillips. Corliss added that there was an outstanding warrant for Drega's arrest, and he had just left the building.

"Come on, John," Phillips said. "Time to get your hands dirty."

The arrest warrant was the latest escalation in Drega's battle with Dan Ouimette. Drega had become enraged when one of Ouimette's workers went into his barn without permission, and had then micromanaged every aspect of Ouimette's work on the riprap and on trenches for electrical lines and drainage. Nothing was good enough. Finally Drega asked Gerry Upton to redo some of that work and refused to pay the balance on Ouimette's bill. When the easygoing contractor came to Drega's place to personally ask for the money, Drega said, "Sure, I'll pay you," all the while stabbing the ground near Ouimette's shoes with the tines of a pitchfork.

That led to Ouimette's small-claims civil suit and a court order for Drega to pay up, but he never did. In 1995 Drega failed to answer a court summons from the Coös County sheriff, John Morton, and a warrant was issued — and back-burnered — for the arrest of a man who was often working out of state and rarely seen.

On this day, Phillips spotted Drega's orange pickup in the parking lot of Prescott Farms, a small grocery store on Main Street at the north end of town. "Look at that thing," Begin said, staring at the truck. "It's almost an antique."

"It wouldn't pass inspection," admitted Phillips. "It wouldn't even move the dial. I've given him warnings on that. So have a lot of guys — and still no sticker. Imagine our surprise."

Phillips said that Drega was set on a hair trigger and went almost everywhere these days with a 9 mm pistol. "So let's just wait for him to come out of the store." Begin noted the arrival of another state police cruiser in the parking lot: inside were Scott Stepanian and Border Patrol agent Paul Dunbar.

Begin was unimpressed when he saw their quarry: a somewhat elderly-looking man of medium build, a gray-bearded farmer type, carrying a bag of groceries. Phillips flipped on his blue lights and they got out of the cruiser. "Excuse me, Carl," Phillips said. "Hi, there — are you aware there's an arrest warrant out for you?"

Drega hesitated, but only briefly. He glanced at Phillips, then at Begin, and was in motion again as he did so, bearing for his pickup. "Carl, did you hear me?" Phillips said. "It's our responsibility to place you under arrest. We'll thank you for your cooperation."

Drega halted only when Phillips grabbed Drega's right arm and Begin his left. By then Stepanian and Dunbar were out of their cruiser as well. "Warrant?" Drega said. "Let me see your goddamn warrant."

"You're under arrest for violation of a court order, Carl," Scott said. "You failed to appear — that was last June — and that's a problem."

"Yeah? Let me see the warrant."

"The warrant is at the station. We'll show you the warrant. We'll make you a copy."

"So you don't even have the warrant?"

"We don't need to have the warrant to make an arrest, Carl. But we'll bring you to where you can see it. How's that?"

"I don't think there is any fucking warrant. Warrant for what?"

"Failure to appear. They expected you in court."

"When? For what?"

"Last June. A civil case. It's on the warrant, Carl."

"And you're just now getting around to it? What a crock of shit. This is really a warrant for asking for those papers at the courthouse — right?"

"I don't know what papers, Carl."

"You wouldn't, you lying piece of shit. You can bring me that fucking warrant at home. That's where I'm going."

"John, let's cuff him."

The groceries had been dropped to the pavement, and Drega's arms had no more bend to them than two-by-fours. Begin was amazed by the man's strength. It took all four officers to pull his wrists behind his back and attach Begin's cuffs. Phillips told Begin to double-lock the cuffs but to make sure they weren't too tight.

Once in handcuffs, Drega went stone silent. Another trooper, Sergeant John Scarinza, had arrived by then. Scarinza dispersed the small crowd that had gathered while Begin conducted a patdown that yielded a canister of pepper spray in a coat pocket, but no handgun. Meanwhile Stepanian gathered the groceries and placed them in the bed of the pickup.

They put Drega into the front seat of Phillips's cruiser, where he slouched in such a manner as to make fastening his seatbelt a wrestling match for Begin. At the Colebrook station, Phillips talked privately with the rookie about whether to charge Drega with resisting arrest. "Well, he didn't cooperate, but he didn't resist in what you'd call an active manner either," Phillips said. "So I don't think it really rose to that level. That would just add insult to injury. Let's let it go."

In filling out the arrest report, Begin met with more passive resistance. Drega refused to answer even the most innocuous questions — name? address? occupation? — responding only with a toxic stare that felt to Begin like it was hollowing its way through him. Finally Phillips put Drega on the phone with Judge Paul Donovan in Lancaster. Donovan set bail at $250 and told Drega it couldn't be posted until the arrest report was complete.

Drega had the cash in his pocket. He answered Begin's questions and was out the door with his pepper spray, striding purposefully past the News and Sentinel, cutting through the old Getty station and up Main Street, within an hour after his arrest.

Before joining the state police, Begin had worked four years as a beat cop in some tough neighborhoods in Manchester. He had dealt with angry people, some of them high or simply crazy, but he had never seen anyone like Drega. "Carl didn't like me because I was a cop, but he hated Scott in a whole different way," he said. "It was personal. It was like he blamed Scott for everything, the civil suit and this whole deal, even though it was me who actually made the arrest, and it wasn't as if this was a major offense. It was an hour out of the guy's life, and we're just cops doing our jobs. But there was something really cold in the way Carl looked at Scott, a different quality of animosity. You had a feeling this guy was capable of anything."

A second hearing on Drega's failure to pay Ouimette was scheduled for June 27. Drega attended, but he didn't pay. On July 19, a lien was placed on his property, and the debt was paid a week later. Drega then filed a civil suit against the estate of John Morton, the Coös County sheriff, who had recently died, alleging that Morton had known he was working in Vermont the previous June and would be unable to attend the original hearing.

Mark Pappas was glad to know there was at least one person in the building interested in his gun.

In February 1997 — a few days before Vickie Bunnell would knock on Eric Stohl's door in Columbia and ask to borrow Eric's Smith & Wesson .38 — Pappas was carrying an unloaded Colt AR-15 assault rifle up and down the aisles of a gun show at the Shriners Auditorium in Wilmington, Massachusetts. He was standing in front of the Bushmaster manufacturer's booth, and the rep there had just said, no, he wasn't interested in the rifle, when a tall, bearded man — someone whom Pappas would remember as a "gray-haired wrinkled old man, a guy who looked like someone's grandfather" — had come up behind him and said he might take a look.

"This made by Colt?" the man asked.

"Made by Colt," said Pappas.

"You sure about that?"

Pappas said he was, that he had bought it used three years before from Roach's Sporting Goods in Cambridge. Pappas was twenty-eight years old, working at a family-owned pizzeria in Brookline, Massachusetts, and part of a circle of friends who were fishermen and recreational shooters.

The man took the rifle, absorbed its weight, and cracked it open to see how clean it was. Pappas watched the way he handled it. He judged that this was a guy who knew his way around this stuff. Around them stretched ranks of folding tables, milling people, and a multitude of rifles laid side by side in rows like fence posts. Most were assault weapons like this.

"Why you selling it?"

"I just don't use it anymore," Pappas said. "Somebody gave me a new gun for a present, and that's what I use now. This has been under my bed for two months."

Pappas had first brought the gun back to Roach's and then to several other gun stores. He wanted a thousand dollars for it, but the most any of the stores would offer was two hundred. Then a friend told him he could get better money at a gun show.

"Is it pre-ban?"

"Yep — I can guarantee it. I got the bill of sale right here."

In 1994 Congress had passed the Violent Crime Control and Law Enforcement Act, which had made illegal the possession of a gun like this — namely, a semiautomatic rifle with a detachable magazine (allowing the option of high-capacity ammo clips) and two or more additional features. These might include a folding stock, a pistol grip, a bayonet mount, a flash suppressor, or fittings for a grenade launcher. The law, however, was toothless. Assault rifles manufactured before 1994, regardless of their features, were exempt from the ban and could still be bought, sold, and possessed. Pappas's gun came with a detachable magazine, a folding stock, and a pistol grip.

"I'd like to change the scope attachment, do some other things. Can it take Bushmaster parts?"

"Hmm — I don't know." Pappas gestured to the Bushmaster rep only a few feet away. "You could ask him. He could tell you."

The bearded man flicked only a glance in that direction. "So how much you want?"

"I don't know. I guess I'd take eight hundred."

The guy had eyebrows, Pappas saw, that pitched teepees over both eyes. These elevated and descended as the man looked up and handed the gun back. "Well, I guess that's pretty high. Thanks anyway."

Pappas let him walk away, but he resolved to keep track of him. If the guy stuck around and if Pappas couldn't get eight hundred from somebody else, he'd catch him before the end of the show and see what happened then.

The AR-15 is sometimes described as a clone of the U.S. military's M16 combat rifle, but it's more accurate to say that the M16 is a clone of the AR-15. Research conducted by the U.S. Army after the Korean War revealed that most rifle hits on enemy soldiers were made at relatively short range (within three hundred meters) and largely at random. What the army needed, then, was not a rifle firing a single large bullet, like the venerable M1, but rather a lighter, smaller rifle that could fire multiple small-caliber, high-velocity bullets — bullets light enough to be carried in large quantities but fast enough to penetrate body armor or a steel helmet at five hundred meters. In 1957 the army asked the ArmaLite Division of the Fairchild Aircraft Corporation to design such a rifle. ArmaLite engineer Eugene Stoner, a former marine and a small-arms expert, produced the AR-15. At the same time Remington produced a new bullet — a .223-caliber projectile — tailored to Stoner's gun.

At five and a half pounds, the weapon delivered to the army for testing was two pounds lighter than anything else under consideration. It was also accurate at both close quarters and its maximum range of six hundred meters, comfortable to shoot thanks to its light recoil, and flexible — a Swiss Army knife of a weapon accommodating a wide variety of barrel lengths, trigger units, butt stocks, and attachments. The gun performed impressively in testing, but a combination of military politics and ham-handed outside tinkering with its design delayed its adoption. By 1959 Fairchild had sunk $1.45 million into the gun's development and was looking to get out of the small-arms business. So it sold production rights to Colt for $75,000 and a small royalty on subsequent sales.

Finally, in 1961, a thousand AR-15s were issued to South Vietnamese troops and their Special Operations advisers. Their battlefield reports so lavishly praised the rifle that within two years the AR-15, rechristened the M16, was standard-issue in all branches of the military. There were losses — jammed guns, dead soldiers — as the military learned how to maintain the weapon, but by 1968 the M16 was an American soldier's best friend. In fully automatic mode it can dispense hellfire at 850 rounds per minute. In semiautomatic, it can shoot nearly as fast as a vintage machine gun, but with much more accuracy. And because photographs of enemy soldiers killed or maimed by M16 fire remained classified for two decades, only GIs in the field knew about the devastating wounds that it inflicted and its brutally efficient kill rate. This was thanks to a bullet that not only tumbles as it penetrates steel and flesh but fragments as well, cutting starburst swaths through muscles and organs.

Nearly half a century later the M16 remains the rifle of choice for the U.S. military and for militaries around the world. A similar if simpler gun, the Kalashnikov AK-47, is still held to be more reliable under harsh conditions, but in other respects the more powerful M16 has to be counted the deadliest handheld weapon ever devised. Stoner's gun is now made by at least a dozen large companies besides Colt, and one civilian who knows how to use an AR-15 could hold off a platoon of Korean War GIs. The gun's .223 "varmint" bullets would crack their helmets like eggshells.

At the end of the day, Pappas still hadn't found anyone willing to pay eight hundred dollars for his gun. But the old guy was still hanging around, empty-handed, and had wandered back to the Bushmaster booth. Pappas waved and went over to him. "What do you think?" he said. "You still interested? You want to make an offer on this?"

They haggled and finally agreed on a price of $575. Pappas took the man's license and wrote out the bill of sale, two copies. "So the name's Drega?" Pappas said, as if it rhymed with "Vega."

"Drega," the man corrected him, pronouncing it with a long "e." "And be sure you write 'pre-ban' on my copy of the bill."

Pappas wasn't sure if that was appropriate, and he wondered if this sale had to be entered into a registry somewhere. The old man became agitated at that point, but Pappas didn't want to run afoul of any gun laws. "Calm down," he said. "Let me just ask this Bushmaster guy about it, okay?"

The rep said it would be legal to specify pre-ban on the bill of sale. "And no, you don't need to do any government paperwork on this," he said. "That's just for handguns. It doesn't cover rifles, so long as they're pre-ban."

They signed their respective copies. Pappas passed the weapon to its new owner, along with a nylon carrying bag and some extra magazines, and the old man pulled the purchase money in cash out of his pocket. Pappas's last glimpse of him was with the rifle already stripped down and its parts spread across the table at the Bushmaster booth.

Among his siblings, Carl Drega was closest to his brother Frank and sister Sophia. By 1997 Frank had retired and left Connecticut for Florida. They spoke regularly on the phone, but Carl had to abide by a rule Frank had laid down: no talk about his personal affairs in Columbia — it got them both too upset.

Drega could be more candid with Sophia Linnane, who still lived near New Haven. In January 1997, before starting a job at the Pilgrim Nuclear Power Station in Massachusetts, Drega went to Connecticut for Sophie's birthday. He told her then that the state police had him under twenty-four-hour surveillance in Columbia, that when he drove home he tried to arrive at two or three in the morning to best elude that surveillance.

In July, on his way back from a job in Detroit, Drega stopped at Sophie's and told her that the state police were now out to kill him. Well, Carl needed to get away from there and unwind, she thought, and they made plans to visit Frank together in the fall. Around that time Drega mentioned to his girlfriend — a woman in Colebrook with whom he maintained a long and very discreet relationship — that Scott Phillips had threatened him. Drega claimed that Phillips had told him to sell everything and leave town before it was too late.

That same month, Drega visited Dr. Bob Soucy in Colebrook for treatment of a sinus problem. Drega was a new patient, and Soucy was surprised when Drega asked, "Do you know who I am?"

"Well, I suppose not," said Soucy.

"It's just that I've got a history here in town," said Drega, who by then had allowed his chinstrap whiskers to spread into a full salt-and-pepper beard. In fact, outside of Columbia town government and some, if not all, in law enforcement, few people in the area knew who he was. Unbidden, Drega launched into a history of his mistreatment at the hands of the Columbia selectmen.

"So do you hold a grudge?" asked Soucy.

Drega nodded and chose understatement. "Kind of. I suppose I do."

"Do you have any problems with the police?"

Drega smiled and said, "No, I have a plan for the police."

Soucy himself did contract work for the police and acted as coroner in incidents of violent death. He knew about a few individuals in town who were on the police watch list, but the list didn't include any Carl Drega. And this man made good eye contact and seemed generally calm and reasonable. Soucy got on with the examination and forgot about their conversation until later.

By then it had been a month since several near neighbors in Vermont — the farmer Bernard Routhier, and also Lance Walling, the manager of La-Perle's IGA supermarket in Colebrook, and Amos Colby, the sheriff of Vermont's Essex County — had noticed all-day reports of gunfire from the Drega property during times when he was home. And it had been six months since Drega had begun occasionally pulling up outside Vickie Bunnell's office in the News and Sentinel Building and staring at her through her office window. The February night that Vickie had appeared on the doorstep of Eric Stohl, begging to borrow a handgun, had been after the first such instance.

On the afternoon of Friday, August 15 — the same day that John Harrigan and Vickie would arrive at the Balsams' together for Ellsworth Bunnell's birthday party — Drega happened to meet Vickie by chance on a Main Street sidewalk. Bystanders reported that he swore and vowed to "get even with her" as Vickie turned scarlet and hastened away.

On Saturday, Drega called Sophie to talk more about the Florida trip.

It seemed to Sophie that her brother was more than usually upset about something, but if so, he didn't want to talk about it.

In his cabin, near the sewing machines that he used to repair his own clothes, Drega kept a calendar upon which he recorded his daily activities. The last entry, on Saturday, the sixteenth, was "PAINT ROOF ON BARN CUT SOME LAWN."

The rest is blank.

THE
REASONS
OF THE
HEART

IN 1869 A PIECE OF LEGISLATION ENTITLED "An Act to Create a State Police in Certain Cases" came before New Hampshire governor Onslow Stearns. At that time many local police departments were choosing not to enforce antidrinking laws, and this new agency was conceived primarily to remedy that. But too many New Hampshire voters feared that state police would also be used in a strike-busting capacity against labor unions, and the act failed to achieve the approval of the necessary two-thirds of male voters.

Attitudes changed in the wake of the Eighteenth Amendment and the federal enforcement of antidrinking laws. The violence of that era raised public fears of crime, while the 1933 repeal of Prohibition pretty well loosened up the antidrinking laws. In the meantime the automobile and improved roads had made it harder for local police to apprehend fugitives within their jurisdictions. The increased fluidity of New Hampshire society also argued for a single agency to keep records, statistics, and fingerprints and to carry out statewide pursuits and investigations.

So it was that in 1937 "An Act Creating a Department of State Police" was signed into New Hampshire law, authorizing an original cadre of forty-eight state troopers. These were issued .38 revolvers that they shared with the National Guard. They were told to get the telephone numbers of gas stations along their patrol routes so that station attendants could put flags on their pumps whenever headquarters wanted to contact a trooper. Bunny remembers the flag that used to fly regularly at Nugent's gas station on Main Street before World War II.

In 1997 there were about four hundred state troopers in New Hampshire. The pay wasn't anything special — "A few years ago there were twelve local police departments that paid better than the state police," said Jeff Caulder, a trooper who attended the New Hampshire State Police Academy in Concord with both Scott Phillips and Scott Stepanian — and the benefits only slightly better. But there was more variety than with municipal work: murder cases, speed chases, VIP security, and so on. And there were special units that did particularly adrenaline-charged work: the Major Crime Unit, for example, and the SWAT teams.

There was also what the New Hampshire Department of Safety's website calls the legacy of those first volunteers: "They were truly a special breed, willing to endure long, arduous tours of duty, meager compensation, and incredible personal risks. As the first New Hampshire State Troopers, they established an *esprit de corps*, a philosophy, and a total way of life that has transcended time and the evolution of social values."

According to Caulder, a former marine and current SWAT team member, it was that legacy and the appeal of the agency's elite image that made it so hard to get into the force. He, Phillips, and Stepanian were three out of a class of twelve at the State Police Academy in 1990, and they were picked from some 2,400 applicants. Getting into the Academy was tougher than getting into Harvard.

In fact it took Phillips two tries. He grew up in Lancaster and went from high school into the Army Military Police Corp, serving four years in Panama. He applied to the state police on his discharge in 1989 and, when rejected, went to work as a security officer at a Concord hospital. He tried again in 1990. "They must have been a little more desperate that year," Caulder told him later.

Stepanian recalled meeting this other Scott at state police headquarters in March that year. "I can remember talking to everyone that day," Stepanian wrote in a 1998 issue of *New Hampshire Trooper* magazine. "I also remember speaking with Scott. Right away, it was obvious that Scott had a 'way' about him. He had charm and warmth. You just felt good being around him."

Phillips had good stories to tell about his military police days, and enough experience polishing leather and brass to help those without previous military experience — like Stepanian — get through inspections. Academy graduates went on probation for a year and were assigned to two different duty stations. Phillips helped Stepanian prepare for a probationary stint at Troop F in the North Country, while he himself reported to Troop D in the Concord area.

There Phillips made a name for himself by daring to arrest a local judge for drunk driving. The judge threatened to have the young trooper fired if the case wasn't dropped, but the charges stuck through a trial and an appeal, and the judge was fined and suspended. "It made the news in a big way," Stepanian wrote. "It is kind of funny, but shortly after that he put in his request to return to Colebrook. I am sure that a lot of people thought that because he arrested a judge he got sent to Colebrook. But Scott wanted to return to the North Country." As did Stepanian, who also requested Troop F as his permanent assignment.

The most widely circulated photo of Phillips is a headshot of a young man who looks more Eagle Scout than trooper. There is the forest-green shirt with its epaulets, brass name tag, and blue, white, and gold badge; the crisp white triangle of the undershirt; the gold-badged Stetson with its black band and its felt brim as flat and stiff as a phonograph record. Softening those angles and planes are the clean, boyish features, rightly proportioned, the black eyebrows and fair skin, and a smile — John Harrigan's daughter Karen labeled it a "smart-alecky grin" — that outshone the spit and polish of the uniform. John liked to call Phillips "Dudley Do-Right" and to point out that the Stetson hid a cowlick the trooper could never quite tame.

There was nothing fraudulent, though, about the Eagle Scout look, the Dudley Do-Right urge to make things better. Karen Harrigan Ladd remembered a Colebrook woman who had moved hastily out of her boyfriend's house and then was prevented from fetching her belongings. Phillips went with her and smoothed things over with the former boyfriend — "That silver tongue of his always came in handy," wrote Stepanian — and helped the woman load a girlfriend's truck with her possessions.

"He just dug in and helped," the woman told Karen in a *News and Sentinel* story. "After we'd gotten the truck loaded, I thanked him and told him he could go, but he said he'd go with us and make sure we got to my new apartment okay. We lost a few things out of the truck on the way, and he'd stop and turn on his blue lights, jump out, and pick stuff up. When he got to my place, he helped us unload too."

Then he stayed to give the woman legal advice on separating her finances from those of the ex-boyfriend. "He knew I had kids and was having a hard time, and he just wanted things to work out for me," she said. "He was a family man, and whatever he'd do for his family, he'd do for anyone else."

Phillips had married his high school sweetheart from Lancaster, and Christine Phillips worked as a secretary at the Balsams. He was an avid skier and runner, and many photos exist of him pushing a baby buggy ahead of him as he jogged around Colebrook during off-duty hours. First it was son Keenan, born in 1994, and then a two-seater buggy for daughter Clancy as well, born in 1996. That year Phillips was the torch bearer for Colebrook's annual Law Enforcement Torch Run, a fund-raiser for the Special Olympics — torch held aloft in one hand, Keenan and Clancy pushed ahead in their buggy by the other.

Border Patrol agent Dave Perry remembered hearing from a grateful citizen how wonderful Phillips had been in providing aid at the scene of a minor accident. Les Lord was there with Perry, and Lord, barely containing that rolling laugh of his, said, "Well, that's just who he is — he's our Mr. Wonderful." So "Mr. Wonderful" duly became Phillips's nickname among his peers, though in fact Lord was repeating a sobriquet previously assigned Phillips by his friend Stepanian.

"I must admit I was kind of jealous of Scott," Stepanian wrote. "I used to ask Scott how many babies he kissed today. When he was hot, he was on fire, like a campaigning politician always trying to get more votes."

And he got votes from his peers because there was more to Phillips than the smooth-talking Mr. Wonderful. Les Lord, for example, was notorious for his readiness to trample on the fussier aspects of state police protocol, as much for its own sake as for a laugh. "But Scott was just as nuts as Les was," said Perry, "only Scott was sneakier about it."

Perry remembered being puzzled one day to get a call from Phillips at his Border Patrol office in Beecher Falls, Vermont. "Hey, buddy, I need some help down here," Phillips said.

The call for help wasn't unusual. In the North Country there are no turf battles between the various law enforcement agencies. With so much ground to cover, they routinely cooperate on even the smallest jobs, and officers socialize without prejudice off duty. "It was this 'buddy' thing," Perry recalled. "He never called me 'buddy.'"

"Just come on down," Phillips said. "I'll buy you some ice cream."

"Scott, what do you want?"

Perry couldn't get it out of him, and Phillips said he was frankly hurt by Perry's suspicions. When Perry got to Colebrook and slipped into Phillips's cruiser, the vehicle's door locks snapped shut. "Did I mention there's a brawl going on down in Woodale Village?" Phillips said.

"No, but you could have — I still would have come."

"Couldn't take that chance, buddy."

Sometimes Phillips needed backup, and sometimes he just wanted company. "He hated to ride alone," Stepanian wrote. "He would always 'kidnap' you and go cruising. It seemed a lot of the times I rode with Scott, something big would happen (i.e., a fatal, a burglary, or something like that). A short ride could easily turn into a complete shift."

Norm Brown, the supervisor of the Coös County Jail and one of Phillips's regular running partners, remembered a young detainee who broke into the jail's laundry room and crawled out a window. "We found out about the break at 5 a.m., and Scott and Sergeant Wayne Fortier of the state police were there within the hour," Brown said.

There were tracks in the snow that vanished onto pavement. Phillips, Fortier, and Brown talked to neighbors, who had seen nothing. They put out a bulletin, and then the three men went to breakfast at a restaurant in West Stewartstown. There Phillips got a call from Dave Perry, who was on duty that morning but returning from a meeting in plainclothes and without handcuffs or a weapon. Perry had been traveling north on Route 102 in Vermont and had seen a hitchhiker thumbing for a ride south — on a remote stretch where it was unusual to see a hitchhiker. Perry turned around, went back, and pretended to be on his way somewhere else. He told the hitchhiker he'd be coming back, though, in twenty minutes. "If you're still here, I'll pick you up, okay?"

Perry had a radio in his unmarked car, but not one that shared frequencies with either Vermont or New Hampshire state police. He sped to a pay phone at DeBanville's General Store in Bloomfield, Vermont, and made enough phone calls to learn about the escape, get a description of the fugitive, and locate the investigating officers. After talking to Phillips, Perry went out to flag down southbound cars: "If you see a hitchhiker, don't pick him up, whatever you do."

Phillips and Brown arrived in Phillips's cruiser, with Fortier following behind. They trailed Perry's car down Route 102 and dropped farther behind as Perry slowed and stopped slightly ahead of the hitchhiker. The cruisers stopped as well. "Scott got out one side, and I got out the other," Brown said. "This kid's running towards Dave's car. We got him by the arms, slammed him against Dave's trunk, and cuffed him. His feet never touched the ground after that."

Fortier left on another assignment, and in the sergeant's absence there was the temptation to just drive across the bridge into New Hampshire, as if the kid had been captured on that side of the river, and so avoid the extradition process from Vermont. "It's a nice idea, but my lieutenant would be bullshit," Phillips said. "If we arrest him in Vermont, we got to process him in Vermont."

Mr. Wonderful had been tempted, but finally the Do-Right side of him prevailed. It might have helped that the lieutenant in charge of Troop F, Leo "Chuck" Jellison, was also Phillips's uncle.

"So we go down to St. Johnsbury, and they tell us they don't have jurisdiction in Bloomfield," Brown said. "We have to go back and way the hell up to Derby Line on the Canadian border. We ended up spending five hours in the car with that kid, who did not want to come back to New Hampshire and who refused to waive extradition. We finally needed a governor's warrant, and I guess it was two or three months before he was back in the jail."

Stepanian wrote, "Scott never took the job dead serious, but just serious enough. He never lost sight of the fact that he was a person too." In fact troopers are wary of those in their ranks who take the badge — and themselves — too seriously, who drink too deeply of the authoritarian, paramilitary elements in the agency's esprit de corps. Les Lord was a walking daily affront to those elements. Mr. Wonderful was more subversive, striking a guarded and personal balance between the philosophy and its statutes, on one hand, and the reasons of the heart, on the other.

John Harrigan was a runner too, and Phillips used to love to creep silently up on John in his cruiser as the newspaperman beat up and down the roads of Colebrook. Then Phillips would pop his siren and lights, and declaim over his speaker-phone, "Come on, pick up the pace!"

Too much pace was the problem one day in 1992 when John had to delay a press run for his newspapers in order to attend Rudy Shatney's wake. John couldn't miss that wake, even for a press run, but he was in a good hurry to get to Lancaster when it was over. He was barreling through Stratford on Route 3 when a cruiser heading north passed him, flipped on its blue lights, and made a U-turn. A moment later Phillips was at his car window, grinning and shoving back his Stetson, said John, "like Andy Griffith."

"Well, well, well — Mr. Harrigan," Phillips said. "Do you know how fast you were going?"

"Um — pretty fast."

"I've got you at seventy-five. So what's going on? What's your hurry?"

John explained the circumstances. Phillips looked down at the pavement for a moment and then said, "Rudy Shatney was the best man who ever walked these woods. Go ahead — get back on the road."

John marveled that Phillips didn't even warn him to slow down. "He knew how much Rudy meant to me," he said, "and he had a real good feel for the culture of the North Country."

"You look at him, and you could see two different futures ahead of him," said Dave Perry. "Either he was going to rise to the rank of colonel and run the whole agency from Concord or else he was going to stay in Colebrook and raise his kids because he loved it so much there. Either scenario was available to him."

Scott Stepanian saw the glimmer of that former scenario almost as soon as he met Phillips: "It was at the academy that I realized Scott was a gifted and exceptional human being. It was there that I told Scott that I would not salute him when he became colonel of the state police."

On the morning of August 19, 1997, Ed Jeffrey needed diesel fuel. The owner and president of the little New Hampshire Central Railroad had a crew of workmen replacing the ties on a length of track, and the machine used for extracting the old ties from beneath the rails and inserting the new had run dry. Ed got a call about it at his office in Columbia. He jumped into a pickup with a fuel tank in the bed and drove to the Blue Mountain Variety Store, nestled on Route 3 between that mountain to the east and Monadnock to the west. He saw that Carl Drega's orange Dodge pickup was already pulled up to the lone diesel pump.

Jeffrey had met Drega in 1995 when Jeffrey was replacing worn crossing planks on track traversing the driveways of private property owners. The planks were actually the property and responsibility of the property owners, but Jeffrey liked to keep an eye on them, and he charged a lowball fee of a hundred dollars for replacing them when he thought it was time. Drega's looked worn, but Jeffrey had had no luck contacting the owner about it — telephone calls were never picked up, mail went unanswered.

Finally Jeffrey stopped with his crew one day at the top of the driveway. He walked down toward the cabin alone, but Drega met him halfway, standing in the driveway with a rifle. "You're trespassing," Drega told him.

Jeffrey thought Drega had a glazed look to his eyes, and he felt chills running in relay down his spine as he explained his concern about the crossing planks. "Those planks look fine to me," Drega said.

"Okay, then, it's up to you," Jeffrey replied. They talked a few minutes more, amiably enough. Drega had several questions about the railroad business, and then Jeffrey walked out over planks that certainly felt punky. Jeffrey had run into Drega once or twice since then and had made a point of being cordial — "The way you handle a pet rattlesnake," he said.

Today Drega — with a darkly gnarled beard, wearing jeans and a blue plaid shirt and a red GMC baseball cap — was both cordial and talkative. The whole bed of his pickup was covered by five-gallon plastic fuel containers, all bound by a single length of clothesline threaded through their handles. That was all that held them — the truck had no tailgate. Jeffrey noticed other pieces of clothesline securing, sort of, the truck's front fenders. Drega was filling each of the containers in turn with diesel fuel. To help speed things along, Jeffrey leaned in and started replacing the caps on full containers.

Drega asked after a used locomotive Jeffrey had just bought, then wondered if it might be possible to reroute the railroad tracks on his land through another part of the property. Jeffrey didn't think so, but he kept that to himself and promised to check into it. He also thought this was a lot of fuel. "Carl, what are you doing with all this diesel?"

Drega laughed. "My tractor's out of gas."

He clipped the nozzle back on the pump and marched into the store to pay. Jeffrey stared after him. He had never seen Drega smile, much less laugh. He glanced at the gauge on the fuel pump — 61.5 gallons — before he reset it, and then watched as the pickup started reluctantly and turned south on Route 3 with its body swaying back and forth over the chassis.

Ed Jeffrey met Les Lord in 1994, shortly after he had moved to Columbia from Meredith, in central New Hampshire. Jeffrey had just finished a meeting with a client at that man's home. He came out the door to find Lord's cruiser parked next to his car and Lord leaning against the cruiser's fender. He held Jeffrey's license plates in one hand, tossed a screwdriver up and down with the other, and said — wearing that chipmunk grin of his — "Well, Mr. Jeffrey, we've been looking for you."

Jeffrey had left an unpaid traffic ticket behind in Meredith. Lord wanted to know where Jeffrey wanted the car parked while it was off the road. The next day Jeffrey made good on the ticket and met Lord at his railroad's gravel yard, where the car had been left overnight. The cop made the event into something of an awards ceremony, shaking Jeffrey's hand and jubilantly presenting the plates while a friend of Jeffrey's snapped a photo.

Jeffrey laughed his way through the whole experience. "Oh, Les Lord was just a peach of a guy," he said.

Growing up in Pittsburg, Lord had been the kind of peach who seemed an unlikely candidate for law enforcement. He was always in trouble, though most often for pranks — once, for example, supergluing his school principal's coffee mug to his desk. Pittsburg fire chief Tom Carlson grew tired of chasing the boy's snow machine off town roads in the winter, but nonetheless he recommended Lord for a two-week summer cadet program for teenagers at the State Police Academy in Concord. The next summer Carlson recommended him again, and Lord got accepted again — which prompted Carlson to dub him "Lucky," a moniker used more around Pittsburg than Colebrook.

That cadet training led to work as a part-time officer in the Pittsburg Police Department, once Lord got out of high school in 1971. Four years later he married Beverly Frizzell, a Colebrook girl who worked as a dispatcher for Emery Trucking and who loved to ride snow machines. That was also the year that the onetime town scamp got promoted to chief of police. Lord was only twenty-three, but people were fine with that.

"Well, Les knew everybody in that town, and he was everybody's best friend," said Dave Perry. Perry remembered a Saturday night on which he and Lord were guests at Tom Carlson's house. The phone rang, and Carlson's daughter answered. After a moment she handed the receiver to Lord with an appalled expression on her face. "I think this is an obscene phone call," she whispered.

Lord got on the line, listened a moment, and said, "Bill, is that you?"

Indeed it was. Lord said that Bill was drunk and babbling, and that was the end of it. The girl wasn't troubled again.

Lord was popular, and he proved himself tough. Perry once went with him on a search warrant into a house on Indian Stream, where they found a number of burglarized goods and an angry suspect with a handgun. "Les had to physically wrestle that gun away from him," Perry said, "and then we put him in the back of the cruiser, where the guy lunges forward, trying to head-butt Les."

Lord reached back and restrained the suspect by grabbing his beard. "Just because your name is L-O-R-D," the man spelled out, "you're not God almighty!"

"He's got a good point there," Perry said.

"Shut up and drive," said Lord, his fist still full of beard.

As the years went by, though, Lord tired not only of being the only full-time officer in the Pittsburg police force and taking too many risks alone, but also of having to play God almighty in respect to some of his civilian friends' failings — and then having to help prosecute them. In 1986 he applied for an opening in the state's Bureau of Highway Enforcement and attended the Police Academy for real this time.

One of his classmates was a young municipal cop from Gorham named Gerry Marcou. "Les had a tough year at the academy," Marcou recalled. "He showed up one Monday morning with a black eye because he'd had to break up a brawl in some club up there, and somebody had cold-cocked him. In a town that small, Les had to go home and work on the weekends while the rest of us could do homework because we were getting time off. So halfway through the year I was assigned to help tutor him, and he made it all right."

Highway Enforcement was not then part of the state police, and once on the job, Lord could pretty much specialize in motorists, truck drivers, and their machines. It was work he enjoyed, and eventually he talked Gerry Marcou into abandoning fourteen years of seniority at the Gorham Police Department for his own cruiser and better retirement benefits with Highway Enforcement. Lord then became Marcou's field training officer.

"I didn't like Colebrook, and I still don't — it's just too cold," Marcou said. "And I was a criminal man. I didn't know a thing about trucks and cars and highways. But on my first night — this was 1989 — I go up there, and park my cruiser, and jump in with Les. It's January, about ten below and snowing, and I'm bundled up like an Eskimo."

They drove to Clarksville, where Lord pulled over a logging truck loaded with a long bed of spruce and fir. "Come on," Lord said. "I'll show you how to weigh a truck."

"We're going to weigh a truck? In the snow? At these temperatures?"

Lord fetched a set of scales out of the trunk, a pair of fifty-pound mechanisms that he positioned in front of the truck's rear tires. "You got to be a little bit careful if the roads are slippery," Lord said. "Sometimes these will kick out."

The snow lay like a layer of grease over the road. The truck eased forward, and Marcou gasped as one scale shot like an artillery shell from beneath its tire, arcing against the trees and landing in a cloud of snow and frozen dirt twenty yards down the road. "He didn't tell me it would come out like that," Marcou said. "The damned thing could break your leg."

Lord told him that some drivers play games with those scales, rolling onto them and then hitting their brakes in a manner timed to kick them out and possibly ruin them. "But I know all these guys — which ones are easy, which ones are jerks," Lord said. "That guy didn't do it on purpose."

Marcou was a man of documented courage, wiry and agile, but he liked heights less than he liked the cold. He remembered the first time he and Lord stopped a logging truck that looked to be piled too high. Lord told

Marcou to climb up there, fourteen feet or so, stand on the outermost log's round slope, and hold one end of a tape measure. With his heart in his throat, Marcou — then in his forties — climbed to the top, but he couldn't force himself out to that edge.

"Les swears at me and tells me to get down off the truck. I told him he knew I was afraid of heights. 'Well, you're gonna have to get used to it,' he says. He climbs up there like a monkey, still swearing — but not really mad, you know, he's always jolly — and says, 'Yep, he's over height.'"

Later Lord gave Marcou an early Christmas present: a four-foot surveyor's stick that could telescope up to sixteen feet and measure with its operator's feet safely on the ground. "I loved him for it," Marcou said. "Immediately everybody else in the bureau wanted one too."

Together they had charge of the North Country for Highway Enforcement, and when they were joined by a third officer — Frank Prue, formerly of the Lancaster Police Department — the men formed a tight-knit trio known variously to their peers as the Three Musketeers, the Three Amigos, or the Three Northern Renegades. On occasions when the Amigos rode a little too deeply into Renegade territory, they were known euphoniously to state police major Dave McCarthy in Concord as "Lord and Prue and that idiot Marcou."

Each of them was assigned to a different part of the region, but they worked together two or three days a week, and — Musketeers-like — each had his respective role. Lord was the front man who had that sweet knack for keeping things friendly. Prue, a brawny weight lifter, was more rules-oriented, the guy more inclined to go by the book and who could play the bad cop when necessary. Marcou liked to keep his uniform clean and handle the paperwork while the others crawled under trucks to check for broken springs.

In fact Lord relished the role of grease monkey, loved diving under trucks, and didn't care for that crisp green uniform worn by Highway Enforcement officers. He preferred to work in fatigues or jumpsuits, even took special pains to avoid being photographed in what Concord wanted him to wear. Eventually the Amigos also earned nicknames pulled from an old Saturday morning cartoon: Lord was the trickster Yogi Bear, Marcou was his wide-eyed sidekick Boo-Boo, and the straight-minded Prue was cast as the Park Ranger.

And Boo-Boo and the Ranger couldn't help but envy Yogi's easy way with their clients. "A thousand-dollar ticket? He'd know everybody in the guy's family by the time he passed it through the window, and they'd both be chuckling," marveled Prue. "If it was me or Gerry and a ticket for a lousy hundred bucks — knuckle city."

All the Musketeers, though, subscribed to the same pragmatic philosophy — even Frank Prue, though sometimes he was in minority dissent. "Concord's mentality was for us to go out and hammer these guys and write a lot of tickets," said Marcou. "But up here it's hard to make a living, and that's all that most of these truckers are trying to do. We knew we had to keep the roads safe, and we also knew who the bad guys were and we targeted them — guys with rocks rolling out of their dump trucks, loggers whose rigs were so overloaded they couldn't control them. But we're not going to ticket somebody who's just missing a fire extinguisher or write such a big ticket that it puts a good man out of business. And it's easier to deal with truckers, you know, than it is with drivers. They understand that we have a job to do, and it's important, and there's more mutual respect. If we break down or slide into a snowbank, we know the truckers are going to be the first guys to help out."

Most of the trouble they got into was at Lord's instigation. Prue remembered a time when too many truckers from Maine were bringing wood chips to a mill in Shelburne, New Hampshire, right near the border, with their plates out of order or their lengths too long. That needed to stop, and Lord saw no call to be sneaky about it. The three set up a table at the side of Route 2, between that mill and Maine, complete with umbrella, a boom box, and extra ticket books, daring the outliers to try a delivery. Yogi Bear picked blueberries from roadside bushes as deliveries to the mill fell sharply enough to disturb management. "Complaints were filed, and finally McCarthy called," Prue sighed. "Things got worked out, but we had to take down that table."

Prue recalled only one occasion when he saw Lord lose his temper. They had stopped a truck on Route 116, near Whitefield, and Prue stayed in the cruiser while Lord went to talk to the driver. "The next thing I knew, Les had that guy out of the truck, and Jesus, he was mad," Prue said. "I got out fast and stepped between them. 'Les, what the hell are you doing?' He just turned around and walked away."

The driver was mad too. "Good thing for him you stepped in," he told Prue.

"No, it was a good thing for you, buddy," Frank said.

Lord was a bear of a man — 240 pounds or so, hard and bulky, "and with hands like baseball mitts," Marcou said. Nonetheless, he had his qualms, enough to ensure that secret sympathy with Marcou's fear of heights. He had a touch of claustrophobia and an Indiana Jones fear of snakes, once resorting to his handgun to defend himself from a harmless species. Nor — for all his fighting prowess — did he stand up well to the sight of blood. Dave Perry got a call from his dispatcher one night. A motorist had hit and killed a moose near Lake Francis and had left the meat to the State of New Hampshire. Tom Carlson, a Fish & Game conservation officer as well as fire chief, needed help dressing the animal off. Perry drove up there and noticed Lord's cruiser parked next to Tom's. "Down here!" Carlson yelled.

Perry descended into some brush and found Carlson with his hands in the moose's gut, pulling out the entrails. "Where's Lucky?" Perry asked.

"Why do you think I had the dispatcher call you?" Carlson said. "He's off in the bushes puking. He's no help."

Nor was he much of a marksman — "He could hit you, but it would take several tries," Marcou said — and lawmen still tell the story of the time Lord set about teaching Brad Presby, who worked for the Bureau of Trails and dealt only rarely with criminal work, how to put handcuffs on a suspect. Lord ended up locking himself into a pair for which he had no key.

But he was a genius at the wheel of his cruiser, a hurtling fusion of man and machine who hated traffic lights for the constraints they imposed, hated straight roads for how little they challenged him. One day the dispatcher at Troop F called Lord to say he was needed at a certain location. Twelve minutes later, Lord reported his arrival. "Jesus," the dispatcher said. "How'd he get there in twelve minutes?"

Scott Stepanian was at the dispatcher's side and offered an explanation: "Well, he must have stopped for a sandwich."

Lord loved it, loved getting up and going to work with soul-mate buddies, driving fast whenever he could, and keeping his truckers in line — until 1996, when Concord took the Bureau of Highway Enforcement out of the Department of Safety and folded it into the state police. The Renegades' primary responsibility remained motor vehicles, but now they got involved much more often in criminal incidents and investigations.

John Barthelmes, the colonel in charge of the state police, was a former North Country trooper. In fact, on his first day of duty there some years before, Barthelmes had made the rookie mistake of asking Lord to show him around the area. Yogi took him on back roads twenty miles over the border into Maine. "Imagine my shock as a young trooper, to find out that not only was I out of my patrol, I was in another state and didn't have a clue where I was or how to get back," Barthelmes wrote in *New Hampshire Trooper*. "When I relayed my alarm to Les, he did what he always did — he laughed and he laughed."

Barthelmes, dubbed Mr. Clean, was enough of a straight arrow to make Frank Prue seem bohemian, but in 1996 Mr. Clean could only laugh himself when Lord — in front of several other troopers — came into the colonel's Concord office, fell into a chair, threw his boots up on the desk, and said, "Well, John, I hear I'm working for you now."

Lord put a good face on it, but he was serious about those boots on the desk. He had little use for the spit and polish of state police culture — if you left your Stetson lying around, Lord would turn it upside down and leave a thumbprint in it; if your shoes were too shiny, Lord would accidentally step on your toes and scuff them — and he took no pleasure in finding himself back in the middle of the criminal stuff he thought he had left behind. One night he was called to a domestic disturbance in North Stratford. An enraged husband had tried to assault his wife and the guy he had caught her with. Lord wrestled the husband into the back of his cruiser, but then the man kicked out a rear passenger window and escaped. Lord chased him down on foot, thinking all the while, "I'm too old for this."

Lord was still driving his cruiser from the Department of Safety, a vehicle that didn't have a cage around the backseat. Nor had any of the Amigos been issued rifles, shotguns, or body armor. "In 1997 the three of us got together on the night of August 18th, Monday, at the Groveton P.D.," Marcou remembered. "We were talking about those very problems, and I'll tell you we weren't happy. Les had just been issued a brand new cruiser, which did have a cage, and he was pleased about that. But none of us had any of that other stuff, and Les was joking around that he could get killed the next day or the day after anyway, cage or no cage."

Brad Presby and his wife regularly rode their snow machines with the Lords in the winter, and he had tried to talk his friend into retiring. Lord was then president of the Pittsburg Ridge-Runners, a snow machine club whose volunteers maintained trails throughout the northern part of the county, and in January he had succeeded the retiring Tom Carlson as Pittsburg's fire chief. Presby told Lord that if he quit the day job, he'd be the most likely choice to head up a new state agency looking after recreational snow machiners.

But Lord didn't want to gamble on that. He preferred to put in a little more time on duty in order to qualify for the next level of retirement benefits. "Besides, this is Coös County," Lord laughed. "What could go wrong?"

Gene Ehlert, the managing editor of the *Coös County Democrat* in Lancaster, knew he wasn't going to get done on time on this Tuesday the nineteenth, the way things were going. So he telephoned the boss up in Colebrook. "Nancy's sick," he told John Harrigan. "Or actually her dad's sick, but she can't come in. Could you get down here and give us a hand?"

John had just finished his editorial column. He handed a printout to Susan Zizza, telling her to do whatever she wanted to it, and explained the situation at the *Democrat* to her and Dennis. In terms of the things that often go wrong on Tuesday, he thought, this was pretty mild.

Then he popped into Vickie's office. "Who's Nancy?" she asked.

"She's the ad manager down there, but she also does a lot of the pasteup work. And that's what they need help with, Gene says."

"So you're gone the rest of the day."

"Yeah, and tell your dad I can't make it for fishing, okay? We'll reschedule."

"Sure."

John had caught her en route to somewhere, and he couldn't help noticing how pretty she looked in that white blouse, how well it set off the chiaroscuro of her eyes and hair. "I'll see you later then," he said.

"More like tomorrow, I guess. I'll be gone when you're back."

They hugged briefly, like siblings, something they always continued to do, even as they grew apart. Maybe this hug lingered a moment longer after their dancing over the weekend. Her shoulders were thin, and she felt frail, John thought. But she still had that scent in her hair of meadow grass and blue sky.

He went out the front door to the Lincoln thinking he needed to get up to her place more often — cook her some real meals and play cribbage.

SCOTT PHILLIPS WONDERED if Les Lord had anywhere he had to be this afternoon. It was 12:45 p.m. in the squad room of the Colebrook police station, which was in the town hall's basement. "Not so far," Lord said.

"You heard about Carl and Vickie?" Phillips asked.

"Drega? I know he likes to sit outside her window in that shit-bucket truck of his. So maybe he's in love?"

No, Lord hadn't heard about that encounter on Main Street last Friday, the threats and obscenities. Drega's pickup was a particular embarrassment to Lord, who still handled a lot of the traffic stops in Colebrook and who was among those who had issued warnings about it. Not even Yogi Bear had ever coaxed a smile out of Drega — or any action on that truck. The next step, pulling its plates and keeping it off the road, had been deemed, by general consensus, not worth the trouble. Drega had another truck in his barn, a new pickup that he used when he traveled to jobs, and grounding the Dodge would just give him one more thing to stew about. On Friday, though, Drega had raised the ante in this poker game they were all playing, and Phillips didn't like this latest development with Vickie. He told Lord, "So she took a restraining order out against him — "

"Oh, well, problem solved."

Phillips smiled. Behind them, Dan Couture — a young Colebrook cop who had recently hurt his ankle and was in civilian clothes that day — came in and occupied one of the empty desks. "Yeah, we know what that's worth," Phillips said. "So I figure I'll just have a little chat with Carl about Vickie and about this situation, and if it sounds like he might be ready to back off and really stay the hell away from her, I'll just give him another warning."

"Sure — as if that'll happen. You trying to scare him or sweet-talk him?"

"I don't know." Phillips shook his head. "Yeah, it probably won't work. He'll just cuss — and I'll pull his plates. Well, that's something. I can't hear about shit like that and just sit on my ass, waiting for a 911 call. I'm tired of getting there too late."

Lord didn't know what Phillips meant by that, but Norm Brown would have. Phillips still felt sick about a recent sexual assault case that had gotten thrown out of court. Maybe there was more, but whatever the trouble, it was enough for Mr. Wonderful to confess to Brown while jogging the day before that he wished he had become a firefighter instead.

"Is Mr. Drega on the watch list?" Lord wondered.

"It might be time to put him there, don't you think?"

"And I take it you're going to look for him today."

"I actually had Steve Hersom lined up for backup, but he's stuck at an accident scene somewhere."

"So I'm not even your first choice."

Phillips smiled again. "You'll have to do. So can I call you if I see him, buddy?"

"'Buddy?' What's up with that?"

Dan Couture, twenty-four, had been a cop for just a year in 1997, and he was still learning, but he could see that it was hard on the whole town for a department with four full-time cops and several part-timers to depend on just one cruiser. If the cruiser was in the shop for an oil change, say, and a call came in for help, the department couldn't respond. He'd seen it happen.

Couture had grown up in a town that straddled the Canadian border — Sherbrooke on the Quebec side, Norton the Vermont. He went to high school in Canaan, drove a school bus for three years for his father's transportation company, and then earned a criminal justice degree at Hesser College in Manchester. Police work seemed like a good way to stay in the area near family and friends. He got hired part time in Colebrook in May 1996 and went full time when somebody quit. He had only a week of field training, and in his second week on the job he found himself in the middle of a disturbing — and delicate — sexual assault investigation. The victim was a three-year-old girl, and the rookie cop knew he was in over his head and asking the wrong sorts of questions. Like a town with one cruiser, he was just trying to muddle through.

In the early afternoon on August 19, that cruiser was getting washed outside the town hall and department headquarters. Couture had sprained his ankle during a foot chase on the night shift, and he was on light duty, dressed in shorts and a T-shirt, handling a lot of department paperwork, and now helping fellow patrolman Steve Breton restore some gloss to the cruiser. Breton was a regular on the night shift, but he was working days now while Colebrook police chief Mike Sielicki was on vacation.

Overhead, what farmers called a haymaking sun hung high in the sky. Couture saw Dennis Joos come out of the News and Sentinel Building and limp — just the way Couture was limping, but this didn't look like an ankle injury — to the Lazerworks shop on this side of the street. A few minutes later the newspaperman limped back with something in a small paper bag. Then Couture saw Vickie Bunnell's dad go into the building with a bouquet of flowers in his hand.

The radio was quiet and the two cops were taking their time. They were only halfway through when dispatcher Lynn Jolin had a call for Steve, a report of domestic violence somewhere out on Route 145, up toward Stewartstown Hollow. Breton jumped into the cruiser and pulled onto Bridge Street with his blue lights flashing and soapsuds streaming from the fenders.

Couture stowed the hose and bucket, limped past two parked state police cruisers, and returned to his paperwork inside. Scott Phillips and Les Lord were downstairs talking about pulling over a guy Couture didn't know. The young cop sat down and held his peace — which he always did with these two. They didn't put on airs — in fact, Phillips was the closest thing to a real field training officer Couture had — but they were each the sort of cop Couture wanted to be someday.

Julie Roy, once her husband had relieved her at the counter of J.R.'s Minimart in Pittsburg, was pleased to learn that her friend Kim Richards had a lot of shopping to do in Colebrook. Julie needed to get some coffee at LaPerle's IGA, and she had other errands to run as well, all of which combined neatly with Kim's. They left after lunch in Kim's husband's Nissan pickup and with her six-year-old son, Cody, and they made the rounds: the First Colebrook Bank, Dickson's Pharmacy, Hills Department Store, and then Collins Video & Photo on the corner of Bridge and Main.

It was around 2:25 p.m. when they turned north out of town to the IGA supermarket. Opposite the Congregational church, they passed Clarkeie's, a much smaller grocery story with parking in front on Main. There Julie noticed an orange, rusting pickup she had seen before a number of times around town.

"Do you know who that belongs to?" she asked Kim.

"That piece of junk? Not a clue."

"I can't believe the cops let that thing stay on the road." Julie gave a short laugh. "Whoever it is, he must have friends in high places."

New Hampshire forest ranger Bert von Dohrmann had come downtown for several reasons: he needed Scott Phillips's signature on some papers about a timber theft; he wanted to ask Vickie Bunnell to write up a deed for some property he meant to buy; and he hoped to talk to Dennis Joos about the manuscript of his novel. Dennis had asked von Dohrmann to check the story for accuracy regarding the logging practices it described, and the ranger had some suggestions to make.

He found Phillips in his cruiser parked driver-side, window-to-window with Les Lord's shiny new rig next to the police department. He got Phillips's signature and learned that he and Lord were on a low-key sort of manhunt. Von Dohrmann didn't know Carl Drega, but he had heard about him from Eric Stohl. "Yeah, you want to be careful with this guy," he said.

Phillips left to run another lap around town, and Lord stayed to chat. "Let's get off the road," Lord suggested. "Want to go to Howard's and get some coffee?"

That was when Phillips broke in on Lord's radio. "Hey, I got him," he said. "He's at Clarkeie's. No, wait — he's just pulling out of Clarkeie's. Heading north. I'll just follow him for a bit. Any time you're ready, we can use you here."

"Duty calls," Lord said.

"You want one more? I'll come with you."

They both looked at Lord's passenger seat, which was always mobile storage space: a cellular bag phone, a portable radio, and piles of forms and documents garnished with old food wrappers. "Not unless you've got a shovel," Lord said.

Von Dohrmann grinned. "No shovel."

"We'll be all right. What time is it? Two thirty or so? I'll meet you at Howard's in twenty minutes."

Von Dohrmann nodded, and as swiftly as that Lord was gone.

Linemen Woody Crawford and Mark Monahan of the New Hampshire Electric Cooperative, both in their forties, were on their way to investigate a power outage on Hughes Road, which branched off Route 3 just north of LaPerle's IGA. Monahan was at the wheel, coaxing the big truck up Cooper Hill. As they came over its crest and in sight of Brooks Chevrolet, they found themselves behind a state police cruiser and — ahead of that — a logging truck. "That's Les, isn't it?" Monahan said.

Crawford smiled as he remembered the time Lord and Frank Prue had pulled him over in this very truck. Lord scrambled under the truck to check the slack adjusters on the brakes and came out dabbing tears from his eyes. "Damn, I just lost five dollars," he blubbered. "I bet Frank this would pass."

They got the brakes adjusted there on the side of the road, and it didn't cost Crawford any money. He leaned forward, but the cruiser didn't look as battered as Lord's. "I don't know. The cruiser kind of looks like Scott's — Scott Phillips, I mean."

Then the cruiser flashed its blue lights. "It must be Les," Monahan said. "He's going to pull this logger over."

"Nope," said Crawford, watching the cruiser glide ahead of the logger. Then its lights went off, and a mile up the road, they saw the cruiser take a right turn behind an orange pickup. At first Crawford thought the cruiser was turning into Hughes. Maybe there was a power line lying across the road? Instead he saw that both the pickup and the cruiser were headed down the entrance ramp into the parking lot of the supermarket. Meanwhile the logging truck and the line truck slowly caravanned in tandem past the Green Mountain Snack Bar — which sat on a bluff overlooking the east end of the parking lot — and a little girl riding her bicycle on the road shoulder.

Crawford watched the girl dwindle in his side-view mirror. Then he cocked an ear toward his open window and looked quizzically at his partner. "What's that noise?" he said.

About thirty miles south of Colebrook, in Groveton, Fish & Game conservation officer Kevin Jordan (no relation to Charlie in Colebrook) was enjoying a day off in the pretty cedar-clapboard house that sat on Route 3 opposite the Northumberland Cemetery and the Connecticut River. His wife, Louise, and their teenage children were working. With the place to himself, Jordan had devoted the day to errands around Lancaster and to sorting out color slides to give to Wayne Saunders at Fish & Game's public information booth at the Lancaster Fair, which was running this week. The slides were shots Jordan had taken of other officers at work, all illustrating the different things Fish & Game did each season. By the middle of the afternoon he was finally outside, washing the new cruiser he had just been issued, a four-wheel-drive Chevy pickup with an extended cab.

The Chevy didn't really need a washing, but Jordan liked to do so on every day off, and this particular day was the sort that had its own chrome gleam to it. Jordan had just finished with the cruiser and moved on to his four-wheeler when Saunders — relieved of his duty at the fair — pulled into the driveway in his own cruiser. Saunders lowered the window of his Jeep Cherokee, just handed down to him from Eric Stohl, and said, "Hey, Kevin, you got your radio on?"

"Nope. Not today."

"I'm not sure, but I think I just heard a Code 1000 come across mine."

"From where?"

"Like I say, I'm not sure, but I think the Colebrook PD."

A Code 1000 signal was for emergencies. Jordan trotted up to Saunders's window, but the signal was fogged by static. They could hear talk from the state police dispatcher at Troop F in Twin Mountain, but they couldn't figure out the content.

A pickup rolled by on Route 3, stopped and turned at the next driveway up the road, and then came back to Jordan's driveway. Jordan recognized the two men in the truck: John Wimsatt and Jim Kneeland, Fish & Game conservation officers (COS) from Newfound, down in central New Hampshire. They pulled in next to Saunders, exchanged greetings, said they were on their way to Quebec for Wednesday's Field Day, a program of competitive events and socializing for the COS of northern New England and Canada. They saw Jordan and Saunders in the driveway and realized they had just passed a house known throughout the agency as the "Groveton substation," so frequently did Fish & Game people stop and congregate there. Today it was their turn.

The men talked about Field Day and the events of the summer while Saunders's radio coughed and gargled in the background. At last something popped clear from Troop F: a stolen state police cruiser heading south on Route 3 in Colebrook, badge number 719. Jordan and Saunders exchanged glances and broke into laughter.

"That's Les Lord's cruiser," Jordan explained. "And let me tell you, that's just the sort of thing would happen to that guy." Jordan suggested that Lord might have left it running while he ducked in for a brownie somewhere, and now some kid was taking it for a joyride. Or maybe someone in law enforcement owed him a prank, and this was payback.

The laughter spread. Would the cruiser get as far as Groveton? Should they set up a roadblock with Jordan's four-wheeler? Saunders described the day last spring when he got his cruiser stuck in mud on a back road in Stewartstown. Lord came to pull him out, but not before snapping a bulletin-board photo of the stuck vehicle. "You got your camera today?" Jordan asked.

"Oh, man, I wish."

Saunders, the only officer on duty, started his motor and prepared to join the hunt for Lord's cruiser. Then another announcement, a correction — the stolen cruiser was not 719, but rather 608. Jordan swallowed his laughter. "Uh-oh, that's Scott Phillips," he said. "That's not something that would happen to Scottie — no way."

"Scott? You sure?" Saunders said. "So what do you think's going on?"

"I don't know. Shit, I can't imagine — but it's got to be serious, knowing Scottie."

"Okay — well, I'd better get going."

"Wait a minute," Jordan said. He stepped up to Saunders's window. "Maybe I ought to come with you."

Saunders was just twenty-eight, sweet-tempered and personable, the perfect guy for that booth at the fair, and brand new to Fish & Game. Jordan was nearly a generation older but in fact was relatively new himself, a CO just since 1994. He had grown up in Whitefield, a little south of Lancaster, had worked as a mechanic twelve years in the family business after high school, and then put in four years as a Whitefield cop. He had made sergeant, and he took a pay cut when he joined Fish & Game, but he was glad to get out into the woods and onto the rivers. He couldn't help feeling responsible for an even newer guy like Saunders, and had taken to him immediately anyway. Other officers used to say that Saunders was at the Groveton substation enough for Jordan to claim him as a dependent.

"No, it's your day off," Saunders said. "Whatever's going on, I'll have help."

Jordan was about to insist, but he didn't want to abandon Wimsatt and Kneeland — or suggest to Saunders that he didn't have confidence in him. Still . . . "Listen, don't go chasing that cruiser yourself, okay? If you see it, just put out a bulletin."

"Got it."

"Hey, I'll have my scanner on in the house. Make sure everybody knows where you are, all right?"

"Yeah, Mom." Saunders laughed and waved, backing out of the driveway, and turned up Route 3 toward Colebrook.

Jordan looked up that way and then said, "Louise made lemonade. You guys want some?" They weren't quite up the front steps before a state police cruiser shot by the house with its blue lights flashing — then two more.

Jana Riley heard it first on the scanner at the News and Sentinel: Code 3, said Colebrook Dispatch, which meant a shooting. Location — LaPerle's trailer park, out near the supermarket, in a lot behind the Chevy car dealership. That was a rough place, prone to domestic violence. A shooting there wouldn't be extraordinary, exactly, but it was still a big story, and one more example of the stuff John Harrigan hated to have happen on a Tuesday.

Claire Lynch wasn't surprised at all, and she was already on her way out the front with her camera and notepad — "Dennis, you want me to cover this, right?" — as several other staffers rose from their desks and gathered around the scanner. Susan was in the newsroom, busy with pasteup, and she wasn't so sure about Claire covering this; she worried about Claire's safety. But Dennis was at the scanner, and on his okay Claire bolted out the door.

Vickie Bunnell was still in her office because that airplane ride with her pilot friend had been pushed back until later in the afternoon. She and Susie Sambito came to the scanner as well.

Someone guessed it was a drunk shooting into the air. After a few tense and quiet moments, there was a correction: "Code 3, Code 3 at LaPerle's IGA. That's LaPerle's IGA. Please note — the supermarket, not the trailer park."

"What?" said Jana. "The supermarket?"

Vickie felt a sudden chill and whispered to Susie, "Sounds like Carl's doing his shopping today."

Then: "Code 3! Officer down! LaPerle's IGA! All units respond!"

Bookkeeper Gil Short used to work at a city hospital, where doors were routinely locked during any sort of police emergency in the surrounding neighborhood. He was in the habit now, and he turned the lock of the Sentinel Building's front door. Then he rejoined the crowd around the scanner. Its silence seemed more fateful with each passing second.

The scanner erupted again: "Officer down — get a fucking ambulance!"

Outside, Claire was barreling up Main Street in her Chevy Blazer with sirens going off in shrieks around her. Near the foot of Cooper Hill, she was surprised — maybe more like shocked — to see Scott Phillips's cruiser heading toward her in the opposite lane, without siren or lights and moving at a wholly moderate speed.

She was even more startled to see that three holes had been punched into its windshield, that the back window had been blown out. Scott had a way of sitting behind the wheel with ramrod posture, just like the military police officer he used to be, and Claire saw through the pocked windshield at least that sort of posture as she whipped past the cruiser. She couldn't imagine why Scott would be headed south right then, and dawdling as he did so, but she'd have to quiz him about that later.

PART
TWO

WHEN
BOTH
ANSWERS
ARE
WRONG

CARL DREGA HAD DREAMED about Rita the night before. The dream, or some parts of it, came back to him as he pulled out of Clarkeie's and headed up Cooper Hill. He was in their house in Bow, but it was different, and bigger, a maze of dark hallways and plunging stairwells. Rita needed him for some reason, but he couldn't find her. Finally he came into a low-ceilinged room that contained a table and an empty chair. Playing cards were spread across the table in an unfinished game of solitaire. There was also an invoice for a payment on Rita's life insurance — stamped "PAST DUE" — and a note signed by Rita: "Don't forget the groceries. I'll see you tonight." He woke with cuts in his palms from the nails on his fingers as they had clamped and knotted into fists.

He glanced at the bag of groceries on the passenger seat of his truck — chicken breasts, a gallon of milk, frozen peas, a bag of red grapes, some cucumbers — and all else heaped on that seat and in its foot well: tools, assorted receipts and bills, a greasy Colebrook House of Pizza box, a manila envelope plumped with his seventy-nine pages of grievances, his 9 mm P85 Ruger pistol and its holster, wrapped in a towel, and the Colt AR-15 he had bought in Massachusetts last February. He was done walking around with just pepper spray, he had decided. No more handcuffs in a parking lot. Drega didn't know, but except for the weapons the front seat looked a lot like Les Lord's.

The AR-15 rested on its stock in the foot well, its muzzle against the door handle. The sun fell in splinters of light along the road ahead, and Drega handled the wheel in something like nervous euphoria. He wondered if it was because he had slept so badly. Nothing different about that, though. There was glare off the grill of the logging truck behind him, off the windshields and fenders of passing cars and trucks. Even with his sunglasses, it all felt like phosphorus in Drega's eyes.

He broke into a cold sweat at the sight of the stabbing blue lights of the state police cruiser that swept into the opposite lane around the logging truck. Then the cruiser snuffed its lights as it came up close on his rear bumper. At first the driver was just a dark form behind the windshield, but then Drega saw the crisp Stetson, the upright carriage, the forehead that flashed in the sun for just an instant like a bleached bone. By then he knew it was Scott Phillips, but he didn't know if Phillips was pulling him over or not.

Drega decided to turn off the road to see what Phillips did, to swing into the parking lot of the IGA, a mile north of the business district, as though he needed more groceries. The cruiser did the same, and as it did so, an odd sort of feeling swept over Carl Drega: a sense that his truck, amid its vapor of blue smoke, was traveling on iron rails, navigating on automatic pilot — down the entrance ramp and straight along the median divider, with its shrubs and stunted trees, and then left and past some parked cars to a stop, straddling two empty spaces near a tan old-model Thunderbird.

The cruiser followed, still with no lights, drawing to a halt twenty feet behind the truck at a diagonal between the lot's first two rows of cars. Drega sat at the wheel of his pickup and took a deep breath — the air was veined with scents of salt and earth. In his rearview mirror, he watched Phillips throw open his cruiser door and in that crisp Stetson take a — swaggering? — step this way, the light prickling in thorns from the handcuffs on his belt.

That feeling — was it Drega's own hand, or someone else's, that pushed the groceries aside and reached for the barrel of the loaded assault rifle? He felt somehow lost to himself, as though he had been the occupant of that empty chair in the dream — and at the same time, after twenty-five years and at this precise moment, never had he felt so true. The pain in his eyes? Their scales had fallen away. Why should he be surprised that suddenly it was now, in a supermarket parking lot with this hammer in his hands?

He wondered at the last moment if he had sent his August check to the

Monastery of the Precious Blood. He mailed twenty-five dollars each month, in good times or bad, to that small order of nuns in Manchester. In his check register he wrote "GIFT" under each such entry. But last month, July, he had written "PEACE OF MIND" instead. It was like a prayer.

A voice from his childhood, a nun's voice pitched to a whisper, rose like the April roar of the Connecticut into his mind: "Holy Mary, mother of God, pray for us sinners now and at the hour of death."

What you thought you heard inside the supermarket at 2:41 p.m. depended on where you were. Head cashier Rachel Hurley thought it was someone pounding on an outside wall. In the produce section, shopper Eleanor Goddard thought someone was using a nail gun, while in the deli section, server Linda Leduc heard banging on the roof. In the bakery, Patsy Smith glanced up at what seemed to be pinging from the metal pipes in the kitchen. Store manager Lance Walling, busy with paperwork in his office, heard a rapid series of thumps.

Julie Roy saw it happen. She was carrying a can of coffee and trailing Kim Richards and Cody through the IGA's automatic exit door. A bearded man in a blue plaid shirt and a red baseball cap stood outside the driver-side door to that pickup she had seen at Clarkeie's. A state trooper, having left his cruiser's door swung open, walked in that man's direction. Julie was near enough to hear them speak — but as she recalls, no one did so. Not a word was exchanged. The bearded man simply hoisted something to his shoulder. It was a small black rifle, with a scope and a sling dangling from its stock, and it was pointed at the trooper — who stopped, lifting his hands, palms out. With no apparent provocation, the bearded man started firing.

This looked like a pantomime of some sort, but with sound effects — some stark and brutal ritual that had nothing to do, certainly, with the world in which Julie or Kim lived. Julie saw the trooper step back, fall to one knee, and reach for his sidearm while the first volley of bullets raked over the cruiser and cut into his legs. The firecracker pop of the rifle could not be linked, somehow, to the leveled flame of pale, forked fire that issued from its barrel. Nothing seemed to connect to anything else or to where she stood stunned outside the exit door of this familiar place at the tail end of an ordinary day.

She saw the trooper's Stetson fall to the pavement. He staggered to his feet, limping around the passenger side of the cruiser, and then crouched behind its trunk. He managed to draw his pistol as more bullets rained over and through the cruiser, punching out its side and rear windows. In that hail of lead he couldn't return fire, or stay where he was.

Julie found herself huddled behind the bulk of a soft-drink vending machine. Kim and Cody had already stepped into the open when the gunfire started. Julie saw Kim's groceries fall and skitter across the asphalt as she snatched Cody and yanked him forward several yards to the cover of her truck. There she pressed herself against its door and wrapped her arms around the boy, Julie would say later, "like a mother bear."

Now the trooper was moving crablike, not toward the store, but instead toward the eastern edge of the lot, using the last row of parked cars as a spotty sort of cover. He was firing his pistol with his left hand, but he was unable to aim, with his right hand down on the pavement to help him stay upright. The man with the rifle took no cover himself. He stood fence-post stiff at the door of his truck, squeezing off rounds at the trooper as if at a duck glimpsed at intervals in a shooting arcade.

The trooper flinched with another hit, maybe another one as well, but somehow he kept moving — to the last of the parked cars, and finally on a covered angle from that car into the high grass fringing the lot. And now the gunman was moving, walking slowly in that direction and firing as he went.

Julie turned and ran, back to the exit door of the supermarket, which wouldn't open from the outside. Another shopper popped it open, and Julie stood on its threshold, screaming for someone to call 911. Faces in the aisles and at the cash registers snapped toward her in unison — "They think I'm nuts," Julie thought. But one of the clerks, Albert Riff, knew better. He had walked outside ahead of her when he had seen a cruiser pull into the parking lot. He ran in and told her to get inside. "I can't," Julie said. "My girlfriend's out there."

Not for long — Kim picked Cody up and dashed for the door. Julie followed her inside, staring back over her shoulder. Her last glimpse of the parking lot was this: the bearded man back at the door of his truck, attaching a new ammunition clip to his rifle, as a second state police cruiser turned off Route 3 and glided placidly down the entrance ramp.

Directly across the road from the IGA stood the New Hampshire Electric Cooperative's Colebrook warehouse and offices, which was where Woody Crawford and Mark Monahan parked their vehicles each morning. As Monahan stomped on the line truck's gas pedal, Crawford wondered about the .243 Browning BLR deer rifle that his partner always kept in the gun rack of his pickup. "You got your gun?" he shouted.

"Nope," Monahan said. "It's home today. Been working on its sights."

No point in pulling into the warehouse, then. Monahan shot the truck past the supermarket entrance and spun it into a leaning, looping turn — and screeching stop — in a swath of empty gravel at the parking lot's west end. Crawford had had no luck in raising the Colebrook Police Department on the truck's radio. Both men leaped out and stared at what Crawford still hoped was a police exercise of some sort: people huddled by vehicles or else running like hell into the supermarket, a trooper in staggering retreat, his pistol flashing, and a man with an assault rifle pursuing him.

This was very realistic — too much so. "Mother of God," Crawford said. "Are you seeing what I'm seeing?"

Yes, and Monahan also saw the little girl they had passed on the road, now coasting down the entrance ramp. He cried at the top of his lungs for her to stop, and the girl braked so suddenly she fell over. She got up gaping at Mark, and he waved her into cover behind a Dodge van parked just off the ramp.

At nearly the same time another vehicle came down the ramp, rolling obliviously past Monahan's shouts. "Oh, Christ, that's Claude Wheeler," he told Crawford. "Claude!" The vehicle kept going, turning beyond the divider and slipping neatly into a parking space that only seconds ago had entertained gunfire from both directions.

By then the gunman had turned around. He was at the passenger window of an old pickup that sat next to a Thunderbird. They saw him reach through the truck's window and take out a new banana clip — as Wheeler strolled past on his way inside. The gunman snapped the clip into place and looked up, directly at the truck and the two linemen, the orbs of his sunglasses like powder pans in the afternoon light. "Woody, shit — get the hell back in the truck."

Their first thought was to park the truck across the supermarket entrance.

But then they saw a second state police cruiser approach from the south and make that turn. "Check that," Crawford said. "We don't want to block those guys. Go to Hughes — we'll stop traffic there."

Monahan swung the truck across the southbound lane opposite Hughes Road. They tumbled out of the doors again, and Crawford said, "Pinch me, will you? I think I'm ready to wake up."

His partner just stared back at the supermarket. Still dreaming, Crawford looked up in time to see the gunman turn in the direction of that other cruiser and once more lift the rifle to his shoulder.

First IGA manager Lance Walling locked all the doors. Then he started herding everyone — employees and customers, food company sales reps and truck drivers — to the back of the building. Among them was a woman who protested that her son was out in the parking lot. Walling refused to let her out, though, and finally the mother and her daughter went to the back with Julie, Kim, and Cody and the rest.

Albert Riff, forty-eight, the clerk who had been outside with Julie, was helping people get in from the parking lot and shooing others away from the window. He was still at the window himself when the second cruiser arrived and then a woman in a Subaru. He saw the gunman drop to one knee and draw a bead on that cruiser, whose driver seemed unaware of any emergency.

Riff saw two holes open like flower blossoms in its windshield. The cruiser jerked to a stop, rocking forward on its springs, as did the Subaru some sixty feet behind it. Then the cruiser snapped into reverse, backing over a curb and onto grass. Meanwhile the gunman was advancing and spraying fire, forty to fifty shots, Riff thought. The cruiser came to a stop, just its rear wheels over the curb, as its windows exploded in shimmering clouds of broken glass.

The gunman kept going, all the way to what was left of the cruiser's passenger-side window. He looked inside, stuck the muzzle of his rifle through the window opening, and fired several more times. Then — in no particular hurry, as though he were a shopper running errands — he started walking toward the grass where the first trooper had fled.

Once the gunman's back was turned, the woman in the Subaru opened her door. Riff saw her run to the shattered cruiser, linger just an instant at its driver-side window, and turn away in distress. Then she saw a child crouching and weeping behind the van parked on the side of the ramp. She beckoned for the girl to run to her.

By then a Ford station wagon had pulled to a stop behind the woman's car. The driver, a middle-aged man, had gotten out of the wagon. The woman shouted a warning as she hustled the child into her car. Riff saw both vehicles back up and speed away at the same time that he heard still more gunfire.

In the backseat foot well of the tan Thunderbird next to Drega's pickup, a thirteen-year-old boy clapped his hands over his ears.

Ian Venne had ridden his bike to the IGA that afternoon from the T&T Mobile Home Park in Columbia, opposite the Drega property on Route 3. In Colebrook, he had paused opposite the Brooks Auto Parts store on Main Street and had recognized the orange pickup parked there as belonging to the guy who had lately taken to carrying a gun every time he checked his mailbox. The boy wondered if he drove around town with a gun as well. In either case, the guy was having a hard time starting the pickup, was still cranking it like an eggbeater when Ian started pedaling again.

Ian's mother and nine-year-old sister were driving the family's '79 Thunderbird to the supermarket. They passed him as he turned into the entrance ramp, and then Ian's mother helped him stow his bike in the trunk. He went to sleep on the back seat while they went shopping.

Then he woke to a popping sound, looked out long enough to see what was happening, and locked the Thunderbird's backseat doors — he didn't dare try to reach the front.

In the foot well, trembling, he stitched his eyes shut and pressed harder on his ears. That shut out the light, but the sound leaked through: shouts, a woman's scream, more gunfire, and then what he knew must be the voice of the policeman who was being shot at.

The boy squeezed so hard that his ears hurt. Still he heard the policeman pleading for help, and then for his life.

In the Colebrook Village Cemetery, sexton Roland Martin, his grandson Mike Martin, and Robert Grassette were taking a break from mowing grass when the shooting began in the parking lot, which was about 150 yards from where they were working.

By the time the second cruiser arrived, they had moved to the bluff on which sat the Green Mountain Snack Bar. They could see the gunman firing at something in the direction of the entrance ramp, but from where they stood, they couldn't see what.

They were spared the sight of that execution, but not this one. They saw the gunman walk from there and into the grass at this east end of the lot. He used the barrel of his rifle to push aside tall stalks of reed and bulrush. The sexton couldn't see the wounded trooper, but he thought he could hear him saying, "No, no," once the gunman found him.

The gunman didn't speak. He pointed the rifle straight down, almost at his own feet, and fired four times.

Patrolman Steve Breton, twenty-seven, had grown up in Colebrook and had studied criminal justice at Champlain College, not for the pay — $9.50 an hour for a beat cop here — but because he liked the idea of a job where every day was different. He especially liked it in a place where the color of your uniform — blue, gray, green — didn't matter, where all the different agencies pitched in and shared a sense of camaraderie. He had brothers, a lot of them, who respected who he was and what he did, no less than he did them. That was its own sort of pay.

This day was sufficiently different: quiet enough at first to wash the cruiser, or half of it anyway; then a domestic violence call that was really just an argument in need of refereeing; a friendly traffic stop in town, warning given, when a salesman from Lewis Ford pulled an illegal U-turn right in front of him. Now this radically day-changing call from Dispatch — shots fired at the IGA, all units respond.

He got on the radio with Lynn, who told him that Dan Couture, light duty or not, wanted to get picked up. That was good, even if it did take Breton out of his way. Shots fired? Yes, he'd want backup.

Because this was a Code 1000, though, he couldn't wait for it. Breton sped south down Main, in the opposite direction from the IGA, and into Bridge Street. There he popped a Y-turn out of the town hall parking lot, squealed to a stop in front, and waited for Dan. A second passed, and then one or two more, maybe five, and still no sign of Couture, so the hell with it. He'd have to take his chances.

Soon Breton found backup anyway. He had gotten as far as Brooks Chevrolet when he saw a Ford station wagon in the opposite lane flashing its headlights at him. Breton could hardly abide another delay, but he had a feeling this was important. He stopped, as did the wagon. Its driver sprinted over to Breton's window.

It was Lenny Dennis, a guy Breton knew from the window factory he had worked at before catching on full time with the Colebrook Police Department in 1994. Dennis was somewhere in his forties and had formerly been a cop in Connecticut. He knew how shorthanded they were at the Colebrook PD, and how cops everywhere got sent into places without knowing what the whole situation was. Dennis's face was grim. "A couple of troopers are down at the IGA," he said. "Did you know that?"

Fuck, no, Breton didn't know it was like that. He tried to talk — ended up staring slack-jawed at Dennis.

"You want some help?" Dennis said, patting his back pants pocket. "I've got a gun."

Breton wanted information and, yes, he did want help, even if backup from a former cop wasn't strictly by the book. He told Dennis to jump in.

No, Dennis didn't know which troopers were down, or who was shooting, or why. He told Breton he had turned into the IGA and seen Amy Hall's car parked on the ramp and a small bicycle tumbled over on its side. He thought there had been an accident with the bike and he got out to help. Amy, whom Dennis knew as a welder at the window factory, was frantic. She told him a trooper had been shot, to get the hell out of there. From the road he saw a second parked cruiser and a guy with an assault rifle openly stalking the parking lot. So he had this bad feeling there must be another trooper down.

Breton couldn't be sure which troopers were in peril — any of several on duty that day. He knew Phillips and Lord had both been around town, but he couldn't imagine either of them getting taken down by anybody.

Breton's tires squealed as they angled into the ramp. The cruiser raced down it and past the discarded bicycle. "Be careful here," Dennis warned. Breton stopped only when blocked by a cruiser as punched full of holes as a pepper shaker. He got out, and he knew it was Lord inside, more from the cruiser's badge number than what was left of poor Les, who lay across a blood-soaked passenger seat and was all too plainly past saving.

Breton couldn't linger. He looked up to see a man with an assault rifle standing in the vicinity of that other cruiser Lenny had mentioned, maybe forty yards away. The man was looking at him. Now he was walking toward him, now raising the rifle to his shoulder and sighting through its scope.

Breton had drawn his sidearm, a 9 mm Ruger, and thoughts were colliding in a pileup inside his head. There were people in the parking lot behind the suspect, or in their vehicles, maybe, who might get hit if he fired and missed. This was just a suspect, might not even be the guy — someone else might have done this to Lord. And if he missed or if this guy was wearing body armor, he was about to be seriously outgunned.

Dennis had taken cover behind Breton's cruiser, and as the rifle came up, Breton backpedaled there as well. But he knew from the ruins of Lord's vehicle that this wouldn't be cover enough. He also knew there wasn't time to get his shotgun out of the trunk.

Breton gestured to their right. Hearts in their mouths, he and Dennis flew up a shrubby slope to the cover of a steel dumpster at the end of the snack bar's parking lot. Breton thought there was a good chance they'd die on that slope, but somehow they got up it without drawing fire.

The bullets came when Breton poked his head out from behind the dumpster to see where the suspect was. The first round exploded like a grenade into metal just inches from his head. That was when Breton entered that odd dilation of space and time described by soldiers in combat — a hollowed-out form of being in which hearing and smell seem to disappear, vision narrows to only the train tunnel in front of you, and time warps enough for seconds and hours to impersonate each other.

No uniform, no badge, and certainly no ballistics vest — Dan Couture got out of his Chevy Cavalier in just his summertime civvies, his Ruger sidearm bouncing around in the hip pocket of his shorts.

When he was at the police station, Lynn Jolin had needed a cigarette break, and that was how Couture — after Breton had gone out on that domestic call — had ended up on the telephone lines at 2:42 p.m., the moment they blew up with calls from the IGA and near neighbors. He took the first several calls and then yelled for Lynn to man the phones as he limped to his car for the handgun kept in its glove department when he was off duty. Then he went back into Dispatch to tell Lynn to have Breton come pick him up.

But Couture didn't know how close Breton already was, and Breton probably underestimated how fast Couture could move from Dispatch to the front door with his bad ankle. Couture got outside in time to see the department's only cruiser swerve onto Main with its wigwags going.

So he took his Chevy instead. He parked on the road above the IGA and stood aghast for just an instant to see Breton and a civilian, both with drawn handguns, taking high-velocity fire from behind that dumpster. Couture ran in his hop-along gait to join them, hoping that he had cover — he couldn't see around the dumpster to fix where the fire was coming from or who was shooting.

Breton poked his head out once more as Couture arrived, and immediately two more rounds slammed into the dumpster. "He's coming this way," Breton said. "Time to get the fuck out of here."

So Couture, more astonished than frightened, turned right around, retreating with the others to a grassy knoll at the south end of the snack bar, a spot that offered less cover but at least a line of sight to any approach from the gunman's direction. They couldn't see the parking lot from there, though.

They waited, listening, their blood and nerve ends singing. The gunfire had stopped, and none could say how long it was — probably thirty seconds or so — before Breton said he was going to circle through the woods and brush below the cemetery and then come up behind the guy.

Albert Riff was still at the supermarket door, opening it when necessary for other ashen-faced refugees from the parking lot and directing them back to the stockroom in the rear of the store. The glass of the windows and doors was like a membrane separating two different universes. In that other universe, a predator stalked as fearlessly as it might in a video game.

Riff couldn't see what happened in the grass at the end of the parking lot, but he heard the four shots. When the gunman came back into view,

Riff saw him climb in a leisurely manner into the orange pickup and try to start it. Riff could hear the motor turning, but it wouldn't catch.

That was when he saw a Colebrook police cruiser speed down the ramp and stop near the second state police cruiser. Riff stared as the gunman got out of the pickup and drove a cop and another man up to the snack bar dumpster. He heard around five rounds whistle into the dumpster, and he didn't know if the cop and the other guy were still alive.

In either event, the gunman was done with that. He started to walk back to the pickup, hesitated, and turned instead toward the first cruiser. That trooper's overturned Stetson lay on the pavement. The gunman stooped to pick the hat up, looked into the cruiser from its passenger side, glanced back up in the direction of the dumpster, and then circled over to the driver's side.

Still carrying the Stetson, he climbed in, closed the door, and started the vehicle. Someone from the J. K. Lynch disposal company had parked a garbage truck across the IGA's entrance and exit ramps, but Riff saw that now the truck was gone. The gunman maneuvered the cruiser carefully past other cars and eased it toward the exit ramp.

Dan Couture would have no memory of Breton stealing away to flank the gunman. He does remember someone saying, "He's getting into the cruiser." He thinks that was Lenny Dennis.

And he remembers thinking over and over, "What the fuck is going on?" In his brief career as a cop, there had been plenty of times already — conducting interviews in that sexual assault investigation, for example — when he felt as he had as a teenager at the wheel of a bus full of school kids in a blizzard: too callow to be good yet at something this important. Now multiply by ten, twenty, a hundred. He only knew that somebody was shooting a gun — he had no idea who or why or at whom, other than at him, Breton, Dennis. He hadn't even caught a glimpse of this guy who for some unfathomable reason wanted to kill him. And nothing in his twelve weeks at the Police Academy had prepared him for a situation in which he was so outgunned and so defenseless.

Couture heard that the shooter had gotten into a cruiser, but he heard it in that fog of war that had wrapped itself around him as it had Breton. The rifle shots had ceased, at least for now, and he was standing on a different part of the knoll. For the first time, he could see the whole parking lot, which was empty except for the vehicles it contained, some scattered groceries, a few plastic bags lifting in the breeze, and a couple of unarmed men, civilians, running toward the lot's east end.

Then he saw a state police cruiser heading south on Route 3, back toward town. The vehicle passed within sixty feet of him, moving at around forty miles per hour. He can still remember noticing that its rear driver-side window was blown out. For a while, he remembered the house he saw on the opposite side of the road behind the cruiser — but later forgot it. He has no memory of its driver.

At the time he thought it was Scott Phillips at the wheel of the vehicle, but then he wasn't sure. The whole sequence seemed bizarre and off-kilter — a cruiser just puttering along, as if this were any other day, but heading away from the scene of a violent crime with a window blown out.

Even at just forty, the cruiser blinked past him like an image in a rapid-sequence slide show. Then he heard a voice he firmly remembers as Lenny's: "That's him! That's the guy — he shot two troopers!"

Co-op lineman Woody Crawford, pushing his way through the grass, was the first to get to Scott Phillips. Sexton Roland Martin arrived a moment later.

Phillips, as usual, was not wearing any body armor. Pale as new snow, the trooper lay on his back with his hands at shoulder height, fingers clenched, palms to the sky, his hands sliced by what appeared to be glass cuts. There were several nearly adjacent bullet holes to the heart, so crisp they looked to have been cut with a drill, and what would be tallied as eight wounds to the hips and legs, which somehow had carried him this far nonetheless. His .45 Smith & Wesson lay at his side in lock-back position, all its bullets expended. Two full magazines of ammunition hung on his duty belt, useless to a man so badly wounded.

He might have had help, Crawford realized, had he run toward the store. But then he would have drawn fire to bystanders. Instead Phillips had fled to a place where no one else would die.

Crawford remembered that it was just last month that a friend on Pleasant Street had hired him to clear a tree limb off his roof. Crawford was having a tough time of it until Phillips — who lived right there on Pleasant — came out of his house to hold Crawford's ladder and pass tools up to him. Phillips and Scott Stepanian used to go jogging past the warehouse across the road, and Crawford and other Co-op men would shout, "You guys ought to get real jobs, so you don't have to run to stay in shape." Phillips just laughed.

Martin knelt and, without a shred of hope, felt for a pulse in Phillips's neck. An ambulance turned into the supermarket entrance and came bansheeing past Lord's cruiser. The two men lingered at the side of EMT Margaret Smith as she bent over the body. Smith had come in her own car, ahead of the ambulance. Crawford overheard little more than a whisper: "Oh, Scott — he's gone."

Two troopers shot — Dan Couture had no inkling of this until Lenny Dennis had shouted as much as the gunman had fled. The dazed patrolman made his way down to Les Lord's cruiser, which was still running. Lord had died with his foot on the brake pedal — which he so rarely touched in life — and it remained there yet.

Couture limped toward where Scott Phillips lay, but by then nausea had nearly overcome him. "I shouldn't go up there, right?" he said to the EMT. She looked at him with eyes like dust and nodded.

Couture turned, and there was Steve Breton. "We're too late," he said.

Another ambulance came skidding into the lot. They're too late as well, Couture thought. Then he thought again about the clear shot he had — how long ago? — at the perpetrator, a killer who was going somewhere else now at the wheel of Scott's cruiser. In a certain way, Couture did have the benefit of a field training officer, at least unofficially. That was Scott Phillips, who had had infinite patience with the dozens of questions about methods, procedures, and protocol that Couture pestered him with. Scott had this habit, though, of never just answering the question outright. Instead he'd turn it back on the rookie — "Well, what do you think? What would you do?" As a rule, this annoyed Couture, but it taught him good lessons about where his instincts lay in relation to that stuff.

So what about that clear shot at the perpetrator — well, the alleged perpetrator — that he had had on the road? Couture thought about what he knew at that moment, which already seemed like it was years ago. There was a shooting in progress. Then someone got into a cruiser, and then a cruiser went by.

What if Lenny had yelled out an instant earlier? What if Couture had known as the cruiser approached that this was the bastard who had murdered Scott and Les? He had a moving target, and behind that a house, maybe with people inside. A civilian had yelled that this guy was the killer, but Couture had no confirmation of that. So — if Lenny had yelled earlier — he would have been drawing his sidearm on a suspect who was fleeing the scene in a stolen police vehicle, certainly, but who may or may not have killed two troopers, who could have been someone else entirely, for all he knew.

At the Police Academy they had hammered this into him, over and over: once you send a bullet on its way, you can't call it back. And then get ready, because there are going to be questions, a lot of them. You're going to go through the wringer. You'd damned well better be sure, beyond the wisp of a doubt, that deadly force was the only option and that no one else was endangered.

Or on the other hand, even with as little warning as he had from Lenny, maybe he could have done the Dirty Harry thing — reflexively drawn and squeezed off a shot. What would have happened then?

Couture could almost hear Scott's voice in his ear again, as if this was all hypothetical — "Well, what do you think? What would you do?"

"What if both answers are wrong?" he asked, nearly whispering it aloud. But Scott wouldn't say anything more.

Steve Breton, picking his way through brush, abandoned his flanking maneuver once he saw from activity in the parking lot that he no longer had anybody to flank. He came out of the woods and scared the hell out of Mike Martin. Martin caught his breath and told Breton that the gunman had gotten into a cruiser and driven away. But Martin didn't know whose cruiser, and Breton knew hardly more than Dan Couture about what exactly had happened.

"Both dead," Dick Marini told him.

"Who?"

"Les Lord, Scott Phillips — both shot to death."

Breton was up near the snack bar, and Marini was a state liquor enforcement officer from Gorham, a thirty-year veteran of police work at various levels. He knew all the Troop F officers and happened to have been working on a licensing investigation in the area. Marini was just nearing the IGA when he heard sounds he thought were backfires from a truck. Then the Code 1000 came over his radio.

Breton shook his head, trying to clear the haze inside it. He walked like a pilgrim to Lord's cruiser and then to that place in the grass where Phillips lay. Roland Martin was still by the body with the EMT, and Roland said that the guy who did all this had been driving that Dodge pickup over there.

Breton had a good idea who that was. After some delay, he managed to get through to Dispatch on his portable radio. He asked Lynn to run a registration check on New Hampshire plate 737243. Lynn confirmed that the truck belonged to Carl Drega.

Marini and Dan Couture met the enraged Breton at his cruiser, just as he was pulling the 12-gauge shotgun out of the trunk. "I know who this fucker is," he said, "and I know where he lives. So let's get the son of a bitch before anybody else gets killed."

They talked. No, they shouldn't take the cruiser to chase him — Drega wouldn't be pulling over to the side for any wigwags today. They'd stand a better chance of approaching him unawares in Marini's unmarked vehicle, a '92 Plymouth Acclaim. No, Dick wasn't packing a sidearm. Liquor inspectors don't carry weapons for routine work. There was no sense in having three guys in the car with just two guns between them, and someone needed to secure the crime scene here. That should be the kid who couldn't run.

Couture fished the Ruger out of his shorts and handed it to Marini. Breton told Dan to report in to Dispatch. Then he jumped into the passenger seat of the little green sedan. He told Marini to turn south onto Route 3. "We're going to Columbia," he said.

At 2:50 p.m., only eight minutes after Dan Couture had received the first call about an incident at the IGA, the patrolman reported in using the radio in the Colebrook cruiser. He wasn't surprised that this took a few repetitions: "Signal 1000 on Colebrook frequency 18B to Colebrook."

At last: "Go ahead, 18B."

"Notify Troop F that the individual — well, he took Trooper Les Lord's vehicle and is heading down South Route 3. Notify all units who might be listening."

"He took Les Lord's cruiser? He's in a cruiser?"

Couture confirmed that, added that an unmarked unit was in pursuit. With his thoughts still ricocheting inside his head, he signed off. By then people were coming out of cars and odd corners of the parking lot like earthquake survivors. An adolescent boy had spilled out of that Thunderbird near Drega's truck and had run like he was on fire into the arms of the first adult he saw, a wide-eyed woman who had wandered out from behind the supermarket. Several others had gathered around Lord's cruiser.

Couture went to shoo them away, and then he knew what he had done. Shit, he thought, Les's cruiser is right here. You just reported the wrong stolen vehicle, you dumb fuck. But in this he forgave himself, thinking it wasn't really that important anyway — it would be the only cruiser in the state of New Hampshire heading south.

It bothered him that Les's motor was still running. He wanted to turn it off, let the cruiser and its operator rest there in peace until the Major Crime Unit arrived, but he wasn't so callow as to touch anything that was part of a crime scene.

Les's radio was running as well. Couture overheard traffic between Colebrook Dispatch and 911: "Yeah, this is operator 113 with 911. That abandoned call came from Ducret's Sporting Goods. He's reporting a shooting as well."

"Could you repeat that, please?"

"Okay. Ducret's Sporting Goods. I took the callback because there was an abandoned phone call. The guy said there's a shooting going on outside the store."

The 911 operator got another call from Ducret's and plugged it directly through to Dispatch. Someone at Ducret's was shouting, "We need some help here now!"

An ambulance driver on his way to the IGA broke in, wondering if the scene at the supermarket was safe yet. After a pause, Lynn replied, "I need another ambulance at the front of the News and Sentinel. We have two people down at the News and Sentinel."

Nightmares happen, thought Couture, going numb. You think you've hit bottom, and it couldn't get worse, it must be time to wake up, but instead — it gets worse. He looked around. He knew he didn't look like a cop, but it was a small town. Some of these people knew him, and others, somehow, could just tell, and they were looking at him. He was a cop — no matter what he looked like, no matter what he had done, or hadn't done, or what was happening somewhere else.

He got a clipboard and some witness report forms out of the cruiser. Then he turned to a woman with raw, weeping eyes. "Excuse me, ma'am — Colebrook police. Were you a witness to what happened here?"

Reporter Claire Lynch of the *News and Sentinel* was among those shooed away from Lord's cruiser by Dan Couture. She had parked her Blazer at the snack bar and then hastened down to the vehicle hung up on the curb opposite the median. She could tell from a distance whose cruiser it was. Were it not for his clothes, she could not have known it was Les inside.

She didn't need to be told to back off. She staggered away, nearly lost her balance. Her notebook fell to the pavement, and she left it there, its pages riffling in a soft breeze. She couldn't take notes on this, nor could she take a photo. John Harrigan's voice, but different, a whisper wrapped in barbed wire, unspooled from the back of her mind: "We can't have this today."

She heard from someone else that Scott Phillips lay dead at the other end of the lot. She had seen enough. She didn't need to go there. The hill up to the snack bar felt like the slopes of Calvary. Her estranged husband, Ken Knapper, stood among the onlookers on the bluff.

Knapper still worked for Claire's father's company, J. K. Lynch Disposal, and he had been the driver of the garbage truck that had sealed off the parking lot. But he and partner Bobby Noyes had stayed only a few minutes. Knapper had looked inside Lord's cruiser in the hope of plucking out his sidearm, but Lord had fallen to his right and lay atop the pistol. Then they drove the truck to Noyes's parents' house, which was nearby, where Noyes begged in vain for the loan of a rifle. Knapper told Claire that he had pretty much seen the whole thing, that the guy was still on the loose, that the Colebrook police force had buckled at the knees and didn't even try to stop him. Claire could tell he was suffering almost as much as she was.

She couldn't help thinking how much both of them could use someone to come home to that night.

A moment later, at the wheel of her Blazer, Claire fought to make the turn onto Route 3, and then to stay on the road long enough to get safely back to the newspaper building, her hands shook so. She tried, but couldn't imagine who in the North Country would want to kill these men. There were enough sirens going off to suggest an air raid. An ambulance hurtled by in the opposite direction.

At work she was in the habit of parking her suv on the side of the building abutting the Getty station, while everybody else on the staff parked in the municipal lot behind the News and Sentinel Building and Memorial Park, a lot that you entered through an entrance between the apartment house and Ducret's Sporting Goods.

Right now Claire wanted to park with the rest of the staff. She forced the Blazer into the alley, and then — wonder-struck, but unable to stop right there — she worked the suv around the form of what looked to be a woman who had fallen facedown on the pavement at the end of the alley. Nobody had come to help her up yet.

9
IN THESE
DAYS OF
CARNAGE

CHARLIE JORDAN's *Northern New Hampshire Magazine* was a magazine in tabloid newspaper clothing, published monthly on newspaper-style paper stock and with longer features than a small newspaper could run on the region's news and cultural affairs — like a tribute to Robert Pike, who had died in July. Pike was the foremost historian of the North Country logging industry, author of classics like *Spiked Boots* and *Tall Trees, Tough Men*, and Donna Jordan needed information on him for the piece she would write for the September issue of the magazine.

So all the Jordans adjourned to the Colebrook Public Library on the afternoon of August 19. Charlie's car was in the shop, and they went in his mother's car instead, an old Plymouth Duster that smoked and rattled and ran as if on dust. Charlie parked it in a lot behind Hicks Hardware on the corner of Main and Pleasant Streets. Then he, Donna, and seven-year-old Tommy crossed Pleasant and strolled to the library, which stood roughly opposite Ducret's Sporting Goods on Main.

Inside, Donna went in search of Robert Pike, Tommy vanished into the children's section, and Charlie passed the time with a volume of Matthew Brady's Civil War photographs. Sure enough, he found himself stunned all over again by Brady's images of the results of this industrial warfare, with its new killing machines — scores of fallen soldiers bloated and ballooning out of their uniforms, the corpses strewn haphazardly behind breastworks or in a shot-apart cornfield. It was death without glory or dignity, and America's first wholesale glimpse of such loss. The images were cruel but necessary, Charlie thought. People needed to be shown what slaughter was really like — though even this hadn't stopped them.

He turned several pages and paused at the crack of rifle fire. He blinked and shook his head. A daydream wrought by force of these photos? Then women's voices, a shout, the distinctive ping of a bullet ricocheting off stone or steel. Julie Colby, the librarian, heard it too.

"Well, what's that, do you think?" she said.

Charlie went to a window facing Main. The sounds were coming from behind Ducret's or else from Bridge Street. Charlie couldn't see anything of Bridge beyond Collins Video and Photo, on the corner opposite the old gas station. A Forest Service cruiser flashed past on Main, its siren wailing, heading north, unconcerned with whatever might be happening on Bridge. Then Charlie saw Sylvia Collins, who worked at the state liquor store next to the library, out on the sidewalk and craning her neck in the direction of Bridge.

Outside, Charlie learned from Sylvia that two people had been shot at the IGA. He sprinted back into the library to tell Donna and Tommy to get down on the floor, Julie to lock the doors. He himself went out the back door, still in a sprint, hastening through the parking areas that backed the buildings on Main, to Hicks Hardware and his mother's Plymouth — where he had left his camera.

Ad manager Jana Riley was the first to see cruiser 608 at the News and Sentinel. Some of the staffers were around the police scanner, but others, still listening, had gone back to their desks. Susan Zizza was staring at the pasteup board, wondering what to pull off the front page to make room for the story Claire would come back with. Dennis Joos was proofing his piece about the Jordans and the 45th parallel sign, while Vickie Bunnell and Susie Sambito had gone back into their offices.

Jana was at the front desk again, but making circuits back and forth to the east-facing window next to the scanner. There she'd lift the blinds and peer at the emergency traffic speeding north. She had already seen Dan Couture hurtle out of Bridge and go drag racing up Main in his little Cavalier.

A little before 3:00 p.m., Jana was startled to see a cruiser going the opposite way, heading south — and more startled to see it make a leisurely turn onto Bridge with all its windows down. She had a queer intuition, immediately confirmed, that the cruiser was coming here. But why not the police department? She felt herself shiver.

Three seconds later, Jana overheard Vickie saying, "Okay, what's Scottie Phillips doing here?"

Inside Lazerworks, Beno Lamontagne's wife, Karen, had called Beno out of the back of the store to help an elderly man with VCR hookup problems. Beno came out in time to see a state police cruiser work its way into a parallel parking space in front of the newspaper building.

The bearded man who got out of the cruiser — carrying an assault rifle military style, at port arms, across his chest — wasn't in police uniform. A young woman, climbing out of the car that the cruiser had parked in front of, did a double take as the man walked with that gun between their two vehicles. She crossed Bridge Street not in a run, exactly, but in a hurry.

For his part, Beno was flashing back to the spring of 1984, the day state police detective Chuck Jellison, now the commander of Troop F, nearly died at the Getty station in a hand-to-hand struggle with a fugitive killer. The like-it-was-yesterday memory of that event and all the sirens going off got Beno thinking some sort of SWAT team exercise was in progress around that haunted spot.

There was something odd in the peculiarly methodical way the bearded man had exited the cruiser, and the slow, even paces he took with that rifle propped across his chest. It was how a priest moved about the altar, Beno thought. But it had to be official business of some kind.

The young woman came into the store looking back over her shoulder. Beno was looking that way too, watching in gathering wonder as the bearded man halted at the Sentinel's front door, rattled its handle, glanced to his right, to his left, and then marched around the building's left corner with the rifle now jabbed straight up in the air.

Bunny was disappointed not to be casting flies with John Harrigan on Fish Pond that afternoon, but he still looked forward to a good meat loaf dinner with the kids, Vickie and Earl, and Earl's wife, Pam.

At two o'clock that afternoon, Irene filled up a shopping bag with ground beef, eggs, tomato sauce, and spices, and they drove in their Buick Skylark to Sliver's old cabin: across the Connecticut to Bridge Street, where Earl and Pam had their house just a few hundred yards from the Sentinel Building and where Bunny waved in the direction of Vickie's office; and then right on Main and south out of town until that left turn into Bungy Loop at the wide lawns of the Shrine of Our Lady of Grace — which looked that day like the set for an old Hollywood musical, its grass was so rich and the sky lifting above it so blue and fair.

The cabin sat above a swale of its own thick grass just off the public access road into the pond. Sliver and Henrietta used to live there from May to October, moving back to their apartment in town for the winter. Sliver rented boats back in the time when seventy-five to eighty vessels would crowd into the twenty-three-acre pond on opening day, and parked cars would choke the launch area. Sliver also sold parking space on his land for fifty cents. Bunny remembers a fisherman who objected to that, a flatlander who wouldn't pay to park because he was sure all this land belonged to the state. Sliver told him to look it up in Concord. In fact he did, once he'd parked and fished and gone home, and he ended up mailing Sliver the fifty cents. "Dad just mailed it back," Bunny said. "He told him they'd start over the next time."

By the 1990s the pond was silting up and weeding over, but Eric Stohl and other Fish & Game COs still stocked it with trout each spring, and it was still good fishing right on Bunny's doorstep. The cabin was expensive, though, with its upkeep and the property tax. Bunny knew that some things that needed doing probably wouldn't get done during his lifetime. He stood on the grass next to a hydrangea in bloom and looked up at some mealy cedar shingles on the roof. "Brother's going to have to replace those when this belongs to him," he said, referring to Earl just as Vickie did. Then he went to turn on the water pump while Irene fiddled with the padlock on the door.

Inside there was a woodstove, a bedroom, a couple more beds in the loft, an upright piano in the living room, and moments of family history on every wall and flat surface: a dapper black-and-white portrait of Sliver, square-jawed and smoking a pipe, like an Oxford don, and another of him on a sled with his best team of Irish setters; Bunny and Irene's wedding portrait, with Irene in a trailing gown and gold ringlets, Bunny in a tux and sporting the natty mustache he still wore; a sampling of the trophies Bunny had won bowling or in sharpshooting contests; a snapshot of Vickie and Brother, maybe aged ten and seven respectively, Earl in a candy-striped blazer and bow tie, Vickie wearing a mischievous glance and a jumper with a puff-sleeved blouse. They looked like Mickey Rooney and Judy Garland.

On a shelf opposite the piano stood a piggy bank in the shape of an owl in cap and gown, a lighthearted gift to Vickie on her graduation from Plymouth State; also a coffee mug she bought for herself on passing the bar. It had "LAWYER" on one side, "JUSTICE FOR ALL" on the other.

Bunny chose a chair on the porch while Irene lit the stove, tidied up the kitchen, and prepared the meat loaf. A breeze sweetened with the scent of pond lilies blew in off the water. The quiet rose up to the sky and sifted like mist into the clouds — until a squall of sirens rose up from town. Bunny guessed that it was some fire he'd read about in the paper the next day. He hoped no one was hurt. He also knew Harrigan well enough to chuckle at how annoyed John must be by a big fire on press day.

At three thirty or so a car turned off Fish Pond Road and came to rest in front of the cabin. Bunny knew the car — it belonged to Paul Nugent, who had gone to Sunday school with Vickie, who was now a near neighbor to Brother and Pam. Paul got out on the driver's side, and Bunny was surprised to see Pam get out on the other, since ordinarily she'd be at work at the First Colebrook Bank. Bunny presumed that she or Brother had invited Paul to dinner, which was fine. There should be plenty. "What are you kids doing here so early?" he asked.

Susan Zizza knows her Bible well, and she would find later that her own story and those of other witnesses were like gospel accounts — each true enough from its own perspective, each limited by that perspective and the tricks of grief and memory, all essential to the apprehension of an event that changed everything. She would find that portions of her own memory, her own gospel account, had been erased or rewritten as early as the next morning.

None of the gospels agree on the exact words of Vickie's shouted warning. Susan remembers a terse, "He's here — everybody get out!" The closest thing to an authorized version appeared in the News and Sentinel's August

27 issue: "My God, he's got a gun! Everybody run!" All accounts agree that Vickie's voice was strident, authoritative, not panicked.

So it began with the clarion call of that shout. Then — after Vickie had called to Tallak and pushed Susie Sambito ahead of her through the door in the hallway near Chandra Coviello's desk — Susan remembers Vickie pausing for an instant in the hallway with her hand on her office door handle.

"I won't forget that look on her face," Susan said later. "There wasn't any panic in it. It was more like a heightened sense of awareness. She just suddenly seemed aware of everything, while my own sense of awareness was already shutting down."

There's no saying what Vickie thought about as she paused outside her door. About going back for Tallak, perhaps, who had scrambled under the couch? Or retrieving the pistol hidden in her filing cabinet? Vickie had a .38, not the .25 that Eric Stohl thought she had bought. But she never liked the idea of a gun in the office, and the weapon wasn't loaded. Or was she simply steeling herself, as she had once before climbing birches with John?

So far as Vickie knew, Drega was coming in through the front door. Jana Riley had cried out almost at the same instant as Vickie, and then the retreat was on through the rear exit. Susan remembers running in eerie, muffled silence. Other accounts described yells and screams, and surely there was the commotion of furniture being shoved aside, shoes scuffling, the back door banging open after someone managed that tricky latch. Susan heard — or remembers — none of that, only the running.

Either Jana or Leith Jones was the first to get outside — probably Jana, who remembers fumbling with the hasp. In the parking lot, Jana literally ran out of her dress shoes and sprinted barefoot for the nearest open door, the back entrance to Ducret's. Leith ran for his car at the far end of the parking lot.

Susie Sambito wasn't so sure about leaving the building. "Is this safe?" she called out to Vickie.

"Probably not," said Vickie. "Go to Ducret's."

Dennis Joos had been talking with Susan about tearing up the front page. He heard the shouts from the front, but not the words exactly, and then saw the stampede through the hallway between Chandra's desk and Vickie's office. "What the hell's going on?" he said.

Susan found herself outside in a world as weirdly silent as the building had been. Had she turned around, she would have seen she was within arm's length of the gunman, who was already at that corner of the building. Susan ran for her car, past two empty parking spaces, and then Dennis's pickup, and then a second vehicle, an SUV. She reckoned that if the man with the gun was coming, he had to be there by then. She dropped to the hardtop and crawled on her stomach under the SUV.

The rest who had gone out the door — Jana, Chandra, Susie, and finally Vickie — struck a beeline past the apartment building to the store, about forty yards distant. There were no parked cars in their way — no was there any cover. Drega shouldered his rifle and took aim at the fleeing women. At the sound of gunfire, Vivien Towle, who had been back by the scanner, stopped in her tracks at the screen door — as did Dennis.

The shots atomized the silence that had wrapped itself around Susan. "And why didn't I get out from under that car?" she would ask herself later, and then ask again — seven times seventy. Her friends were dying around her, and she would accuse herself of St. Peter's cowardice. At the same time she concedes that she never really had a choice. Everything happened so fast that she was never really there — her body just went about its motions on autopilot as it sought to remain the sort of breathing husk to which a blanched soul could eventually return.

She would recall each shot like a storm's only thunderclap — or would until the next day. She would feel angry, even violently angry, reading and hearing about the differing numbers of shots reported by some witnesses, in some gospel accounts. Leith Jones would tell the police there were two, Jana Riley four or five, Richard Paquette (a clerk inside Ducret's) a hailstorm of at least thirty.

Susan would be angry until she realized that her own exact sum had melted away, that she no longer had any idea how many shots were fired. A freeze-frame image of Vickie crumpling and falling to the pavement — described that same day in her police statement — would also have disappeared. But she still remembers thinking at first, because they were dressed similarly, in white blouses and long print skirts, that it was Vivien Towle who was falling. She doesn't remember when she knew instead that it was Vickie.

Jana Riley looked back over her shoulder at the first crack of the rifle. She saw Vickie's face, saw the light being snuffed out of it even as she fell. Chandra Coviello screamed at the splintering pop of several rounds into the frame of Ducret's back door, which still seemed miles away. Susie Sambito, with the scent of gunpowder in her nostrils, kept following Chandra and Jana toward that door.

Inside the Sentinel Building, Vivien Towle saw Vickie fall, and turned around, back to the shelter of a storage room inside. Dennis Joos showed no such prudence. Instead the former seminarian launched himself through the door and at the gunman.

Jeannette Ellingwood was behind Dennis, and she watched it begin. She saw the gunman pivot with Dennis wrapped around his back and shoulders. Drega's GMC baseball cap fell to the ground as the two men tipped together onto the hood of Jeannette's car. Then they were on their feet again, lurching out of Jeannette's sight to the grass of Monument Lot.

Susan Zizza's world had shrunk to the same narrow tunnel described by Steve Breton and Dan Couture at the IGA. Through that tunnel and from under that SUV, she saw the gunman shake Dennis off like a house cat. They stood face to face, each with his hands on the rifle, but Dennis's were on the barrel, which was as hot as a branding iron.

Three times he lost his grip, and each time Drega squeezed off a shot. The first went through Dennis's ear, ricocheted against the building, and was heard by Charlie Jordan. The second buried itself in his arm. Dennis still kept grappling until the third, square to the midsection. He staggered backward, then fell forward like a cut tree.

Susan wanted to turn away. Instead, awestruck, she watched, turning about under the SUV, as the gunman walked to where Vickie lay motionless on the pavement and then back to Dennis. By this time Beno Lamontagne was out in the street, shouting at the gunman, telling him to stop.

Drega instead stood over Dennis as he had Scott Phillips. "You should've minded your own fucking business," he said. Holding the rifle as if it were a pistol, he drilled, in rapid succession, four bullets into Dennis's back. Then he changed the ammo clip on his rifle in motions that struck Susan as "very controlled, well practiced."

At some point Susan scrambled out from under the suv — without ever deciding to, exactly — and then she was next to Dennis, but still deep inside that tunnel. She remembers a series of faces, one after the other, glimpsed as though from the bottom of a well: Charlie Jordan, and then Karen Lamontagne, and then Yvette Collins, the wife of the pastor of the Baptist church across the street.

Susan was the first to reach Dennis, at his side before Drega had left the area, and she doesn't remember what she said to him, but it's there in other gospel accounts and the newspapers: "Don't go, Dennis. We love you. Please don't leave us."

Karen Lamontagne had been trying to reel her husband back into the store. She had no success until the gunman had attached that fresh clip and taken a step in Beno's direction. She and Beno locked the doors and got down on the floor with their two customers. But Karen kept an eye above the windowsill, watching the movements of a man she recognized as a previous customer, someone who had come in a few weeks before, who refused to believe that Lazerworks didn't carry any of the early satellite television dishes just starting to appear in the North Country. He more or less accused her of lying. At last Beno had to come out of the back to get rid of him.

Karen noted the unruly beard, the blue jeans tucked into his boots, the plaid shirt that was unbuttoned and flapped as he walked, the blue denim shirt he wore beneath it. "He moved gracefully," she said later. "His face was calm and alert. I thought there might be a trace of a smile on his lips."

The inventory of Ducret's Sporting Goods is devoted almost entirely to the North Country's two most popular sports, hunting and fishing, with target shooting not far behind. Its pegboard aisles were hung with lures and reels, vests and ammo belts, backed by glass cases of handguns and deer rifles. The store only rarely sells an assault rifle. Owner Phil Ducret had taken charge of the store in 1985 from his dad, who started the business and who used to shoot with Bunny on Colebrook's pistol team in contests against other towns.

Clerk Dave Robidas was from southern New Hampshire and had worked in a housepainting business Phil had going while the elder Ducret still ran the store. Vickie had recently done wills for Robidas and his wife, and last winter it had been Dave who suggested that Vickie buy a Taurus .38, a good value for ease of use and reliability. Vickie didn't say why she wanted a handgun, and Robidas didn't ask.

Ducret was at home that day, and Robidas was manning the store with another clerk, Richard Paquette. There were two customers out front — John Brunault, who was a guard at the Coös County Jail, and his friend Matt Rosi — but the staff was in the back. Paquette was listening to reports from the IGA on the store's police scanner, while Robidas was on a backdoor cigarette break.

The cigarette must have dropped from his lips at this explosion of people out the back door of the Sentinel, the four women who ran straight toward him as though their lives depended on it. Immediately — from the shriek of those bullets hitting the doorframe above his head and the women's screams — Robidas understood that this was just what it looked like. He backed into the doorway as Vickie staggered, rose, and fell. He threw the door open for Jana, Chandra, and Susie.

He and Paquette followed the three survivors into the store. Robidas called 911 and then called Phil Ducret, as Brunault and Rosi herded the women into a place behind a table in back. Meanwhile Paquette started loading handguns from the store's inventory. Once the four men were armed, they ranged themselves on either side of the back door as more shots came from the parking lot. They could see where Vickie lay motionless on the pavement, but not the blood rising in a rose-colored pool on her other side. They assumed they were under attack by a second gunman, maybe allied with the one they had heard about at the IGA.

They waited and heard no more gunfire, but they could hear people yelling and moving about. A Chevy Blazer, Claire Lynch's, eased through the alley between the buildings, past Vickie, and into the parking lot. Once the car went by, the men, one by one, slipped out the door and ran to Vickie.

From the rectory kitchen of the Baptist church on Bridge Street, next to the town offices, Pastor Charles Collins stared like Blake's Los, howling in fire, as the gunman walked across the grass of Monument Lot to the driver-side door of a state police cruiser. The killer walked with the stock of the rifle on his hip, the barrel pointed to the sky, the gun's sling over his shoulder. He slipped his arm out of the sling, entered and started the cruiser. He pulled it slowly forward until he was opposite the town hall and police station, and nearly opposite the church. There he stopped to put one hand out the window and wave two westbound cars on ahead of him.

Collins also saw Susan Zizza kneeling by a man who lay facedown on the grass. Susan had appeared as soon as Drega had finished with Dennis. She didn't know that the gunman had arrived by cruiser, and when the vehicle pulled into sight from behind the building, she thought Les Lord had come to help. She nearly called out, but something stopped her. Later she would believe that Drega had paused in front of the town offices in the hope of picking off whatever policemen came out.

Perhaps so. By then Collins had joined his wife, Yvette, on the front steps of the church. He and the gunman locked eyes for a time that stretched, Collins said, to "some fifteen or twenty very awkward seconds." If so, this was a length of time nearly as great, it would be determined, as that which separated the first shot Drega had fired at Vickie and the last he fired at Dennis — thirty-five seconds.

Yvette thought at first she recognized this man, thought him the butcher who cut meat at the IGA, but then she knew he was a stranger to her. The killer stopped, stared at her husband for that awkward, pregnant moment — the minister and the devil, the temporal world like a bone between them — and then he steered the cruiser in a slow U-turn in front of the church. The vehicle eased past the town offices, past Lazerworks and the camera shop. At the corner, it flashed a right turn signal, waited for a break in traffic, and then swung south.

Afterward the pastor was nearly as shaken by that encounter on the steps, by the rank pitilessness of that gaze, as he was by the events across the street. "God help us in these days of carnage," he would write at the end of his statement to the Colebrook police, "when man kills without conscience."

Karen Lamontagne, a registered nurse, had no idea there was another victim besides Dennis. She was by Dennis's side just seconds after Susan, and she saw that among his multiple wounds — seven — was an exit wound to the spine, which made her reluctant to turn him over. She clawed at the grass and dirt around his face, clearing a trench through which he could breathe. She heard someone, probably Yvette Collins, say, "Oh, my God, my God — it's Vickie."

Karen left Dennis, thinking that Vickie might have a better chance. Vickie was still breathing when Richard Paquette reached her. Paquette had knelt by her side while Robidas, Brunault, and Rosi fanned out into the parking lot with handguns drawn — just as Drega was completing that U-turn. Yvette had heard Vickie gasp for air, seen her eyes roll white and vacant. Karen saw that among Vickie's several wounds was one to the neck, a sliced carotid artery. It was already too late, and Karen ran back to Dennis with a hollow wind blowing in her head.

Beno was by Dennis as well, and so was Charlie Jordan. Then Charlie was up taking photographs as a Colebrook ambulance arrived in front of Monument Lot, as a pair of EMTs hurdled the low stone wall that fronted the lot. Soon there were others: Cherie Leavitt, an RN who had been using the ATM at the First Colebrook Bank when she heard gunshots; Bill Bromage, president of that bank, also an EMT and volunteer fireman; Brenda Marquis, an EMT who had been paged to go to the IGA but then told no, go instead to the Sentinel — who feared she had been given the wrong location when she saw a state police cruiser driving south out of Colebrook; and several others.

Leavitt and the EMTs confirmed that Dennis was running a pulse, but it was way too low. They had to turn him over, and did so as if they were handling a soap bubble. Karen sent Susan running into the Sentinel Building for paper towels to sop up blood. They saw that Dennis's eyes were open and dilated. There was not nearly as much blood as they anticipated.

Charlie Jordan never saw who had shot Vickie and Dennis. He arrived just as the cruiser was turning onto Main, during a lull in which a pedestrian strolled alongside the wall and then a cyclist pedaled by.

He knew immediately that Dennis had better help than he could provide. He could endure only a glance at Vickie. Almost twenty years before, he had seen Bunny and Irene sharing a booth at Howard's Restaurant with a young woman and, after introductions, been charmed to learn that he and Vickie both had Hungarian blood on their mothers' sides. Now all that blood had been emptied from her.

He understood no more than anyone else why this had happened, and to these two, of all people. He shared with everyone else the dread that whoever did this might be back for more — or that someone else might be coming, if there was more than one killer on the loose. He was glad to see that Brunault and Rosi had weapons and were searching the bushes around the area. But here we are right in front of the police station, he thought, and there's not a cop in sight.

On the grass, Brenda Marquis and Cherie Leavitt were performing chest compressions on Dennis. Paula Chapple, who had arrived with the ambulance, was trying to get a breathing tube down his throat while Bill Bromage held an oxygen mask to his face. Dennis was struggling, and Beno had to hold his legs.

Charlie got shots of that, and everything else too. He was turning like a windlass, shooting in all directions, shell casings crackling under his shoes, because a news photographer had told him once to do it like that, to make sure he didn't miss anything — and also, he said, because "the camera viewer gave me a distance from the reality I found myself in the midst of. It was my 'protection,' such as it was."

Margaret Smith, a volunteer EMT for fourteen years, was still at the IGA when she was paged for two subjects down at the News and Sentinel. She left Penny Henry, another EMT, with the body of Scott Phillips, and she arrived on Bridge to find several people already at work on a man lying in the grass, but no one tending to the woman on the pavement.

Alas, Vickie Bunnell was an old friend — just as Scott Phillips had been. Margaret swooned and fell to her knees. She lingered that way a moment, overcome not just by sorrow but by the nothingness that lay beneath it, these many years of finding the flesh of her friends and neighbors broken and bloodied. She had never seen anything as bad as this, though — or so inexplicable. When she got back on her feet, she went to the other victim, who by then had been hooked to a defibrillator, and she recognized Dennis Joos as well.

Margaret had nothing to do there, and she went back to Vickie, just to be with her. That was when Steve Breton, with an older man in civilian clothes — she didn't know him — arrived on foot. They stopped at where

Dennis lay, hurried over to her and Vickie, and just as promptly turned and disappeared across the street. She had hoped that Breton was there to provide security, but soon Chief Mike Sielicki arrived, in civilian clothes, and also Phil Ducret, who was carrying a handgun.

From where she stood, Margaret could hear Brenda Marquis say that the defibrillator's readings weren't making any sense. "That's enough," Brenda said. "Let's get him out of here."

Dennis moaned as hands, many pairs of them, lifted him from the grass and into a gurney. They put him into the ambulance just as a second one arrived. Margaret saw Bill Bromage climb into the first ambulance with Dennis, along with Paula and the EMT who had come with her. Then the ambulance peeled away, wheeling left on Main for the Upper Connecticut Valley Hospital, just a few minutes distant.

Once the ambulance was gone, Margaret saw Susan Zizza go weeping into the Sentinel Building, come out again a moment later, climb into her car, still weeping, and drive out of the parking lot, also turning left on Main. So she's not going home, Margaret thought.

Then she wondered about disturbing Vickie, about performing CPR on her corpse for no other purpose than to get her onto a gurney, loaded into the back of the second ambulance, and taken away. She hated to think of Vickie just lying here, as if abandoned. She saw Paul Nugent, who lived on Bridge Street, who often brought drinks and appetizers to Vickie's office at cocktail hour, walking this way. Other people besides Susan were starting to come out of the Sentinel Building.

Just the same, Margaret was about to go to work on Vickie when her pager toned again at 3:10 p.m. She was needed in Bloomfield, Vermont, across the river from North Stratford, where, God help us, another officer was down.

In the parking lot of the Upper Connecticut Valley Hospital — just off Route 145, on the way up South Hill to John Harrigan's place — Bill Bromage watched as Dennis was hustled through the doors of the emergency room. That's when he was paged to respond to a house fire in Columbia.

10
KILL
YOUR
BLUES

STILLNESS REIGNED at Vickie's house on the slope of Blue Mountain — no vehicle in the driveway, no sign of disturbance or forcible entry. Forest ranger Bert von Dohrmann, wielding a shotgun borrowed from Chief Sielicki, knocked on the front door. Deputy ranger Scott Owen provided cover.

Von Dohrmann had been using the restroom at the fire station on Pleasant Street when the scanner went off. He saw Scott Phillips's cruiser coming the wrong way, saw in his mirror that its rear window was gone. He parked by the other cruiser in the IGA parking lot. EMT Margaret Smith had to tell him that this was all that was left of Les, that Scott lay over in the grass.

Von Dohrmann thought he was the only law officer on the scene. He hadn't noticed Dan Couture taking the names of witnesses in his civvies. Others came: Sielicki and Jules Kennett, a part-time Colebrook cop; Troopers Scott Stepanian, who was Phillips's best friend, and Tom Yorke; Border Patrol agent Dave Perry; and Scott Owen.

Someone — Stepanian? — said that Drega might be looking for Vickie Bunnell, that someone should get to her house ASAP, provide protection if she was there. Von Dohrmann was unarmed, and Sielicki gave him that shotgun. Owen climbed into the passenger seat of von Dohrmann's cruiser, and they drove past some sort of commotion on Bridge Street. They heard nothing on the radio about trouble there, and for Vickie's sake, they couldn't stop. They turned left on Parsons Street and east on Route 26, to a northern access road to the Bungy Loop, a more likely route for Drega if he didn't want to be noticed on the way to Vickie's.

There was no answer to von Dohrmann's knock. From here the sirens in Colebrook were barely audible. They walked to the back of the house, and from the fire pit von Dohrmann could see church spires and the southern spine of Monadnock. "Not unless you've got a shovel," Les had told him, and that was why von Dohrmann was still alive to gaze at Monadnock. A telephone, a radio, a pile of papers, and some food wrappers — that was why Liz, whom von Dohrmann had called from the IGA pay phone, still had a husband.

How much sense did that make? Not enough.

Dick Marini and Steve Breton weren't strangers to each other. Marini got around, and recently he had ridden as backup with Breton to some place he remembered only as a swamp somewhere around Colebrook. A woman had gone there to commit suicide, but Breton talked her out of it. The young cop did a good job, Marini thought.

Breton had a feeling Drega was headed straight home to Columbia, but just in case Drega was waiting in ambush instead, he had Marini edge the Plymouth slowly into each intersection on the way into the Colebrook business district — even Edwards Street, where Breton, his wife, Christine, and four-month-old Nicholas lived a few doors away from Audrey Noyes.

Past Clarkeie's, they saw people walking the sidewalks as usual, going in or out of stores, in what struck Breton as some lewd imitation of normal life. Something abnormal, though, was happening at Bridge Street — there was an ambulance, a crowd of people. Whatever it was, they didn't want to drive blithely into the middle of it, like Les had. They drove one more block, entering the parking lot for the town hall and police station from the backside.

They crossed Bridge on foot. EMTs were ministering to a shooting victim Breton learned was Dennis Joos. The woman facedown in the parking lot was Vickie Bunnell, and the EMT with her said she was gone. Someone else said that the gunman had turned around on Bridge and headed south on Main. Breton noticed two empty banana clips of ammunition on the ground and asked a bystander, a friend, to make sure nobody touched those.

The two men checked the perimeter of the town hall and the court chambers.

No one was in the police station except Lynn Jolin, the dispatcher, who said that Mike Sielicki was on his way from the supermarket. Lynn was working hard to hold herself together. "Drega's headed down Route 3, and we'll be in pursuit in an unmarked car," Breton told her. "Make sure everybody knows that, okay?"

As they passed the Shrine of Our Lady of Grace and then Dan Ouimette's logging and excavation business, and as the road opened up, Marini pushed the Plymouth to seventy-five. He heard Lynn announce to all units that they were in pursuit of cruiser 719, and Marini radioed a correction: "That's 608 — repeat, cruiser 608."

Meanwhile Breton went undercover. He unpinned his badge and slipped it into a pocket. He thought about taking off his blue shirt as well, but decided against it. Instead he slid down far enough in his seat so that the blue shirt disappeared, so that only the top of his head appeared over the dashboard. "Can this go any faster?" he said to Marini.

COLEBROOK DISPATCH, 2:53 P.M.

Caller 8: I know that there's an emergency. This is Lori Berry. I just wanted to let you know that Trooper Phillips's car 608 just went through my driveway, and it wasn't Scott Phillips that got out of the car.
Dispatch: Okay, all right — thank you, Lori.
Caller 8: At Owen Park, at Kenneth Parkhurst's.
Dispatch: Okay.
Caller 8: Thanks.
Dispatch: All right.

COLEBROOK DISPATCH, 2:57 P.M.

Caller 12: Hi, it's Lori Berry again. I just went over to my uncle's house next door. The house has — the door's been kicked open.
Dispatch: Okay, who's your uncle, Lori?

Caller 12: Kenneth Parkhurst.

Dispatch: Okay.

Caller 12: That's where I told you I just saw the cruiser leave — the 608 cruiser.

Dispatch: Uh-huh.

Caller 12: And I went over there, and I called, and nobody answered, and I just saw that the door's been forced open.

Dispatch: Okay.

Caller 12: And I didn't dare go in.

Dispatch: All right, I will tell them, but you need to stay in.

Caller 12: Okay, I'm going up the end, but there's — it was unusual for them not to answer their phone.

Dispatch: Right, right. And it's very — well, don't be out there.

Caller 12: Okay.

Dispatch: All right — bye-bye.

Caller 12: And you're gonna send somebody? I know everybody is busy, but —

Dispatch: Yeah, um — we've got people down.

Caller 12: Okay, well — I'm scared.

Dispatch: Lock your doors and stay inside.

Caller 12: Thank you.

Dispatch: Okay — bye-bye.

He cut off most of his beard with scissors. Then he lathered and shaved. The face that was revealed to him in the mirror, he thought, was that of a stranger, a pasteboard mask that would serve well enough. He wanted to keep cutting, to angle the razor so it bit into his skin and peeled it like wood shavings away from his skull, to let the eternal part of him come clear. But there wasn't time. He had more to check off on his calendar before he met Rita.

Still in the cabin's basement living quarters, he donned the police surplus ballistics vest he had ordered from a dealer in Miami. He could have sworn he heard one of his sewing machines running, a foot on its treadle, as he climbed the stairs to the ground floor, but at the top everything was still. He stood there a moment in that quiet, on that plywood floor, the light slanting in from the west over the river, the motes of dust like broken glass in the air. Now that his ears no longer rang with the reports of his rifle, whose barrel was now a few inches shorter, he could hear the murmuring tick of the clock on the wall. He noticed he'd left his coffee mug on the workbench next to where he'd hung laundry this morning. He admired that bench he built, its heft and squareness and finish.

He walked over to the picture window and looked at the Connecticut, its water a loamy green, moving in its imperceptible way past the ramparts he had raised against it. He wondered where Eric Stohl and Dan Ouimette might be. Parkhurst hadn't been home, and neither was Ouimette at his shop. The Columbia town hall had been vacant as well. Stohl could be anywhere — but maybe the CO would come to him today. He drank in the beauty of the river and reproached himself for not calling Gerry Upton about that canoe trip down the Allagash.

Now he'd need some kerosene — or diesel fuel, if he was short on kerosene. He had plenty of diesel and probably enough ammunition. With a sigh, he abandoned the coffee mug, the ticking clock, the sewing machines, the clean laundry, the sturdy benches. He went forth from the cabin into the blessed light and air.

Kenneth Parkhurst might have died at fourteen, when he fell to the road out of his parents' car on a trip to Groveton. He still has headaches to remind him of that. He might have died a few years later in Korea, on a freezing night in which he slept sandwiched between two air mattresses. These saved him from the artillery shell whose debris crushed the other four GIs in that foxhole. And he might have died a few minutes after Vickie, had he not had a dentist appointment that afternoon.

Perhaps his wife, Isabelle, survived as well because of Kenneth's preference for a dentist in Canada. The Parkhursts live in a one-story ranch home at the end of a cul-de-sac off Route 3 just south of Colebrook. Isabelle Parkhurst is an amateur musician, and on Tuesday afternoons her sister comes to play duets with her on portable electric keyboards. On that particular Tuesday, however — since Isabelle's sister lives right on the way to Canada — they played at her sister's house.

During that week in August, Parkhurst had taken his screen door off its hinges to do some work on it. That left just the front door, which was stout and securely locked, but it took Drega only a minute to kick that in. He found the house empty, and there was no damage besides the ruined door that Lori Berry found. Lori was Isabelle's niece and their neighbor across the road.

"Drega was mad, though," Parkhurst said later. "He drove out into the field, spun that cruiser around, and then took off out of here like a shot. You could see the tracks in the lawn."

Parkhurst considers his wife's survival no less miraculous than his own. Isabelle demurs. "I don't think so," she said. "I don't think he would have shot me." In fact the former Columbia town clerk was one of those rare officials to whom Drega was usually civil.

"He'd have done it just to spite me," Parkhurst said. "You know that."

Steve Breton's first thought was to disable the cruiser. He had told Dick Marini to slow down as they approached Drega's place in south Columbia, and then Breton broke into a cold sweat to see 608 at rest at the top of the driveway, waiting to make a turn back onto Route 3. "Okay, let's ram it," he said.

To the west a plume of smoke billowed into the sky. Something was burning on Drega's land.

Marini wasn't so sure about a collision. "Then we're out of action too," he said, thinking this little Plymouth would crumple like a soft-drink can against that heavy Crown Victoria. "Maybe it's just us out of action."

Instead they slowed enough to allow the cruiser to ease out ahead of them and to continue south. They followed at a distance of five or six car lengths. Drega observed the speed limit — fifty-five miles per hour — and drove with his right arm stretched over the passenger-side headrest. "Not in any hurry, is he?" Breton said.

Marini was on the radio again: "This is Liquor 13 to Colebrook Dispatch. We've got 608 right in front of us. We're following the suspect on Route 3, south, leaving Columbia — "

It occurred to them both at once that Phillips had probably left his radio on, that the suspect could well be listening to this. Marini clicked his microphone off with a nervous glance at his partner. Up ahead, Drega still drove at an easy pace with his arm over that headrest. "Maybe we're okay," Breton said.

As they approached North Stratford, Breton got to thinking about the bridge there into Bloomfield, Vermont — and they decided to risk the radio again. Marini couldn't get through to either Colebrook Dispatch or Troop F. Finally he tried the dispatcher at the Lancaster Highway Department. Lancaster answered, and Marini reported their position and situation.

Sure enough, in tiny North Stratford, the cruiser blinked a right turn onto the bridge. At the same time, Breton saw a Fish & Game cruiser approach from the other direction. Whoever was in that green Blazer popped his blue lights as he prepared to follow the stolen cruiser across the bridge. "Oh, shit," Breton said. "I don't like Drega knowing he's being chased yet. This could get him shooting again."

Marini picked up his mic. "I'll try Channel 2, see if I can tell him to snuff those."

COLEBROOK DISPATCH, 3:17 P.M.

Dispatch: Colebrook emergency line.

Caller 15: Hi, this is John calling from Channel 7 in Boston, Mass. How're you doing? Is there something — hello?

Dispatch: No comment.

Caller 15: All right, well.

Dispatch: Colebrook emergency line.

Caller 16: Yeah, this is Dan Shallow at the Academy. Is it all right for people to leave the building?

Dispatch: Um, I would — oh, gosh. I don't know. Hold on.

Caller 16: Are you there by yourself?

Dispatch: Hold on — yes. Hold on.

Caller 16: When was this? I haven't heard about it.

Dispatch: Hi, Dan.

Caller 16: Yeah.

Dispatch: If I — I think if I were you, I'd hold them for a while.

Caller 16: Okay.

Dispatch: He may be headed back this way. We're not sure.

Caller 16: Okay — you haven't apprehended the suspect yet?

Dispatch: No, we haven't.

Caller 16: Do you know the suspect yet?

Dispatch: Yes, it's Carl Drega.

Caller 16: Okay — all right. Thank you very much.

Dispatch: Colebrook emergency.

Caller 17: Hi, this is Associated Press. We heard word that there was —

Dispatch: No comment.

Caller 18: Hi, this is *Channel 7 News* calling. Is there —

Dispatch: No comment.

Caller 19: Hi, it's Donna calling from WBZ.

Dispatch: Yes.

Caller 19: You guys have two state troopers down somewhere?

Dispatch: Ma'am, we have every emergency line lit up. I can't talk to you right now.

Caller 19: Thanks.

Dispatch: Colebrook emergency line.

Caller 20: Hi, ma'am. I know you're busy. This is [inaudible] with Fox 25 in Boston.

Dispatch: Bye. Colebrook emergency. May I help you?

Caller 21: Yeah, this is Vern Reynolds down in Columbia. Has anybody called in a fire down by the T&T trailer park?

Dispatch: Yes, sir, they have.

Caller 21: Okay, thank you.

The business center of Bloomfield, Vermont, begins and ends with DeBanville's General Store, which, like the Green Mountain in Colebrook and the Blue Mountain in Columbia, is a combination snack bar/convenience store with gas pumps — except DeBanville's also offers outside dining at umbrella-shaded tables. The store and its small parking lot sit opposite the bridge from New Hampshire and on the intersection of Vermont Route 102, which runs north-south along the Connecticut, and Route 105, which bears northwest to Newport and the Canadian border. A railroad trestle arches over 102 as it runs south out of Bloomfield, and a sprinkling of maple-shaded private homes spreads along both roads within walking distance of the store.

Sharlyn Jordan had gone to DeBanville's around two thirty that afternoon to pass some time with her friends Junior and Rose DeBanville. From the parking lot, she waved to George Nugent, who was up on a ladder against the second story of his house. "Painting up a storm, are you, George?"

"Might as well," Nugent said. "Good day for it, don't you think?"

Inside the store someone called to say that something was going on over in New Hampshire and that Junior should turn on the store's police scanner. Junior got around to that once someone else called with the same advice.

When the scanner said that the suspect, a Columbia resident named Carl Drega, was heading toward North Stratford, Sharlyn said, "Well, if I was being chased by the law, I'd cut right over into Vermont."

The store was busy that afternoon. Rose was talking to a fisherman from Connecticut who wanted some live bait. The fisherman's wife and two little boys were looking at a table full of sale items outside. Rose directed the guy to a store in Island Pond, a town twenty miles up Route 105. But the wife wasn't ready to go yet. Other people were outside as well, and a few more inside the store.

Sharlyn thought that with a shooting suspect on the loose, she ought to at least pull the keys out of her Ford Explorer. She fetched the keys and wound up leaning at the sill of an open window with Junior and Rose. Within a couple of minutes, Rose said, "Well, here comes a New Hampshire trooper right now."

"Wonder which way he's headed," Junior said.

Sharlyn watched the cruiser bear left down 102 South, and then she knew. "That's not a trooper! That's the guy — look, he's got no uniform on!"

The cruiser, at moderate speed, disappeared under the railroad trestle. The next vehicle across the bridge was a green New Hampshire Fish & Game cruiser, also moving at moderate speed, as if nothing much were going on.

This cruiser paused at the intersection of 102 and 105, and then turned south on 102. It slowed to a halt on the grade leading down to the trestle. Then its blue lights came on, like embers bursting into flame.

Wayne Saunders was six when his father took him grouse hunting and they were met by a game warden in the woods down in New Hampshire's Lakes Region. The ranger checked his father's hunting license and wished them luck. The boy liked the hat the warden wore, similar to the Stetsons he saw in cowboy movies, and also the badge. He liked the woods too, with their unfenced whiff of the frontier he saw portrayed in those Westerns.

Saunders was wearing just such a hat and badge right now, though instead of hiking through the woods, he was on a stolen-car chase, and the quarry had just popped up like a grouse in front of him. He didn't know there were officers down. He shared Kevin Jordan's concern, however, that this was Scott Phillips's cruiser he was chasing. He had worked with Scott just last week, investigating a camp break-in down a dirt road in Stewartstown. As impossible as it seemed that anyone could make off with Scott's cruiser, it seemed equally unlikely that harm could have come to a smart, affable cop like him.

When Saunders caught sight of 608 — a couple hundred yards ahead of him, too far to see the driver — he was surprised that the thief was traveling so slowly. He radioed Fish & Game in Lancaster that he had the suspect in front of him and flicked on his light rack — with scant expectation that someone in a stolen state police cruiser would pull over and show him his license. Before he turned left toward the bridge, Saunders heard something on his radio about lights, but he didn't know what or from where. As he approached the river, a shout arrived through the half-open window on the passenger side: "Hey, kill your blues!"

Saunders didn't know where that came from either, but he was edgy enough to do just that. By the time he got across the bridge and in front of DeBanville's, where there were about half a dozen people on the store's outside deck, he'd lost sight of 608 and wasn't sure which of three roads the suspect might have taken from there. But he saw dust floating in a cloud beneath the railroad trestle, as if a vehicle had just passed that way.

He turned left again, pointing south, but with a feeling that something was going wrong. He eased the Blazer down the slope to the underpass. Route 102 went straight from there, and he should have been able to see the cruiser at that point. But the right lane was empty.

Saunders remembered he was required to show his lights when chasing a felony suspect across a state border. He moved the Blazer into the middle of the road and flicked his blues on again. A Chrysler minivan came the other way, squeezing past him as if the cruiser were a stalled car in the road. Typical Vermonter, Saunders thought.

He advanced a few more feet and then stabbed his brakes at this: a Toyota sedan stopped in the left lane on the far side of the underpass, the driver-side rear fender of Scott's cruiser, which was pulled off to the right of the underpass, and a man standing next to the cruiser in a black ballistics vest and a state trooper's Stetson. The guy in the hat was pointing the muzzle of a rifle square at his windshield. Distance? About twenty feet.

Saunders experienced no pain as such. Instead — simultaneously — he heard the report of the rifle shot, felt the force of such a mule kick to his chest that he was sure he'd been hit by a shotgun slug, and felt his left arm go limp and numb.

At the Police Academy, they had said the engine block is your best friend if you're taking fire in your cruiser. Saunders fell to his right, behind the engine block and the dashboard. He took his right hand off the steering wheel to shift into reverse, then put it back on the wheel. He backed quickly, but under control, to DeBanville's and its parking lot. Still pitched over on the passenger-side seat, he raised his head just high enough to see those people on the deck of the store and at the sale table. They stood frozen, as if enchanted. Saunders shouted as loud as he could, "Get the fuck out of here!"

But they didn't move. Not until the next instant, when six shots rang out in rapid sequence, leaving a spray of holes like carnation blossoms across the Blazer's windshield, jolting the vehicle itself with the force of those mule kicks.

Outside the store, people screamed and ran for cover. Saunders stomped on the gas pedal and sent the Blazer barreling blindly in reverse through the intersection, still taking fire. Glass burst from it like confetti as it hopped the curb, then churned across George Nugent's lawn. The Blazer careened over the riverbank and would have fallen into the Connecticut were it not for the bank's lattice of cottonwood, paper birch, and red maple.

The vehicle bounced off a twin-trunk birch, bumped against a cotton-wood, and hung in the brush, halfway down the embankment, with its front wheels off the ground and its lights still flashing.

Junior DeBanville could set his watch by retired Vermonter Joe Lizzie, who lived five minutes down 102 and who arrived at the store at precisely 3:15 each afternoon to buy a newspaper. That day — at 3:14 — Lizzie braked to a halt as he approached the railway trestle. He saw a New Hampshire State Police cruiser pulled off to the left and a man by its driver-side door, someone wearing a Stetson but not otherwise in uniform. He had a rifle trained at a New Hampshire Fish & Game cruiser only a short distance away.

Once the shooting was over, and the other cruiser had backed out of sight on the other side of the intersection, the gunman turned and looked at Lizzie as he sat at the wheel of his Toyota.

"Was that the bear?" Lizzie turned to see an old woman standing on the other side of the road. "Did you get him?" she said to the gunman. "The bear that's been bothering people around here?"

The gunman ignored her. He stowed his rifle, climbed into the police vehicle, pulled onto 102, and proceeded south as if sightseeing.

On the other side of the underpass, a heavyset man in a button-down shirt was crouched behind a Plymouth sedan with a shotgun in his hands. The guy was waving his shotgun in the air and yelling at Lizzie to get the hell out of there.

Lizzie put his car in drive, climbed a little more briskly than usual to the intersection, glanced at the green cruiser snagged in the shrubs and trees along Nugent's riverbank, and turned east over the bridge.

That day he bought his newspaper in New Hampshire.

From where they were on the bridge over the river, Steve Breton and Dick Marini could see that 608 had never come out the other side of that underpass. As soon as they were across the bridge and near the intersection, Breton said, "Stop the car. He's got to be right here somewhere."

Marini pulled to the left shoulder and they both jumped out. Marini stayed behind the Plymouth, in a spot that gave him a clear line of fire with his shotgun through most of the underpass. Breton thought it likely that Drega meant to climb to the top of the trestle. From there, he could rain fire down on the whole area. Breton sprinted across the intersection, conspicuous in his blue shirt and pants, with his Ruger drawn, making for the nearest corner of the store. His plan was to scramble up to the tracks some distance west of the trestle and see if he could get Drega flanked this time.

Meanwhile the CO whom Breton had recognized as Wayne Saunders was edging his cruiser down the slope. Breton didn't like the looks of what Wayne was up to. He tried to signal him to back off, but he was behind the Blazer and Saunders never saw him.

Then the first shot, the warning to the bystanders, the second flurry. The Blazer narrowly missed a Jeep Cherokee as it rocketed diagonally through the intersection and onto the lawn. Oh, God, he's gone too, Breton thought.

Marini would have had a shot at Drega had it not been obstructed by the man in the Toyota. Nor was further pursuit possible now with another officer down, an unsecured crime scene, and a lot of panicked bystanders on the loose. Breton saw 608 continue south as Marini backed his car into a roadblock position across the ramp to the bridge. Then Marini set about clearing the intersection and the store grounds, and Breton went after Saunders.

This didn't make sense to Wayne Saunders: he had just taken a shotgun slug to the chest, he must have, and yet he felt like he was still alive. If he wasn't, then this wasn't heaven. If he was, he might not be alive much longer if the gunman — whoever it was, for whatever reason — was coming to finish him off.

Saunders's shotgun was in a boot on the left side of his seat, but he couldn't move his left arm to get it. He struggled to quiet the roar of his breathing, his gasping, fearful of the racket it made. With his right hand he popped his seat belt, and then, reaching across his bloody shirt, he managed to find the door handle.

The door fell open, and the cruiser was pitched enough for Saunders to feel as if he were dropping out of an airplane. He slid and fell several feet down the bank, almost into the water. With his one good hand he worked his sidearm, a .40-caliber Sig Sauer P229, out of its holster. Then he lay still a moment, gasping.

At last he began climbing up through the underbrush, on his knees and one hand. He was like a drowning man struggling to the surface, and with no sense of how far that was. Eventually he heard someone — who was that? Steve Breton? — calling his name.

Vickie Bunnell and Tallak in Vickie's office at the News and Sentinel Building. Fred Harrigan's law books line the bookshelves behind Vickie. Photo courtesy of the *News and Sentinel*, Colebrook, New Hampshire.

Donna Jordan, Charlie Jordan, Vickie Bunnell, and John Harrigan on vacation in Halifax, Nova Scotia, during the 1980s. Photo courtesy of Charles Jordan.

Dennis Joos interviewing presidential candidate Pat Buchanan and his wife in the newsroom of the *News and Sentinel* during the 1992 New Hampshire primary. The door through which Vickie Bunnell and newspaper staffers would flee in 1997 is in the background. Photo courtesy of Charles Jordan.

Trooper Leslie G. Lord in a photo taken by Charlie Jordan for an Upper Connecticut Valley Hospital advertisement. Photo courtesy of Charles Jordan.

Trooper Scott E. Phillips at an accident scene. Photo courtesy
of the *News and Sentinel*, Colebrook, New Hampshire.

Where the shooting began: LaPerle's IGA supermarket in Colebrook.
Photo courtesy of the author.

Carl Drega, in the driver's license
photo that was circulated to law
enforcement agencies and media
outlets. Photo courtesy of the
New Hampshire Office of the
Attorney General.

Dennis Joos attended by emergency medical personnel moments after being shot by Carl Drega. Photo courtesy of Charles Jordan.

The remains of Vickie Bunnell lying beneath a blanket in the parking lot behind the News and Sentinel Building. From the left, standing vigil, are John Brunault, Dave Robidas, and Paul Nugent. Photo courtesy of Charles Jordan.

The Bloomfield, Vermont, railroad trestle, from behind which Carl Drega ambushed Conservation Officer Wayne Saunders. Drega stood to the left. The bright photo tents on the right side of the road mark the locations of ejected shell casings. Photo courtesy of the New Hampshire Department of Fish & Game.

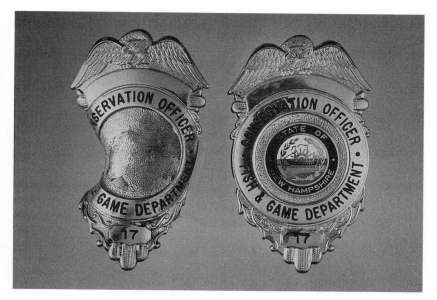

The badge that saved Wayne Saunders's life, now on permanent display at the Concord headquarters of the New Hampshire Department of Fish & Game. Photo courtesy of the New Hampshire Department of Fish & Game.

Wayne Saunders's bullet-pocked cruiser. The white rods indicate bullet entry points. Photo courtesy of the New Hampshire Department of Fish & Game.

A wounded Jeff Caulder, clutching Todd Bogardus's shotgun, being carried out of the woods at Brunswick Springs. Assisting the EMT are, left to right, Sam Sprague, Bogardus, and Steve Brooks. Photo courtesy of Toby Talbot and the Associated Press. © 2015 The Associated Press.

John Harrigan being interviewed by Fredricka Whitfield of CNN in the aftermath of the shootings. Photo courtesy of the *Coös County Democrat,* Lancaster, New Hampshire.

The front door of the News and Sentinel Building draped in black. Photo courtesy of the *Coös County Democrat,* Lancaster, New Hampshire.

Funeral procession of law enforcement personnel for Scott Phillips and Les Lord led by Governor Jeanne Shaheen and her husband, Bill, Saturday, August 23. Photo courtesy of Charles Jordan.

News reporters gathered for a press conference around a display of the pipe bombs and other weapons and explosives recovered from the ruins of Carl Drega's barn. Photo courtesy of the *Coös County Democrat*, Lancaster, New Hampshire.

The name that Carl Drega had blocked into the foundation of his barn in 1971, partially eradicated by gunfire. Photo courtesy of the *Coös County Democrat,* Lancaster, New Hampshire.

The monument to Vickie Bunnell, Dennis Joos, Scott Phillips, and Les Lord that was raised next to the News and Sentinel Building in 1998. Photo courtesy of the author.

Earl (Bunny) and Irene Bunnell, with a friend, as they sell Kiwanis raffle tickets on Main Street at the 2008 Moose Festival. Photo courtesy of the author.

GOING
TO WAR

IT'S NOT JUST MARGARET SMITH — all emergency medical technicians (or cops) in a small town are harrowed by work involving people they know and the laments of those people's friends and family. Upper Connecticut Valley Hospital doctor's aide and volunteer EMT Penny Henry, twenty-eight, had heard the shots at the IGA from the nurse's station at the hospital, which is not far from the supermarket as the crow flies. She and Barbara Daley, another young EMT, raced there in the Colebrook 1 ambulance. Margaret Smith had arrived just ahead of them.

Penny knew from the badge number of the stranded cruiser that it belonged to Les Lord, a family friend. "You can't help him," someone told her. "He doesn't have a head."

She had come to know and like Scott Phillips from his visits to the hospital on casework. In death his skin was as white as a Styrofoam cup — Margaret said she had never seen such a ghastly white before. Penny bent to lay a stethoscope against Scott's chest, working around the hollow wounds, simply because she wanted so grievously to hear something.

They had been there only three minutes when they were paged to yet another emergency in progress, this at the News and Sentinel. But here the parking lot was still in chaos, and Penny couldn't bear to leave Scott to the gawkers arriving from all directions. So Margaret and Barbara drove away in Colebrook 1, and Penny stood vigil.

Chief Mike Sielicki arrived at the supermarket in his civvies, and then some other officers showed up, and crime scene tape went up around Les's cruiser. Soon Sielicki came over to this plot in the grass. "He became very emotional," Penny would say in her witness report. No less emotional was Scott's neighbor on Pleasant Street, Jules Kennett, who came after Sielicki.

When the fire truck arrived, Penny begged for a tarp that she could use for covering the body, and the crew produced one, but they warned her not to use it until Bob Soucy, the medical examiner, said so. Then the fire truck was called away to a structure fire in Columbia. Penny went to her knees to brush away ants, the occasional fly.

Scott Stepanian was off duty that day, and he arrived, like Sielicki, in his civvies. Stepanian "lost it," Penny would report, mourning loudly enough to turn heads in the parking lot. At last Stepanian left, vowing to come back, doing so just as Dr. Soucy approached from the direction of Les's cruiser and as a helicopter came churning up over Route 3 from the south.

The left side of Wayne Saunders's blouse was drenched in blood, and Steve Breton presumed he had been hit in the shoulder. "Wayne, put your gun away," Breton said. "He's gone."

"Who's gone?" Saunders said. "Who is that guy? What the fuck's going on?"

Breton helped the wounded man get the Sig holstered. Then he and George Nugent pulled him up the bank, out of the brush, onto Nugent's lawn. Breton told him that the guy in the cruiser had also shot Scott and Les, but didn't mention they had died. Saunders himself didn't look good, Breton thought. His face had gone pale and he might be slipping into shock. Saunders didn't seem to be in pain — in fact seemed oddly euphoric. Breton made him sit down on the grass, though Saunders protested he was fine.

Dick Marini was in his Plymouth and on the radio. He had gotten through to Troop F, reporting that there was another officer down, that the suspect was again mobile, heading south on Vermont 102 toward the Maidstone Lake or Lancaster areas.

"Wayne needs a hospital — fast," Breton said to Marini. "I don't know if there's time for an ambulance or if there's even one available with all the shit going on."

"Sure, and now there's another crime scene to secure," Marini said. "We need my car here to keep a lid on the traffic."

They decided to commandeer a civilian vehicle. The driver of the Jeep Cherokee that Saunders had nearly hit in the intersection was Vermonter Harry Stinson, who had just come back from the New Hampshire side with his wife, Christiane. Now the couple was among the onlookers on Nugent's lawn and the first to whom Steve Breton turned. "Sir," Breton said to Stinson, "do you have a valid driver's license?"

Later Breton would remember that question — in all its officious vacuity — as a sign he wasn't thinking clearly. Nor was Saunders. When Breton told him that they'd be riding in Stinson's Jeep to the hospital, Saunders looked at DeBanville's — where people stared in ranks from the deck and parking lot, ignoring Marini's demands that they go inside — and said, "Can we stop there for a soda first?"

Stinson was told to drive north up 102, which would have less traffic than Route 3, and to cross the river at Colebrook. He left Christiane at the scene and pushed the Jeep as fast as he dared, its hazard lights blinking. A Vermont game warden flashed by them in the opposite direction, and once they had crossed into Lemington, Breton noticed that same pillar of smoke he had seen just a few minutes before on the opposite side of the Connecticut.

Saunders was in front, bleeding copiously over Stinson's passenger seat, while Breton, using a rag from the Jeep's trunk, applied pressure to his shoulder from the rear seat. Breton was also slapping him on the back of the head, hard, and shouting into his ear to for him stay awake, not to die on him.

In Colebrook, they found people and cars clotting up Bridge Street in front of the News and Sentinel. Breton put his head out the window and yelled for them all to get the hell out of the way.

Dr. Bob Soucy had grown up in northern Maine and gone to medical school in Iowa with Bill Gifford, the son of Doc Gifford and Parsie. Bill talked warmly about Colebrook and would put issues of the *News and Sentinel* in Soucy's mailbox. In 1988 Soucy visited the hospital Bill's dad had founded, and the next year he joined a medical practice based there.

By 1997, as Coös County's medical examiner, Soucy was familiar with violent death, and the frequency with which he knew its victims. Nonetheless, he was shaken to find Les Lord dead in that cruiser at the IGA. Lord had been a patient of his. Soucy was treating him for hypertension, had told him to lay off junk food. "There are worse things than Twinkies," Lord said.

Indeed there were. Soucy put on his gloves and battled his emotions as he went about his task amid that carnage. He didn't like it that the vehicle was still running and in gear, that it might take off across the parking lot if the dead man's foot happened to slip off the brake. "We can't turn it off," one of the investigating officers told him. "We've got to leave everything just as is until all the evidence is collected."

Soucy worked carefully, mindful of that foot and brake pedal. Then he had to go to where Scott Phillips lay. Mike Sielicki walked with him across the parking lot. They glanced up at the chopper in the sky and Sielicki said, "Probably news media."

Penny Henry was there with Phillips, who lay in a contorted position, Soucy noted, on his back and on top of an anthill. The examination took only a moment, and Penny pleaded permission to lay a blue tarp over Scott. "They're probably up there taking pictures," Soucy said. "Go ahead."

But Sielicki said no. Again, nothing could be disturbed in any way for the sake of evidence and its integrity. "Evidence for what?" Soucy asked.

"The prosecution — once we catch this asshole."

Soucy boiled at the mere thought of that. "I'm doing my job," he snapped. "If you guys do your job, there won't be any prosecution."

He said he'd be back to make out the death certificates and hoped these men would be covered by then. He went back to his car steeling himself for another dose of bitters downtown. He thought back to his one meeting with Drega, that office visit two months ago, and the hair lifted on the back of his neck as he recalled the particulars of that odd conversation.

Prosecution? Well, he didn't think Mr. Drega was the surrendering type anyway.

Steve Hersom, New Hampshire trooper first class, thought that in the morning he'd deliver some reports, forms, and supplies from Troop F to Scott Phillips up in Colebrook. Then they'd have lunch and work some traffic patrol together. Instead Hersom spent much of the day at the scene of a traffic accident near Mount Washington.

By midafternoon he was at Troop F headquarters in Twin Mountain working on a diagram for his accident report. Then — like Dan Couture at the Colebrook Police Department — Hersom was asked to take the place of the regular dispatcher on the telephone for a moment. That was when the call came from Colebrook Dispatch that two troopers were down.

Troop F commander Chuck Jellison was off duty, but everybody knew what to do: get in a vehicle with some weapons and ammunition, head north, keep your ear to the radio — but stay off the air unless you have something of Code 1000 priority. Troopers flew out of the building like it was on fire.

Hersom drove up Route 3 as fast as he'd ever pushed a cruiser — "at warp five factor," he said — with Detective Chuck West, thirty-nine, following in an unmarked car. Hersom didn't like not knowing who was down, but he feared Scottie had to be one of them. He didn't think about Les Lord. Lord had been with Highway Enforcement for so long that Hersom still didn't quite think of him as a trooper — which was fine with Les. But he remembered Lord when the radio said the suspect had stolen cruiser 719.

In Lancaster, Hersom waved West over to the road shoulder. They decided that West would take the Lancaster bridge across the river and go north on Vermont 102. Hersom would continue up Route 3, and that way they'd cover both arteries to the south, with only two crossing points — Northumberland into Guildhall, Vermont, and North Stratford into Bloomfield, Vermont — between Lancaster and Colebrook.

Hersom had just cleared Lancaster when he heard that shots had been fired in downtown Colebrook. Nearing North Stratford, he heard someone identified as Liquor 13 report that another officer was down, that the suspect had just left Bloomfield, driving south on 102. Hersom answered and got Liquor 13's location.

He slowed, perhaps, to warp three across the bridge into Vermont, confident that either he or West would soon meet this fugitive. He was about to veer past the sedan blocking the intersection after the bridge when he was waved to a stop by a man he recognized as Dick Marini. "Jesus, I can't get anybody to answer at Troop F," Marini said. "I'm glad somebody's finally here."

"You got everything under control?"

"Well, no, I could use some help with this fucking crime scene. Everybody's just standing around gaping, won't clear the area. But that's all right — you better get after that guy."

Hersom himself couldn't help but gape at the Fish & Game cruiser with its lights still popping on the riverbank. Marini told him that there were at least three dead, and who they were, and that Wayne Saunders might not make it.

Hersom was about Scott Phillips's age, the son of a rescue paratrooper who trundled his family around the country until he retired to Pittsburg in 1972. Hersom was an athlete, and he might have had a career in baseball had he not partied too hard at college in Louisiana. He got straightened out in the U.S. Army, and was a cop in Nashua until nine years ago, when Chuck Jellison suggested he try the state police.

He knew Carl Drega well enough to say hi, had considered him just a grouch — by no means a killer. Vickie Bunnell had drawn up Hersom's parents' will and counseled him through a divorce. He'd be the first to admit he wasn't good at keeping his family and professional lives separate — as Scottie had been. Troop F was the first place that really felt like home to him, mostly because Jellison ran it so well, and guys like Scottie and Les made it so much fun to work there. If Troop F was home, they were his family.

Hersom took leave of Liquor 13 and steered under the railroad trestle. He felt he was doing what he had prepared to do in the army — go to war.

Penny Henry was still with Scott Phillips when Stepanian returned, now in uniform. He asked her if he could sit with his friend alone for a while. By then Penny had learned that two other shooting victims had come into the ER.

"I think they need some help at the hospital, and I should probably get over there, if I can find a ride," she said. "Is it okay if I go? You'll stay with him?"

Stepanian said that he would. He settled himself down in the grass and the ants next to Scott, and Penny heard Stepanian speaking softly to him as she left. "Hey, buddy," he began.

Word had gotten around the IGA crime scene that Wayne Saunders had been shot in Bloomfield and taken to the Upper Connecticut Valley Hospital. Dan Couture asked Chief Sielicki if he might go there to check on him, and Sielicki told him to hurry.

If Kevin Jordan in Fish & Game could have claimed Saunders as a dependent in Groveton, Sielicki could have done the same in Colebrook — could have claimed both Couture and Saunders, in fact, since the two of them ate so many meals with him and his wife. The young men had been roommates at the Police Academy. Now they shared a little A-frame in Dixville Notch, went barhopping together in Canada during their off-duty hours. Saunders's happy-go-lucky temperament always left Couture feeling better about things.

In a hallway outside the emergency room, he found Steve Breton sitting butt-end on the floor, his back against the wall, feet splayed out in front of him, face bleached of color. Breton had gone into the ER with Saunders and had helped cut off his clothes. "Those are new boots," Saunders had said. "Don't cut those."

Once the blouse was gone, Breton had seen what looked like a constellation of wounds to the chest and left arm, a chunk of bloody gristle right over his heart.

And no, Couture couldn't see Saunders just then. "He's in critical condition," a nurse told him, adding that Wayne was being prepared for medevac transport to an operating room at the Dartmouth-Hitchcock Hospital in Lebanon.

COLEBROOK DISPATCH, 3:55 P.M.

Dispatch: Emergency.

Caller 28: Yes, is this the Concord barracks, or — ?

Dispatch: No, no — this is Colebrook.

Caller 28: Oh, this is Colebrook.

Dispatch: Yeah.

Caller 28: Oh, hi. This is Anne Defresne at Channel 5 in Boston. I know you guys are very, very busy.

Dispatch: We're out straight — yes, ma'am.

Caller 28: Do you have any information whatsoever?

Dispatch: We have a multiple shooting — five people anyway.

Caller 28: Five people?

Dispatch: Yeah.

Caller 28: Two troopers, one district judge, one civilian.

Dispatch: At least, yes, and a conservation officer.

Caller 28: A conservation officer?

Dispatch: Yep. That's all I can give you right now.

Caller 28: Was this at District Court?

Dispatch: No — within the street.

Caller 28: It was on the street? On Main Street, or — ?

Dispatch: No, on — well, it was all over the place. I'm sorry. You'll have to call me again.

Caller 28: Is the person in custody?

Dispatch: No, he's not.

Caller 28: He's not.

Vermont game warden Paul Fink, fifty-five, had just gone off duty at 3:00 p.m. — and was in New Hampshire, buying some drywall screws at Columbia Home & Building Supply — when the clerk at that store stopped in mid-transaction and went to listen to a police scanner in a side office.

He got to the IGA knowing only that there had been a shooting. He rolled slowly along Route 3 in his Chevy pickup cruiser, past lines of people on the road shoulder gazing into the parking lot. He saw Bert von Dohrmann's red Forest Service cruiser in the lot and von Dohrmann himself talking on the supermarket's outside pay phone. Fink continued north to West Stewartstown, hearing from his dispatcher that two New Hampshire troopers had been shot, and a cruiser — 719, she said — stolen. He knew that felons on one side of the river liked to flee to the other, and he crossed into Canaan at West Stewartstown, turning south on 102 on BOL status — Be on the lookout.

By the time Fink reached Bloomfield, he had stopped to report a house fire on the Columbia side of the river, been passed the other way by a Jeep Cherokee with its hazard lights going, and been told by his dispatcher about shots fired at DeBanville's General Store. When he rolled past the store with his blues flashing, he decided the dispatcher must have been mistaken — he saw no one outside, no emergency vehicles in front. He went on below the underpass, would have kept going had not Dispatch added that an officer had been wounded in front of the store.

Fink turned around, and this time, as he pulled into the store parking lot, Sharlyn Jordan came out the door. "Paul, some guy shot a game warden," she cried. "The warden's truck is over there."

Only then did Fink look in the opposite direction and see the stranded, bullet-ridden New Hampshire Fish & Game cruiser. He recognized it as belonging to Wayne Saunders, the friendly new guy in the Colebrook patrol area. Several people stood around its grille, headlights raised to the sky as if in sorrow, and one said her husband had taken Saunders in their own vehicle to the hospital in Colebrook. Fink looked at the Blazer's windshield, was amazed that Saunders was alive enough to be taken anywhere. He didn't think much of his chances.

George Nugent — Fink knew him as Bloomfield's fire marshal — said that a plainclothes New Hampshire cop was in the store on the telephone, that the cop had charged him with keeping people away from the cruiser. But the Blazer's motor was still running, and Nugent was worried about a fire if the gas tank was leaking. Fink told him to shut it off just as a Vermont state trooper in an unmarked car stopped in front of the store.

Sergeant Tom Roberts knew less than Fink did. "He bombarded me with questions I had no answer for," Fink said later. Behind them the disabled cruiser groaned and shifted as Nugent climbed into it. The fire marshal bailed out, landing safely, as a birch trunk gave way and the Blazer — its engine stopped — slid and settled another two feet down the bank.

By then Fink was on the radio to Dispatch: he and Roberts were heading down 102, and New Hampshire Fish & Game needed to find someone to secure this cruiser. The game warden led, and the trooper followed: under the trestle, across a small iron bridge spanning the Nulhegan River, over the Bloomfield line into New Brunswick, past dairy farms and fields of high corn. Their lights were flashing, their sirens mute. Two vehicles came and went the other way: people on errands as routine as buying drywall screws, Fink thought.

"Soon we entered the long straightaway on VT RT102," he wrote in his report. "We picked up speed. At the end of the stretch, the highway bends to the left, and halfway through this curve, I came onto a marked New

Hampshire State Police cruiser burning its tires as the operator attempted to execute a U-turn and go back south. . . . I increased speed to cut the distance between my vehicle and the one in front. As I did so, I craned forward and tried to read the plate number to ascertain if it read '719' while my body began to tense in preparation for a high-speed chase."

12
BY THE
GRACE
OF GOD
AND
VALHALLA

THE AUGUST 20 EDITION of the *Coös County Democrat* was just about wrapped up. The reporters had gone home. Editor Gene Ehlert and some production staff were still in the building. John Harrigan still had more pasteup to do, but they were all on the downhill slope of a good Tuesday afternoon. People were giddy, jokes were flying back and forth — no different from the *News and Sentinel* on a good press day. Laughter reigned until the police scanner went wild with scrambled information about shootings in Colebrook.

John went to the phone and called the *Sentinel*, expecting a sober to-the-best-of-our-knowledge journalist's enlargement on what had happened and where. Vivien Towle answered and was nearly hysterical. "Vickie's been shot," she cried. "Dennis has been shot." Then she hung up.

John stood with the dial tone buzzing in his ear and five people in the newsroom looking at him. When he spoke, it was in a whisper to himself, but it came out louder than he meant. "It's that bastard Drega."

By then Ehlert was at John's side. "Who's Drega? What happened?"

There was too much to explain and no time to do it. "I'm going up north," John said. "You're all done. Just put the paper to bed and get out of here."

"Well, no," Ehlert said. "If there's been a shooting in Colebrook, we're not all done. We're starting over."

John was at the wheel of his father's Lincoln within a minute, steering it like a mad Zamboni through a slalom course of Lancaster traffic. Once he hit North Main — the last place he could get a signal between there and

Groveton — he devoted one hand to dodging other vehicles while he dialed the *Sentinel* on his car phone with the other. Gil Short answered and told John all that had happened. "It doesn't look good for Dennis," Gil said. "Vickie, well . . ."

John careened past the courthouse on North Main, then veered right with Route 3 past the fairgrounds, where heavy traffic into the fair gridlocked the Lincoln for a few frantic moments. The road opened up north of the fairgrounds, and John slammed the Lincoln into the first straightaway. Its big V-8 drove him like a nail head into the springs of the split-bench seat. With sirens keening in the distance and the speedometer yearning to the right, he steered with nearly a death wish through the road's riverbank bends, around the station wagons and pickups of people who had no idea yet that everything had changed.

It's thirty-six miles from Lancaster to Colebrook, but just five to the village of Northumberland, with its convenience store and post office and bridge over the Connecticut into the Vermont town of Guildhall. John was there within a few deep breaths. There were sure to be roadblocks on Route 3, and there was always less traffic on the Vermont side anyway. He decided to cross the river, go up 102, and come into Colebrook from the Lemington side.

The Lincoln fishtailed onto the bridge, swung right on 102, and then stretched out again, accelerating to nearly a hundred miles per hour through road-hugging ranks of pine and hemlock, their trunks and branches blurring into finger paints. The first mile clicked off in seconds, but only that mile, since suddenly John had to brake — hard enough to set his tires smoking. He fought to rein in the Lincoln before it slid across the spike mat that a group of New Hampshire and Vermont troopers had spread across the width of the road.

Les Lord's friend Frank Prue — the Park Ranger among that trio of animated characters — had met Gerry Marcou for lunch that day in Groveton. Prue had gone off duty that afternoon and was pulling into his driveway when Code 1000 broke on his radio. He hadn't been able to get through to Troop F for a full situation report and knew only that a stolen New Hampshire cruiser was traveling south on 102. With a felony in progress,

Prue had jurisdiction in Vermont, and he crossed to 102 from Lancaster while John was just hanging up the phone at the *Democrat*. At a little more than a mile past Guildhall, Prue met Corporal Mike Doucette of Troop F coming the other way.

Doucette had no more information than Prue about what else had happened. Nor did the pair of Vermont troopers who came down 102 on Doucette's heels, but their rendezvous seemed like a good spot to set up a checkpoint and watch for a suspect who could be driving a different vehicle by then. Doucette took a spike mat out of his trunk, but before they had stretched it across the road, a New Hampshire Fish & Game cruiser sped past. They waved to the two men inside. A civilian pickup followed on the heels of the cruiser, and this they flagged to a stop.

Its operator was in civvies, but he was a Fish & Game CO from southern New Hampshire, John Wimsatt. Wimsatt explained that he and partner Jim Kneeland had stopped at Kevin Jordan's house in Groton. This was Kneeland's truck, but since Wimsatt had packed his duty belt and a .40 Sig Sauer pistol, he had taken the wheel of the truck, while Kneeland — with weapons borrowed from Jordan — had jumped with Jordan into the cruiser that had just whipped by.

Wimsatt was still there when a black boat of a car from the '80s slid to a hairpin stop in front of the spike mat. The vehicle was coming from the south, the less suspicious direction, but nonetheless nobody liked the look of a car traveling that fast without emergency lights.

They relaxed when they saw who the driver was. Prue used to be a beat cop in Lancaster, and he and John had become friendly then. Doucette and Wimsatt both recognized Harrigan from the photo on the banner of his columns in the newspapers.

Prue smiled as he scolded John for speeding. Then, "I'm sorry we can't let you through. You're going to have to turn around, and then take it easy, okay? We're trying to catch up with a bad boy who's borrowed one of our cruisers."

"A borrowed cruiser?" John said. "That's what you're worried about?"

Prue blinked in surprise. "Well, that does get our attention."

"People are dead in Colebrook, at least one of them at my own place of business," John said, "and you're chasing a lost cruiser?"

"People are dead?" Prue said. "In Colebrook? Wait a minute — what the hell are you talking about?"

For a sanctified instant, with all these cops gathered around his window, John thought, okay, Vickie is alive, Dennis unhurt. The stuff on the scanner had been piped in from some other universe, was else a bad joke, a colossal misunderstanding of some sort. And sure, no sooner had Vivien hung up than John had questioned the possibility of something like this really happening — in Colebrook, of all places. No sooner had he grasped that straw, though, than he let it nearly fall. He remembered the fizz of terror in Vivien's voice, the anguish choking Gil's. John told the cops what he had heard in Lancaster.

"You say two troopers were murdered?" Prue asked.

"Yeah, that's what I heard. That's what he told me."

"Like who? Did you get the names?"

One of the reasons Frank Prue took the role of bad cop when he worked with either of the other two Musketeers was that he so readily looked the part, with his nicked-up prizefighter demeanor and plough-horse shoulders. He looked like a tough guy, and if he had to be, he was. But the first syllable that John pronounced hit him like a blow to the kidneys, and at the sound of "Lord," he staggered backward.

The other cops were skeptical, and Doucette was angry, telling John he shouldn't be joking about shit like that. "You think I'm kidding?" John said.

"I don't know," Doucette said. "But we haven't heard anything. So it's a rumor — and let me tell you, this isn't a good place to repeat that sort of rumor."

John was furious himself by then. "Jesus Christ, people are dead or dying, and they were killed by that nut Drega, and you guys knew something like this would happen, and you never did anything about it. Now you just want your fucking cruiser back."

Doucette stood firm. "We don't have a report on any shootings."

Then John Wimsatt spoke up. "We heard on the Fish and Game channel that Wayne Saunders got shot — in Bloomfield. That's just up the road from here, right?"

Doucette stared at Wimsatt and fell silent. Prue had stepped away from the group, out into the middle of the road, and as Wimsatt's words hung in the air, John witnessed in that sheet-metal version of a man the most explosive onslaught of grief he had ever seen. It was like watching a building hung with dynamite collapse in on itself. And as Prue shrieked, beating his skull with his fists, John abandoned the last thread of hope he had in his heart for Vickie, the last fond thought that he might yet wake up from this.

He nearly went biblical himself before turning around for Guildhall and flying back to the bridge and Route 3.

Susan Zizza described herself later as "a wild woman" at the Upper Connecticut Valley Hospital. After trying several times to telephone Polly Joos from the Sentinel Building — and getting no answer — she had wept and leaned on her horn, frightening children and other cars out of her way, as she drove to the hospital.

She was told that Dennis had already been taken into intensive care. At that point nurse Julie Riffon took the wild woman in hand and settled her in a waiting room. Someone at the hospital had contacted the ministers of all the churches in town, and several were there already, including Charles Collins of the Community Baptist and Bud Hulse of St. Stephen's Episcopal — but not Peter Dyer of the Monadnock Congregational. The Bunnells were members of that church, and Dyer was at Earl and Pam's house on Bridge Street, where Bunny and Irene had been taken. Each of the ministers at the hospital took a turn trying to calm Susan, but none succeeded. "I heeded them not," she said later.

No one at the hospital could say with certainty that Polly knew what had happened. Susan found a telephone and rang her again — still no answer. Well, there wouldn't be if Polly were outside in her garden, as no doubt she would be on a day like this. Susan did manage to reach her husband, Mark, at work. "Has this guy been caught yet?" Mark asked.

"No, he hasn't," Susan said. "I haven't heard that he has."

"Wait there. I'll be right over."

But she couldn't wait. She got off the phone and told Julie Riffon she was driving up to Dennis and Polly's house in Stewartstown. "Oh, no, girl, you're not," Julie insisted. "Not in the condition you're in — you're not driving anywhere."

Circumstances conspired. Bill Bromage, the bank president who had come to the hospital in the ambulance with Dennis, had been paged to a house fire in Columbia, but he didn't have any way to get there. Susan offered him the keys to her car once Julie agreed to drive Susan to Stewartstown in hers. Someone else then volunteered to give Bromage a ride to the fire, but Julie stuck to her offer.

The two women went up Route 145, then up South Hill Road, over the hill, and across the line into Stewartstown. They cut east on Chet Noyes Road, higher into the hills and away from the sirens, into country still nearly as wild and empty as it had been two decades ago when Dennis and Polly had found a raw parcel of land on which to build their stone house, grow their gardens, raise a child, and live, as the Nearings had urged, in a "decent, simple, kindly way."

Up there the summer was already in eclipse, the tamaracks and red maples starting to turn. Susan imagined that Polly's lettuce and beans must have gone by, that the first kissing frost would dispatch her cukes. But after Julie turned into the long hidden driveway that led through wild shrubbery to the house, they saw that Polly's flower gardens were still riotous with late-season blooms whose allegiance was all to the summer: chrysanthemums, black-eyed Susans, showy asters, and beauties that Susan couldn't name.

Polly had always preferred her flowers to the vegetables, and they found her on her hands and knees in the midst of what Susan always thought the Garden of Eden must have looked like. Polly glanced up with a look of concern at the arrival of a car she didn't know, but she smiled and waved and struggled to her feet once Susan got out.

Julie went first, telling Polly that something had happened and that Dennis was badly hurt. After a few moments, Julie went inside to make a call to the hospital. Susan was left to offer what comfort she could to Polly, which was hard because Polly was already swooning and Susan was so comfortless herself.

When Julie came out, Susan knew from the tread of her foot on the stone steps, like the slow clicking shut of a door, that there was no longer any cause to hurry.

County jail director Norm Brown knew just a little more than Frank Prue about what was happening. His radio at the House of Corrections had reported an armed robbery at the IGA. Familiar with the behavior of fleeing felons, he had gotten in his car and driven directly into Vermont from West Stewartstown. He cruised south down 102 from Canaan to Lemington, and its bridge into Colebrook, without seeing anything.

He turned there and was passing the Sentinel Building only a moment after the gunman had fled. Matt Rosi waved him to a stop and told him that two people had been shot, a cruiser stolen. Brown drove on to the stop sign, then down Main Street to the edge of town, and turned back. There would be a lot of cops on the gunman's trail, he figured, and he had only his side-arm, as good as a water pistol against the sort of weapon Rosi mentioned. Brown returned to protect the crime scene at the Sentinel.

He was sure somebody would arrive from Troop F to do that, but he didn't know who or when. In the meantime this was a tough exercise in crowd control, and Brown was glad one of his guards, John Brunault, had been in Ducret's when hell broke loose, and was still here. They still had help as well from Rosi, and also Phil Ducret and Dave Robidas. They were keeping most people at the edge of the premises and already stringing up yellow caution tape taken from the shelves in Ducret's. At the same time they scoured bushes for any sign of Jana Riley, whose shoes had been found in the parking lot and who was still unaccounted for.

Vickie's friend Paul Nugent stood guard at Vickie's body. Ducret had given Nugent a camo-pattern blanket from the store, and he had laid it across her. Dr. Bob Soucy arrived a little before four, and it was from Soucy that Brown learned what else had happened. Brown and Scott Phillips, besides being running partners, had shared the same birthday in January and the same background in military police work, Scott in the army and Brown in the air force. Since they had ended up in different branches of civilian law enforcement, they could talk frankly with each other without fear of it bouncing around the workplace. They were supposed to run together the next day.

Bob Soucy had come to know Vickie working with her on the board of trustees at Camp E-Toh-Anee. He grieved audibly as he lifted the blanket, as did Brown as Nugent turned away. The examination was swift. Soucy saw that Vickie lay as she had fallen, without subsequent movement. "Well, she died almost instantly," he said. "At least there's that." He filled out his report and went back to the IGA, where he said he had unfinished work.

Vickie was left alone again with Nugent — at least until the arrival of her brother. Earl ducked under the caution tape and walked heavy-footed in the direction of where she lay. Brown intercepted him, however, and guided him to a quiet spot behind a parked car. "What do you want?" Brown said. "You want to live with the memory of how she looks now? Vickie wouldn't want that — for you to see her like this."

Earl was tall and rangy and strong, and there was no stopping him if he wanted this memory. But he hesitated — turned away — nodded his head. Brown called Nugent, and Paul and several others took Earl in hand. They walked him back to his house, where the driveway and curb were jammed with cars, including those of Earl's friends Woody Crawford and Mark Monahan. The electric linemen had gone on to fix that power outage on Hughes Road. Then they heard about this next catastrophe.

Brown stood near Vickie and looked up at the sound of a medevac rig coming from the hospital and sweeping downriver to Dartmouth-Hitchcock. Inside the Sentinel Building, Claire Lynch heard it also and rose to stand at a window. She whispered a prayer for Dennis, whom she thought must surely be aboard.

John Harrigan's daughter Karen had grown into a reporter, a destiny nearly as unforeseen as John's. "Dad never made any attempt to cram the family business down our throats," Karen said later. "In fact, he might have overcompensated in the other direction."

Once John won his custodial share of the children, Karen had split her school years between New Hampshire and New Mexico. Then there were different jobs: four years in the U.S. Army, intercepting and translating North Korean radio signals; waitressing in Texas; cleaning rooms at the Balsams. She tried college in Idaho while waitressing full time at an Olive Garden franchise. She lasted only a semester, but she met her first husband, who was a chef at the restaurant.

Just before she went to college, John took her on briefly as a reporter at the *Democrat*. She was surprised by how much she liked finding out about the way things worked and writing stories about it. The couple moved to New Hampshire in April 1997. Russ found a job at a restaurant in the state's booming Seacoast Region, and Karen landed a reporting job at the *Union Leader* in Manchester. She covered the outlying towns of Newmarket, Newton, and the Rockingham County Court.

On August 19, she was working on a story at her desk at home when the phone rang. It was John, on his car phone and hurtling up Route 3 again after being turned around in Guildhall. He had to hang up after just a few words to put two hands on the steering wheel. But those few words were enough to yank Karen out of her chair. John called again a moment later. "You're not kidding, are you?" Karen said.

"They're still working on Dennis. I don't know about him."

She was a reporter, so she wrote the names of the three murder victims on a pad of paper, including the one who had been nearly a second mother to her. Karen had once spent a summer living with Vickie on Bungy Loop. She sat motionless for some time after John had hung up. Then she stood and paced the empty house.

Her brother, Mike, was visiting — he was between jobs and had stored his belongings in their basement — and he and Russ were at a nearby driving range. She went back to her desk and called the driving range, asking that someone find Mike and Russ and send them home. Her next call was to Charlie Perkins, the executive editor of the *Union Leader*. "Charlie, I just heard that four people have been shot up in Colebrook."

"Yeah, we've just gotten reports on that. We're getting someone up there."

"Charlie, I know these people." The tears came upon her unawares, and the fishhook catch in her voice.

"Okay, yeah — you go on up there too, then."

She heard a helicopter outside her window as she hung up. She didn't even need to look. It was the WMUR-Channel 9 helicopter, and if she had known just a little earlier, she could have hitched a ride on that. She rushed to pack some things for a stay of more than a few days, including clothes for a funeral — for three of them, at least.

Mike decided to come as well. The radio in Karen's car was tuned to New Hampshire Public Radio, and its first report on the incident was both a personal and professional affront to Karen: "Bunnell" was said with an accent on the second syllable, Dennis's last name was pronounced as though it went with "orange" or "grapefruit," and Carl Drega was identified as Vickie's ex-boyfriend.

"Oh, Jesus, that's so fucked up!" Karen cried. "We've got to stop at that radio station."

Mike persuaded her otherwise. It wasn't easy.

The law offices of King and Waystack occupy a small brick ranch house facing Route 3 in Colebrook. This house was first the home in which David King, the son of longtime New Hampshire state senator Fred King, grew up. Then it was David's and his wife's home in the first years of their marriage, and finally the house was bought by the law practice.

The building sits opposite Brooks Chevrolet, north of town, and near enough the IGA for King to hear what he thought were firecrackers. Twenty minutes later, a colleague, a lawyer with an office in Lancaster, called to ask him about the shootings up there. King said he wasn't aware of any shootings. Fifteen minutes later she called again, this time from the county sheriff's office. She listed the victims and named the alleged perpetrator. King felt a snake crawl down his spine.

He knew from the Lancaster police about Drega's request for his tax assessment cards. These included a sketch of his house and property. As soon as he got off the phone, he sent his secretary and clerk home — Phil Waystack was on vacation in Cape Cod. Then he called his wife and told her to lock the doors, take their two boys down to the basement, and stay there. Finally he knocked on his next-door neighbor's back door.

He returned with a borrowed 12-gauge shotgun, which he laid across his desk. The gun was loaded with buckshot, and King had a Ziploc bag filled with more buckshot. It wasn't that much by way of firepower, but better than nothing, and it was all his neighbor had.

King realized that Drega had driven past his office at least twice that day already. He didn't dare go home, and so tempt Drega into going there to look for him. He thought Drega would come here first, and King would rather be found here.

The phone kept ringing, but King let the answering machine take the calls. One was from the Colebrook police. Somebody had reported seeing

Drega hiking on foot up the railroad tracks, traveling north. That sighting was unconfirmed, but since those tracks ran right behind the King and Waystack office, David should keep an eye out.

Another call was from the *Boston Globe*. They had heard that Mr. King was familiar with Carl Drega. Could they get a little background information on him, please?

Word got around fast, thought King, who found the irony of an interview request about the man who might be coming to kill him to be, well, piquant.

Nobody on the *News and Sentinel* staff could tell Charlie Jordan who the gunman had been. He had swiftly used up the roll of black-and-white film that was already in his camera. Then he had run to Collins Video and Photo on the corner. Charlie burst through the door, made hand gestures to a wide-eyed Michael Collins that Charlie hoped would suggest a shooting in progress, grabbed a fistful of boxes of color film off the rack, and raced out.

Then, once the ambulances had left, nobody could tell him who was guilty of all this. Jeannette Ellingwood, Leith Jones, someone else he had asked — they all felt they should know, but they were in some sort of haze, some sealed-off vestibule of the trauma ward, that prevented them from calling up that name or face. Eventually the scanner near Gil's desk had reported a fire at the Carl Drega residence in Columbia, and someone had shouted to Charlie, maybe it was Leith, "Oh, yeah, that's the guy."

That didn't make the killer's motives any clearer to Charlie. One thought was that Drega had a grudge of some sort against newspapers, and therefore might be on his way to the *Coös County Democrat* office. So did John Harrigan know about this? Charlie got on the phone with Gene Ehlert, who told him that John had left twenty minutes ago and that Lancaster police had posted an armed guard at the door.

Then he called Charlie Perkins at the *Union Leader* in Manchester to say that he had photos of the immediate aftermath. Charlie said he was sure John would want the *Union Leader* to have some of the shots. Perkins said he could give them to the reporter coming on the WMUR helicopter.

Charlie was still on the phone with Perkins when he saw the Lincoln pull up in front of the building. John had covered the thirty-six miles between

Lancaster and Colebrook in twenty-six minutes. The front door was locked, and Charlie hurried to let John in. "I want to help," he said.

John nodded a greeting to the people around the scanner, a group that now included Monty Montplaiser, a customs agent and Vivien Towle's boyfriend; and Kenn Stransky, the *Sentinel's* Essex County correspondent in Vermont. Kenn had gone to the hospital and come back with the news — shared at that point only with Claire Lynch — that Dennis had died. When they had opened him up in the intensive care unit, Kenn told her, they had found his body cavity awash in blood. Dennis had bled to death internally.

On the scanner, reports of Drega sightings were popping up all over the map: on a motorcycle on Route 3; stowed away on a northbound freight train; driving through Jefferson; fording the river at a shallow spot between Groveton and Stratford. One report had him circling back to Colebrook. That was why Gil Short had locked the front door again.

John walked around the front desk and peered down the hallway past Chandra's desk into the newsroom. Jeannette Ellingwood was at work again there. Jeannette looked like a prim Yankee granny in her white hair, spectacles, and print blouse, but she had an earthy sense of humor, loved a fast snow machine, and wore monkey-themed socks every day of her life. She had been cutting out columns of newsprint for pasteup when Drega arrived, and she was doing so again, as if none of this had happened, as if Dennis had gone out for ice cream. But the scissors shook in her hands.

Norm Brown crouched at the back door, stretching a length of caution tape across its width. John looked like a man who had come home to find his house on fire and his family inside. "Well, I'm going to need some help," he said to Charlie.

"I've got pictures."

John turned and stared. "You've got pictures?"

"I got here just a minute after he left. I shot — I don't know — half a dozen rolls maybe."

"Where are they?"

"Leith's developing the black-and-white stuff now. I took the color rolls to Collins. I also talked to Charlie Perkins and told him he could have some photos. I figured you'd want that."

"Oh, sure." John looked up the hallway again. "Where's Vickie?"

Charlie led John down the hallway, past Vickie's door and Dennis's empty desk, and through the newsroom — Jeannette glanced up, murmured a greeting to John, returned to her work — and then Charlie stopped. "Norm's going to have to let you through," he said.

Norm looked up and said something about a hell of a bad day, John. He undid enough tape for John to open the door. Norm followed him. His first glimpse was of a small, lifeless foot, wrapped in pink tights and extending from one corner of the blanket, and, near it, the shoe it had donned that morning.

Charlie waited inside. In his recollection of that moment, he heard a sound that ordinarily he wouldn't have recognized as human, that he might have deemed an animal's in its last extremity. John would have no memory of such a cry. Norm Brown would only say, "Lots of emotion."

Jeannette's scissors came to a halt, and for a moment she sat still. Then the blades completed their cut and another swath of paper fell to the floor.

That rumored Drega sighting at the old river ford between Stratford and Groteton? Eric Stohl could have told you it wasn't true. He'd been watching.

Stohl had been off duty and working — felling trees, cutting brush — at his son's new place in Columbia. The house was on Route 3, and Stohl had noticed neither the orange pickup headed north nor the stolen cruiser coming south. He did see the fire trucks race past. He followed one to an assembly of trucks parked at the top of Drega's driveway. Smoke plumed into the sky above the bluff as Stohl heard what had happened.

He arrived at the hospital before Saunders was airlifted to Dartmouth. There he was told the CO needed surgery for the repair of extensive vascular damage. Stohl went on to Bloomfield, where the cruiser he had driven just a few months ago still lay snagged on the riverbank, cordoned off by tape. Dick Marini had been relieved at last and was being debriefed in Colebrook by somebody from the state attorney general's office. Vermont authorities were in charge of the scene, and from them Stohl heard that New Hampshire troopers Steve Hersom and Chuck West, traveling in opposite directions on 102, had met in the middle. Vermont's Paul Fink wasn't far behind Hersom, and Fink had been put much on edge by a high-speed U-turn Hersom had made.

So the fugitive had ducked down a dirt side road somewhere between Bloomfield and Guildhall — either a short dead-ender to the east and the river or else into those winding nests of roads around Dennis Pond or Maidstone Lake. Only the Maidstone roads offered access to another paved road to the west, but a cruiser might not have enough road clearance to get through.

Or Drega might have ditched the cruiser by then and be on foot. One of the Vermont troopers had suggested posting a pair of snipers at the only nearby place on the river where a man might wade across. Stohl was in his civvies, driving his pickup truck, but he had a spare uniform jacket in his truck — albeit his winter wool one. Someone loaned him a .308 rifle, and he went with that trooper to the New Hampshire side of the ford.

They slipped into a thicket of sumac and settled down to watch. Stohl was soon swimming in sweat inside that jacket, but it was better than being mistaken for Drega by someone else with a rifle. He thought about who had died, and who might yet die. He remembered loaning his .38 to Vickie last February, on what must have been the first day that his old friend Carl showed up outside her office window. He wondered if Drega thought it was he at the wheel of the Fish & Game cruiser in Bloomfield. Drega would have hoped so. He thought about Bunny and Irene and wondered who was with them.

A good part of the river in front of Stohl was dimpled with rocks and the featherings of stones just below the surface. That much was ankle-, knee-, thigh-deep. There was a channel closer to the Vermont side, though, where the water would come to shoulder height or so, where a man, if he were carrying a rifle, would have to raise both arms above his head in the manner of someone surrendering himself. Drega wouldn't be doing that, though.

Stohl wiped sweat from his eyes. Then he lifted the .308 to his shoulder and sighted through its scope to a point in the channel. It wouldn't be a difficult shot, a man's head at this distance. Stohl was a God-fearing man, and he dared not pray — that might be blasphemy — but he hoped it was God's will that he might have that shot.

Dispatch: Hello — hello?

Caller 33: Hey, who's this? Hey, John, how are you doing? Is Pickering there?

Dispatch: He's at the scene.

Caller 33: He's at the scene?

Dispatch: Yeah.

Caller 33: All right, listen — here's some information from Captain O'Brien. Can you pass it on to the guys?

Dispatch: Sure.

Caller 33: A guy by the name of Gerald Upton.

Dispatch: Okay.

Caller 33: U-P-T-O-N.

Dispatch: Sure.

Caller 33: He lives in Hardwick, Vermont. That's all I know about him.

Dispatch: Okay.

Caller 33: He's Drega's best friend. The last time Drega gets arrested, this Upton bailed him out. We're passing this on — have somebody maybe find out where this Upton lives in Hardwick. It might be a good check.

Dispatch: Okay. And the photo — can you kick somebody in the ass down there?

Caller 33: I got it coming. I got it coming right now. I just got it off the license.

Dispatch: Okay.

Caller 33: We'll fax it up to you.

In Hardwick, Gerry Upton parked his pickup near the outbuilding that served as a garage, workshop, and warehouse for his heavy machinery. He had been running a bulldozer for the town that day, shoring up a recently washed-out section of road.

He went up the driveway to the house in nearly a run. He wanted to tell Margaret about something on the radio, something about shootings in Colebrook. He didn't know the details yet — but Margaret did. She came racing out to meet him. "Gerry, my God, come in and watch this on the TV," she cried. "Something terrible — awful — has happened in New Hampshire, and they're saying Carl's responsible. Hurry!"

Upton had not spoken to Carl since he had asked two months ago if he could use Upton as a reference in applying for work at a nuclear plant. Then Carl wanted to get together with him and Margaret as soon as that job was done. Upton had never objected to Carl using him as a reference, and Carl had done so often before, but he always called each time to ask. Go ahead, Upton told him, and then yes, whenever you're free, come on over.

Inside, Upton stared at news images of familiar places: LaPerle's IGA, Bridge Street, DeBanville's, all of them now swept by flashing lights, cross-hatched by yellow tape, crowded with cops and weeping people. The most disturbing image was shot from the head of Carl's driveway. Fire engines were at rest, firefighters standing around and fidgeting, as smoke billowed from the roof of Carl's cabin. The firefighters were there only to make sure that the fire didn't spread, the news anchor said.

Then appeared an image, in scratchy black and white, of the alleged perpetrator, a fax of a photocopy of a license photo. At that point the image was almost abstract. But Carl confronted the camera like he was standing for a mug shot. His eyes were hidden by his dark glasses, which he had probably refused to remove, and his right eyebrow arched sardonically higher than his left. The mouth looked thin and cruel, seemed to be flirting with a sneer. This was central casting's mold for a pitiless killer. To Upton, it was just Carl looking like Carl, for Christ's sake.

The news anchor mentioned that the fugitive was last seen fleeing across the Connecticut River into Vermont. Upton turned to look at Margaret. "Oh, my God," she said. "Do you suppose he could be coming here? Oh, my God."

The door was locked, the lights off, at the headquarters of the Hardwick Police Department. A handwritten sign said that the department was closed and offered a number to call in the event of emergency. Upton might have guessed — every cop in town had joined in the hunt for his best friend.

The Uptons returned home, locked their own doors, turned on the TV again, and dialed that emergency number. This had to be a case, Upton thought, of mistaken identity.

John Harrigan got help from Norm Brown in getting back on his feet. He looked around as though surprised to find himself where he was. Someone came from up the street to tell him that Bunny and Irene were at Earl's house, and they wanted him to come over. "They're asking for you," John was told. He wanted to do that and promised to be there soon, but first he had to walk back through the door into the newspaper building again.

Charlie Jordan was still in the newsroom, and so was Jeannette. John looked over her shoulder at the story she was cutting into strips. It was the one about last week's restoration of the first settlers' gravestones in the Canaan Village Cemetery. John rubbed salt from his eyes and took a slow, deep breath. "Who else is here?" he asked.

"I heard Chandra went home," Charlie said. "Susan went to the hospital with Dennis. We don't know what happened to Jana. She must be all right, wherever she is. Everybody else is here, along with Monty and that guy from Norton — what's his name? — Stransky. Kenn Stransky."

"You said you've got photos?"

Charlie nodded.

"You gave them to the *Union Leader*?"

"No, not yet. I told Charlie Perkins he could have a few of them. But nobody from the *Union Leader* has gotten here yet."

"Vickie?" John didn't recognize the sound of his own voice. "Did you take photos of Vickie?"

"I did, a few — but I made sure she was covered. You only see the blanket."

"Where are they?"

"Like I said, Leith's working on that first roll right now."

John remembered that even in a normal week — like this was until an hour ago — press day at a weekly newspaper was, to his mind, like the last leg of the Dixville Notch Race, a half-marathon event he used to run in each year. You start at the peak of the Notch, and you hope that you're still running a good pace, seven minutes or so per mile, as you come into Colebrook on Colby Street. By then your mind has shut down, even though there are still decisions to be made about positioning and the timing of your kick, if you even have one. You just hope, by the grace of God and Valhalla, John would say, that your decisions are good ones.

That point in the race is right about where his staff would have been now if this week had ended the way that it started. But now this.

John wasn't sure if he was thinking right, but maybe what he thought had nothing to do with it. Charlie shot those photos, and nobody else had them yet. In the darkroom Leith was up to his elbows in developing fluid, stop bath, and fixer. All these columns Jeannette had cut out should be waxed and pasted up. His daughter Karen, a good reporter, was coming up from Newmarket. Almost everybody else, and an extra body or two, was still here — waiting for what?

"All right — can you tear up the front page?"

"What?" said Charlie.

"Claire can go out and get the rest of the story. Karen can help. If I write it up and write a new editorial, can you run the production stuff out here? Can you get it all put together?"

Charlie thought about this. "Well, we'd have to hurry."

"Susan's probably got the front page all done. Pick two stories to pull off of there — I don't care which two — and move them to the middle. Then make a jump page in back for the rest of this story. Tear me a hole in the editorial page and leave room for sidebars."

Charlie said, sure, he could do that. Then John started rounding up people for a meeting in the newsroom.

13

NO
INKLING
OF CAT
AND
MOUSE

KEVIN JORDAN could think of a couple reasons he might get drummed out of Fish & Game once this day was over. That might be for the best, he thought, given how he had let Wayne Saunders go off alone in pursuit of that cruiser.

Jordan, John Wimsatt, and Jim Kneeland had still been at Jordan's home in Groveton and talking about the dog days of summer — and a deer poaching bust Jordan and Saunders had made the previous week in the Stratford Bog — when they heard Saunders's voice on Jordan's scanner: "Yeah, I've got 608 right in front of me — turning west on the Stratford Bridge." A moment later they heard some other unit shouting that Saunders was down.

Wimsatt had meant to compete in one of the shooting contests at Field Day, and his duty belt was in Kneeland's truck: pistol, handcuffs, knife, pepper spray, extra magazines. But Kneeland was unarmed. Jordan shared with both men the heavy weapons he'd been issued and was officially qualified to use: a 12-gauge shotgun and a .308 deer rifle. For himself, from his own gun collection, he grabbed a Ruger Mini 30, an assault rifle like the AR-15 and a weapon he knew very well how to use — but for which he had no permission to use on duty. Well, he didn't want to find himself, or either of these two guys, outgunned in a firefight. He also knew that if he ended up firing the Ruger, there would be hell to pay with the brass in Concord.

Kneeland jumped into Jordan's cruiser while Wimsatt, with his duty belt, followed in Kneeland's pickup. They crossed into Vermont at Guildhall, but then the pickup got stopped at a roadblock set up a mile north of the bridge. Jordan and Kneeland had flown through, continuing up 102 and expecting at any instant to be met by 608 and its gun-wielding occupant.

They had traveled ten miles north of Guildhall, nearly to Bloomfield, when they were met instead by a convoy of law enforcement vehicles. Jordan learned that Saunders, still breathing, had been taken to the Upper Connecticut Valley Hospital by a civilian, that Scott and Les and Vickie Bunnell were dead, that the assailant, probably, was hiding somewhere off this road.

Inside Jordan's cruiser, all twelve of its radio channels were jammed with competing traffic, and opportunities for contact occurred like quick breaks in cloud cover. Jordan couldn't get through to his lieutenant, Eric Stohl. But he heard from Wimsatt — John had left the roadblock and was driving north. The two vehicles rendezvoused at the wooded entrance to one of the many old logging roads branching off 102, this one about a mile south of Bloomfield, just over the Brunswick town line and almost kitty-corner to the turn into Dennis Pond. By then other vehicles were stopping at roadside homes or dispersing down other side roads.

At the Brunswick line, Kneeland and Wimsatt switched places, with Kneeland taking his pickup north to the hospital to check on Saunders. He took Jordan's deer rifle with him, just in case, and he reached Bloomfield in time for Dick Marini to tell him to hurry. "Wayne wasn't looking too good," Marini said.

Meanwhile Jordan and Wimsatt prepared to join the search on 102. Jordan had done some nighttime deer-poaching stakeouts with Scott Phillips before Saunders came aboard, and as he tried to work the radio, he felt his emotions roiling in his gut: guilt and shame about what had happened to Saunders; wonder that a couple of pros like Scottie and Les could be taken down by anybody; grief and the muffled rage with which a cop pursues a cop killer; and a sharp unease about his role in this pursuit.

"Are you sure it's okay for us to be over here?" Wimsatt asked. "I mean, in Vermont?"

"To tell you the truth, I'm not," Jordan said. That was the other thing, besides his illegal Ruger. In general terms, conservation officers have the same right as other cops to pursue suspected felons across state lines. But with Fish & Game there were always restrictions and procedures to observe, and they kept changing.

Jordan tried once more, in vain, to get through to Stohl. "Well, we'll probably all get fired," he sighed, throwing his cruiser into gear. "But first let's get this son of a bitch."

The clear-cut summit of Carlton Hill, with its panoramic view to all corners of the compass, is close enough to Columbia for Vickie Bunnell to have thought it was on her side of the town line when — once she was named an associate judge in 1995 — she asked her friend Steve Brooks, fifty, to take her place on the Columbia Board of Selectmen. Brooks had a house on the top of that hill, but as a Colebrook resident he couldn't stand in for Vickie. Instead he became a Colebrook selectman in 1996.

Brooks had grown up on a Colebrook dairy farm, working 365 days a year, attending school a couple years behind Vickie, and determined to live in the North Country as anything but a farmer. After college at the University of New Hampshire, he drove trucks for the Tillotson Rubber Company and worked part time for the Colebrook Police Department. In 1982 he joined the Border Patrol, serving a long stint on the Rio Grande before transferring back home in 1988.

He was home that day on annual leave, enjoying the view, when the scanner in his kitchen went off. There was no time to get into uniform. He grabbed his gun belt and badge and dropped his nine-year-old daughter off at the Colebrook Police Department. Brooks's wife, a schoolteacher, arrived within a few minutes to take Erica back home. Brooks drove first to the IGA, where Lord's cruiser had been blanketed with a blue tarp. Bert von Dohrmann told him what had happened there and who had done it.

Brooks knew where Drega lived. He parked at the head of the driveway, where several people had gathered to look at the smoke rising from down near the river. One of the bystanders, a neighbor of Drega's, told him that a state trooper had come out of the driveway just a short while ago. "Yeah, but that was no trooper," Brooks told him.

Keeping his head down, Brooks advanced to the crest of the driveway, just to be sure that Drega was gone. The cabin was almost entirely engulfed in flames, and one corner of the barn looked to be smoldering. There were no vehicles in sight. Brooks lingered a moment at the spectacle, at the almost biblical vision of this pillar of flames.

A fire engine pulled into the driveway and wheeled through the grass around Brooks's pickup. The crew wanted Brooks to go down there with them, but Steve saw Denny Welch, his commanding officer at the Beecher Falls station, headed down Route 3 in a marked Ford Bronco.

"It's safe," Brooks said. "There's nobody there."

Brooks waved the Bronco down and left his pickup parked in the driveway. "We're going to Bloomfield," Welch said. As they pulled onto Route 3, Brooks saw in his side-view mirror that the fire truck wasn't moving.

Once Jim Kneeland had left for the hospital and Kevin Jordan had given up on trying to get orders or authorizations of any kind, he and John Wimsatt turned around on 102. "We'll just join the gang checking out the dirt roads," Jordan said.

They would have started with the road at which they had rendezvoused, but Jordan remembered there were three farmers at work haying a riverside meadow just south of that entrance. He stopped in front of the meadow with his blues flashing. Then he and Wimsatt got out and waved the men over. The farmers climbed off their tractor and baler and approached — two middle-aged men in plaid shirts and covered in grass, one of them in a trim black beard, and a young guy in his twenties.

Yes, they had seen a lot of cruisers, but they hadn't noticed one with broken windows or seen anybody on foot. Jordan said this was a manhunt for an armed and dangerous fugitive and to please get inside. "And whatever you do, don't go looking for this guy, okay?"

Inside the cruiser, as he pulled away, Jordan remembered that he had said almost the same thing to Wayne Saunders a long time ago, or so it seemed. He shook his head. "Those guys were staring at me like I was nuts — like I had two heads on my shoulders."

"You've got to admit it's hard to believe," Wimsatt said.

Dean Hook represented the second generation of his family to work 365 days a year on this tidy dairy farm abutting the Connecticut and straddling Route 102 in Brunswick, population a hundred or so. Dean's son

Dan, working at his side that day in the hay meadow across from the farmhouse, would be the third, if he kept with it. And it was a good day for haying — bone dry and no rain in the forecast.

The Hooks had help from their friend Dick Moulton. By late afternoon a good portion of the meadow was dotted with sweet-smelling and evenly spaced bundles of timothy, rye grass, and clover. They were curious about all the police activity, but too busy to pause — until a New Hampshire Fish & Game cruiser stopped in front of the meadow.

Both men who climbed out were in plainclothes, blue jeans and T-shirts. Dean Hook couldn't hide his disappointment at being told to shut down. He hated to leave that much hay in windrows under this sun, but he promised to do so and get his machinery out of there.

As Hook watched the cruiser pull away, he gave his beard a thoughtful tug. He was, after all, constable of the Town of Brunswick. And to reach the road, he'd have to drive the tractor and baler back through Brunswick Springs, that fifty-acre patch of woods on the north side of the meadow. Just to be safe, he thought, maybe he and Dan should take a look around in there first.

By 4 p.m., Julie Roy, Kim Richards, and other customers at the IGA had been freed from the supermarket's stockroom, but none were free to leave until the police had taken down their statements. Some would be kept until eight that evening.

Ian Venne, the boy trapped in the Thunderbird parked next to the gunman's abandoned pickup, had been tearfully reunited with his mother and sister. The Vennes joined the people waiting to submit statements, some of whom were making phone calls. Kim Richards tried without success to reach her husband. Then Guy LaPerle said he had a call for her. Kim went to the manager's office expecting at last to speak to her husband. Instead it was a reporter for *Channel 9 News* in Manchester. Someone had given the reporter Richards's license plate number in the parking lot, and her name had been obtained from that. Kim wept as she declined to be interviewed.

Julie Roy wished she hadn't been present for the arrival of Bev Lord, a woman she admired as someone "strong as a threefold brick wall." Chief Sielicki had tried to keep her away from Les's cruiser, but Bev, frantic, broke away and ran to its window. "To hear someone like Bev break down like that," Julie said later, "well, I don't know — that was a sound I never want to hear again in my life. That was about when it all sunk in."

The man who had vanquished Christopher Wilder thirteen years before was enjoying a day off and on the back nine of a golf course near Mt. Washington. Chuck Jellison had been a state police detective in 1984, while Wilder was a wealthy, charismatic thirty-nine-year-old business-man, photographer, and sometime Formula I race car driver. Found to be a murderer as well, a predator who tortured young women before he killed them, Wilder had kept murdering as he fled from Florida to New Mexico and then back across the country and into the Northeast, aiming for Canada. The fugitive had stolen a Pontiac Firebird in New York, and on an April afternoon Jellison happened to notice such a car pulled up to a gas pump at the Getty station in Colebrook.

When Jellison approached, Wilder drew a .357 Magnum from a jacket on his car seat. The ensuing hand-to-hand struggle ended with Wilder shot through the heart by his own hand. A previous bullet had passed through Wilder and lodged near Jellison's liver. Beno Lamontagne heard the two gunshots from Lazerworks, and when he arrived at the Getty station, Doc Gifford and Eric Stohl were already tending to Jellison, who lay bleeding on the pavement. Wilder lay stretched across a car seat. Jellison looked up at Beno, his face gone white, and said, "That idiot just shot himself and me."

Jellison, now the lieutenant in charge of Troop F, had nearly died of that wound. On this day he almost wished that he had as he sped west from Mt. Washington, picking up information in bits and pieces along the way.

At DeBanville's, Vermont State Police officers directed him down 102. A mile later, he saw an unmarked New Hampshire State Police vehicle parked at the right-hand turn into Dennis Pond. The operator turned out to be Chuck West, who showed Jellison a set of tire tracks in the intersection's gravel. West said the tracks had to have been made by a vehicle traveling at a high rate of speed, and maybe not long ago.

Everything was not long ago. It had been only ten minutes since West had met New Hampshire trooper Steve Hersom at just that point on 102. Hersom had turned around and then had spun around again when he saw a Vermont Fish & Game officer — Paul Fink — coming south. Hersom led Fink and Vermont trooper Tom Roberts back to Dennis Pond Road. Roberts continued south, Hersom and Fink went up the dirt road together, and West stayed to secure the intersection.

Vermont State Police lieutenant George Hacking arrived moments later, and this wide turnoff, far from any houses and bordered by woods on all sides, seemed a good spot for a command post from which to coordinate some complicated search patterns. Dennis Pond Road has spurs that go off to several smaller ponds: Tuttle, Big Wheeler, and Little Wheeler. Maidstone Lake is about four miles to the south — it's bigger and there is a more extensive knot of roads wrapped around it, along with spurs to South America Pond and Notch Pond and a backdoor outlet to the west over a mountain.

The problem of too much traffic on all radio channels was compounded by the fact that New Hampshire and Vermont law enforcement shared very few channels. Jellison and Hacking managed as best they could by parking their cruisers side by side and reversed, with their windows open, allowing their radios to be in the most literal sort of audio contact.

Then Jellison set about dispensing assignments. He made contact with Kevin Jordan, assuring Jordan of his right to pursue and telling him to join the several units circulating through the Maidstone area. When Border Patrol agent Steve Brooks arrived, jumping out of Denny Welch's cruiser, he was paired with Chuck West in checking houses along 102. Gerry Marcou, ashen-faced from what he had just learned from Frank Prue, was sent with a partner to scour some of the many short spurs off 102.

It took Fink and Hersom half an hour to follow each road to its end in the Dennis Pond area, to survey the various camps and houses. When they came out, Jellison was at the door of Fink's cruiser before it had come to a stop. "Talk to me — talk to me," Jellison demanded.

Fink said he doubted the suspect had gone up this road, no matter the tire tracks, though there was still one stretch, a spur along the west side of Wheeler Pond, that needed checking. He also confessed himself still ignorant about much of what was going on. Fink would write in his report, "I was saddened to hear him say four people had been shot/killed in cold blood. I knew all four. Lt. Jellison became choked when he added, 'Scott Phillips was my nephew.'"

Between twenty and thirty miles of dirt road wind around Maidstone Lake, and so many cruisers were pounding them that Kevin Jordan felt like he was part of an invading army. Several of these vehicles looked just like 608, and all were coming suddenly around corners and tight bends in these narrow, leafy roads — around bends where radio communication would blink from nearly useless to completely so. And who was to say Drega was still driving a cruiser?

Around the pond, people came out of their houses to gaze in wonder at the fleets of cruisers. Some were on their porches brandishing shotguns. Others were being hauled out of their trucks or cars by nervous lawmen with their sidearms drawn. Most of the lawmen were in uniform, but some — like Jordan and Wimsatt — were not. Sooner or later, Jordan thought, somebody was going to pull a trigger before enough questions got asked.

He and Wimsatt were working their way down a stretch of road with a number of hunting or fishing camps, going into each to look around and tell the occupants, if any, to stay inside. One camp gave them pause. "It looked empty, but its door was open," Wimsatt said. "We approached on foot, very slowly, using trees for cover. But it looked like whoever owned it had just been careless. We cleared it and moved on."

They were still moving when they overheard a broadcast from Sam Sprague. Sprague, thirty-two, was a Fish & Game co who had been cleaning a live bear trap in Twin Mountain. The agency had just relocated a bear grown too fond of the chicken fingers fed it by tourists at the Mt. Washington Hotel, and it had fallen to Sprague to hose out the trap's residue of bear shit. But when the scanner started squawking, he quit that to help at the roadblock near Guildhall and then to join the forces deployed around Maidstone.

Sprague was on his own, and he had announced over the radio, to whoever might hear, that he had pulled into a camp and seen a white Cadillac with New Hampshire plates. Then he saw a tall, bearded man in a plaid shirt standing at the camp's picture window — a man who had backed suddenly away at the sight of the Fish & Game truck and its emergency lights. Sprague had paused, backed out, and decided to solicit advice.

Jordan answered immediately, telling Sprague not to go in there without backup, to meet him first at the junction with 102. So far as Sprague knew, they were chasing a guy who was joyriding in a cruiser. Sprague would remember listening to Jordan and thinking, Jesus, what's this guy done besides that? And then he began to worry.

At the junction, Sprague, Jordan, and Wimsatt were joined by Gerry Marcou and another Fish & Game CO, Todd Bogardus. Sprague was quickly briefed. They caravanned in several vehicles back to the camp and parked at the bottom of the driveway. Then they crept into the site on foot from several directions.

Bogardus would summarize the incident in his report: "We found the guy inside the camp, secured him, and found it wasn't the guy we were after."

New Hampshire attorney general Philip McLaughlin looked down from several hundred feet at the crisp greens and emerald fairways of the Concord Country Club. Two men on one of the greens looked up into the sky and waved. McLaughlin couldn't help raising a hand in response.

Earlier, McLaughlin, only a few months into his job, had received a call from the secretary of Dick Flynn, commissioner of the Department of Safety. "Commissioner Flynn is heading to the airport," the woman said. "The commissioner thinks that you should get somebody from the Homicide Unit and meet him at the airport now. He hopes to be up in the air in a couple of minutes."

Mike Ramsdell of the Homicide Unit took off in the first helicopter. McLaughlin and Flynn traveled together in the second. In a column in a 1998 issue of *New Hampshire Trooper* magazine, McLaughlin would write, "The mountains are beautiful on a clear day. From a helicopter at a thousand feet, it's difficult to understand why anyone worries about creeping development when almost all that you see north of Tilton is the beauty of New Hampshire's endless forests and the clarity of its lakes. Rocks are visible twenty feet below the surface of Squam Lake."

McLaughlin and Flynn were able to chat through their headsets. "We talked about the headwinds, the updraft as we cleared Waterville Valley, the mountains of the Kancamagus," McLaughlin wrote. "We spoke about the beauty of the Presidential Range, the green of the valleys, the black of the mountains."

They chatted as well with Ramsdell in the chopper twenty miles ahead of them. "We talked about everything and about nothing. Franconia Notch was stunning. Cannon Mountain to the left, the small airstrip at Twin Mountain. Then came flashing blue lights on a road below and a question as to whether the cruiser or helicopter was going faster."

As they flew higher into the North Country, the talk faded away. "The line of smoke to the left by Columbia was noticed but ignored. The bends in the Connecticut were beautiful and gave no inkling of danger, of pursuit, of cat and mouse, of ambush."

Finally they heard a voice from the ground telling them they were in sight and to come in straight. "And there it was — a supermarket, a large parking lot, the other chopper, and the voice, muddled with static," McLaughlin continued. "Engines, voices, and static. That's what you hear in a chopper. It's easier to see than to hear, but Dick Flynn was heard, 'There they are.' There they were. A blue tarp on a knoll to the right, a blue tarp over a cruiser to the left. A single police officer in the doorway of the store. A hundred yards from the touchdown and a group of men to the left approaching the chopper. Mike Ramsdell I knew, Chief Mike Sielicki of Colebrook and Sergeant Howie Weber I came to know."

McLaughlin was already putting out of his mind the splendor of that journey up the Connecticut, and so was Flynn. "It's going to be a hard day," Flynn said as they trudged toward the parking lot.

Amos Colby, sheriff of Essex County, Vermont, lived in Bloomfield in 1997, on the banks of the river and within sight of the Drega property. "I thought he did just a super job on that waterfront of his," Colby said later. "He hired an excavator, put those stones in. People should be doing more of that. It was the feds who set him off."

According to an Associated Press newspaper clipping that Colby keeps framed on his wall, Essex County — statistically — is the safest county in the United States. So far as that goes, it's just a matter of the right approach, Colby says.

His family had run a sawmill for several generations. "But then logs from subsidized mills in Canada drove us out of business in the '70s." Colby sold logging and snow-grooming equipment, and then trucks and log loaders until he got fired, he says, for not lying to customers about the condition of

certain used trucks. He also served a nine-year stint in the Vermont legislature and for fun went riding on patrol — when invited — with a friend in
the Vermont State Police. In 1986 a neighbor, who happened to be the local
chairman of the Democratic Party, suggested Colby run for sheriff. Though
Colby was a Republican, he won against several experienced candidates in
a predominantly Democratic county.

"This really is a safe place, but all the same people get upset sometimes,"
he says. "There have been several times when there could have been gunshots fired. You'd have a guy with a gun, and he'd be yelling, 'The troopers
won't take me.' Well, I'd show up instead. I'd holler at him, tell him who I
was, run my mouth a while. It takes time. It might take several hours. But
eventually people settle down."

Colby and his neighbors had been hearing gunfire from the Drega property all that month. On the nineteenth, Colby was home doing some main-
tenance work on his Jeep Cherokee cruiser, a vehicle he kept in showroom
condition. He sped down to Guildhall, where he recalls preventing local
police from setting up a roadblock at a dangerous point in the road and
then found his way back to the command post on Dennis Pond Road. He
was unimpressed by the tire tracks at the junction. "They were made by
someone coming out in a hurry," he said, "not going in."

Chuck Jellison was poring over topographical maps and had a call out
to the area's chief landowner, a paper company, to confirm that no new
logging roads had been put in off 102 or around the ponds. He also kept
Colby close at hand as his best authority on local roads.

By this time the sheriff was among those suspecting that Drega had
ditched the cruiser off one of the eastbound roads from 102 and forded the
river back into New Hampshire. But which road? Paul Fink remembers
Colby coming up to him and saying, "You know, that cruiser could be down
there in Brunswick Springs, right across from us."

Fink went alone to check the two more northerly of the area's hidden
entrances and found both blocked with cables and undisturbed. He was
on his way to check the third, the one that local farmers used, a half mile
south of the command post, when he stopped at the post to check for news.
At that point Jellison sent him and Tom Roberts to clear that last spur of
road along Big Wheeler Pond.

Ten or fifteen minutes later, at 4:52 p.m., Colby, and everybody else present, was astonished to see a civilian vehicle, a gray Chevy Cavalier sedan, approach the command post from the south. The man in the passenger seat — bearded and wearing a plaid shirt — had a rifle held across his chest.

Pistols were whisked from holsters. Safety catches were clicked off. The car slowed, and lawmen raced to its side. Several thrust shotgun barrels through the Chevy's open windows. Colby brought up the rear in a dead sprint, shouting, "No, no! Don't shoot!"

TROOP F RADIO LOG, AUGUST 19, 1997: NO TIME GIVEN

Unit 500: Troop F.

Troop F: [responding to another caller] I didn't know if anybody would be there.

Unit 500: The vehicle, the cruiser, has been located on the Vermont side. Everybody's going near the river — the river.

Troop F: Are you still with me? Okay, 500 — you broke right out. You said you located the cruiser? Which is on the Vermont side, just over the river? Okay, what route? Do you know what route number they are on, and the town?

Unit 500: It's between 102 and Route 3, 102 and 3, near the river.

Troop F: 10-5. Troop F to all units. Troop F to all units. Vehicle located. The vehicle has been located on the Vermont side, intersection of Route 102 and 3, just over the river.

Unit 500: Not the intersection. There is no intersection. It's sort of between 102 and Route 3.

Troop F: Between 102 and Route 3. All units — between 102 and Route 3.

14
LIKE THE
BRUSH
OF A
WING

YOU COULD ARGUE that Dean Hook was just being prudent, checking out his route through the Brunswick Springs woods before he took his tractor through there. But he was also acting on a hunch, a tingling in his bones, that this guy they were all looking for might be holed up in there. Certainly these woods were eerie enough for that to happen.

If you take the most northerly of the three entrances into the area, one that Paul Fink found cabled off in 1997, and that still is, you'll have to fight your way through the deadfall trees crisscrossing the abandoned tote road behind the cable. Eventually you'll reach a road that is clean and still used, that will take you on an easy walk around Silver Lake, which lies at the heart of these woods. At the southeast corner of the lake, you'll be surprised to see — unless you're looking for it — a weed-choked concrete staircase climbing inexplicably out of the woods and up a steep bluff that overlooks the lake. At the top of those stairs, on the bluff's other side, you'll gaze upon a wide stretch of the Connecticut River. You'll also catch a whiff of sulfur in the air.

Another weedy staircase descends this other side, but only halfway to the river. It stops at a concrete slab jammed like a wafer into the slope. Water issues as if from a tap out of five separate iron pipes jutting from the slab, and another water source seeps from the earth nearby. At the foot of the slab, where it joins the slope, you're liable to find a cloth spread with offerings from people who still visit this spot, some to draw water: coins, fishhooks, cigarettes, Christmas bulbs, ribbons, and so on.

Once these six springs were sacred to the valley's Native American tribes for their healing powers. In 1748, during the French and Indian War, a wounded British soldier was brought here by his Abenaki allies. The soldier came away so much improved, and so impressed, that he returned after the war with the intention of bottling and selling the water. When the Abenakis objected, a struggle broke out in which a man and child were killed. According to North Country legend, the child's mother, a shaman, then pronounced a curse on anyone who tried to profit from the springs.

In 1860 a local dentist bought a hotel near the springs, added a bottling plant, and offered the "curative waters" to the tourists who stayed at the hotel. The hotel burned to the ground in 1894, was rebuilt and bought in 1910 by local businessman and politician John C. Hutchins — who would be the Democratic Party's failed candidate for governor in 1916 — and burned down again in 1929.

Hutchins decided to replace the building with something like the Balsams, a vast luxury hotel of the sort once common in the North Country. No doubt he was looking to capitalize on the mystique that Robert L. Ripley, of *Ripley's Believe It or Not*, had lent the springs in one of his early columns, one in which Ripley dubbed them "the Eighth Wonder of the World." Local historian Joseph A. Citro explains: "Ripley deemed the six springs a wonder because they all flow from a single knoll, forming a semicircle of about fifteen feet. Though nearly as close together as spigots on a water fountain, the mineral content of each is completely different from that of its neighbor. Moving left to right, they are: iron, calcium, magnesium, white sulfur, bromide, and — if you are brave enough — arsenic."

Hutchins's new hotel, the Brunswick Springs House, was four and a half stories tall and featured what was trumpeted as "the Mineral Waters of the Great Spirit" piped into every bath and shower. But while the building was still under construction, fire struck again in the spring of 1930, and fire crews couldn't get enough water to stop it, despite the proximity of a lake, a river, and the mineral waters of the Great Spirit. "New Brunswick Springs House a Total Loss on the Verge of Its Opening," lamented the *Coös County Democrat*.

Hutchins rebuilt the whole thing within a year, but once again the structure burned to the ground on the eve of its opening. Whether he suffered from arson, bad luck, or an ancient curse, Hutchins had had enough. Remnants of the great hotel's cement foundation can still be found near the middle entrance into the woods.

Some of the local people still swear by the water as a cure for a variety of ills. It has a metallic, though not unpleasant, taste, but the alleged diversity of elements in each of the six springs has not proved out, with the water displaying uniform levels of sulfur dioxide. In the years since 1997, there have been two suicides in the woods: a logger who hung himself in a tree and a woman who drove her car into Silver Lake.

On the day of the manhunt, Dean Hook wasn't looking to tempt fate in a place he considered haunted. But he had to go through there anyway, and he did have that tingling hunch. He sent his friend Dick Moulton home, and then he and his son Dan went across the road to the farmhouse to fetch a pair of deer rifles, just in case.

They went in on the road out of the hay meadow with Dennis Pond Brook running briskly on their left. Within a quarter mile or so, that road comes to a tee. You can go left to a frayed but sturdy wooden bridge over the brook and out to Route 102 or right, along a road that follows Black Creek, a slow little rill that seeps from Silver Lake. Soon that road fades into a footpath to the side of the lake opposite the springs. A ridge of high ground, blanketed in hemlock and pine and mixed hardwoods, borders the road and creek on their south side, but the Hooks never came to the tee. Instead they abandoned the road along Dennis Pond Brook and bushwhacked up the back of the ridge to high ground. Even before they had reached the summit, they could hear the sound of a police radio rising from the other side.

They crept a short distance down from the ridgetop and saw the cruiser through a lattice of trees at a distance of forty yards. It had been driven along the creek for as far as that section of road was passable and then had been turned around in the tight quarters of a small clearing to face out again toward 102. "It looked like it was pointed so it could leave fast," Dean Hook said later.

They could see the bullet-pocked windshield, and the open driver-side door, and what looked like a pair of shirtsleeved arms stretched forward on the dashboard ahead of the steering wheel. The radio had been cranked to maximum volume, or near to it. Voices were flying back and forth, all talking about the search for this very thing the two men were staring at. It was loud enough that the Hooks knew they wouldn't be able to hear anybody moving in the woods behind them. And it was a spooky thing to see in a place like that. "It looked like the end of civilization," Dan Hook said.

Father and son jacked shells into the chambers of their rifles and — moving quietly as Abenakis, scanning the woods in all directions — retraced their steps up the ridge and down the other side. They avoided the road on their way back to the hay meadow, preferring to slip through the woods that hugged the Connecticut. Then they hurried across the meadow, back to the house, and into Dan's Chevy Cavalier. They had to go only half a mile up 102 to Dennis Pond Road and Chuck Jellison's command post — where an armed, bearded man and his similarly armed companion were nearly shot by a posse of very edgy Vermont and New Hampshire lawmen.

Border Patrol agent John Pfeifer, thirty-three — an economics major at Vermont's St. Michael's College before being recruited directly into the Border Patrol, now with a wife and ten-year-old daughter at home — was becoming a little more nervous with each step down this road and into these woods.

Pfeifer had been getting first-aid training at the agency's Newport station when calls for help came in, and he thought things probably would be wrapped up by the time he got down to that stretch of 102. Not so — he met fellow agent Dave Perry at the turn into Maidstone Lake. There they debated who would help search the lake roads and who would secure the turnoff. "This is more my fight than yours, John," said Perry, distraught in particular over Phillips. "You stay here, and let me go in."

Then Pfeifer had been at the command post, the CP, when that little Chevy and its two farmers had come out of nowhere and scared the bejesus out of everyone. That was how he found himself part of the entry team, what had become a six-man detail walking along this creek on their way to the stolen cruiser's reported location. And the ground was rising sharply on both sides. They were marching into a valley, Pfeifer realized. Tactically, this wasn't good.

The team had taken shape at the CP, when Captain Mark Metayer of the Vermont State Police ordered one of his K-9 units, Russ Robinson and a

German Shepherd named Major, to go in with a Border Patrol agent —
Eric Albright — and secure the cruiser. Chuck Jellison pitched in with his
own K-9 unit, state trooper Rob Haase and Rowdy, with backup from Jeff
Caulder, thirty-four, the SWAT team member who had attended the Police
Academy with Scott Phillips. Haase and Caulder had been on separate
assignments below the notches and had driven up I-93 in tandem at 105
mph. They stopped at Troop F in Twin Mountain, where Howie Webber
told them that Scottie and Les were dead. "And watch yourselves. This guy
is a real badass."

Amos Colby was added to the team because of his knowledge of the area,
and the team was completed by the nearest at hand, all of whom happened
to be Border Patrol agents: Pfeifer, Steve Brooks, and a third, Ben Batchelder. They drove in convoy to the area's southern entrance, the one that
led directly across the bridge over Dennis Pond Brook. Colby led the way
in his Jeep, which he drove across the bridge and parked a quarter mile in
at the intersection where the road split, either straight ahead down Black
Creek or off to the right and the hay meadow.

Dean Hook remembers advising against a direct approach to the cruiser,
that rather they should go over the ridge, as he and Dan had. But there
was no one formally in command of the detail, and that advice — if it was
heard — was only partially adopted, with Brooks and Batchelder splitting
off from the rest and heading to the right, behind the ridge. Pfeifer and the
other five followed the creek.

Nor was there thought to be much probability of trouble. Rob Haase
remembers Caulder telling him this should be a Sunday stroll. They both
knew that, in the usual run of cases like this, the perpetrator would be found
to have committed suicide, and the Hooks' report of arms stretched out on
the dashboard seemed to suggest that. If not, then the guy would have fled
on foot, and Major could track him.

Pfeifer reminded himself of all this, took comfort too in this detail's being
well armed. Russ Robinson had only his sidearm, but Caulder packed an
M16 assault rifle and had loaned a Remington .870 pump-action shotgun
to Eric Albright. Haase and Colby carried shotguns as well, while Pfeifer
had his M16.

They set off in pairs from the crossroads. Robinson and Haase had decided that two K-9 units were redundant. "It was their state, so we used their dog," Haase said later. He locked Rowdy in his cruiser, and Robinson took the lead with Major. Caulder, who was on his first hot call since qualifying as a SWAT team member, and whose SWAT-issued tactical vest boasted a one-inch steel plate in front, followed a short distance behind. Twenty feet behind Caulder, in staggered formation, one on each side of the road, came Pfeifer and Albright, and finally Colby and Haase.

The woods were silent except for their own rustlings and the faint buzz of radios from the CP. The trees grew thick as jail bars on either side, with patches of blue showing in streaks through their branches. Black Creek is aptly named, a crooked ribbon of darkness winding between shoots of pickerel weed and sedge. Caulder, the former U.S. marine, scanned the ground as it rose on both sides, and Haase kept an eye on the woods behind as they advanced, step-by-step, up the road.

A hundred yards in, Major hit a scent. Five gun muzzles swung in front of the dog as it buried its nose in something at the foot of a maple. Robinson pulled the dog off, inspected some tissue that might have been left by a hiker. The handler shrugged and marked the spot.

They were three hundred yards from the fork when they rounded a bend and caught their first glimpse of the cruiser, some ninety yards ahead. Caulder didn't know that the vehicle had been parked facing out, and he felt the hair lift on the back of his neck to see its grille and open door and hear its radio. Somebody just looking to kill himself, he thought, wouldn't trouble to arrange things like that. Pfeifer was close enough to see those arms flung across the dashboard. He relaxed, until he saw that the blue flannel shirtsleeves were empty.

Robinson and Major were still ahead of Caulder and had advanced beyond that bend. By then, so had Pfeifer. Caulder raised his hand — the team halted.

Then Major alerted a second time, more vigorously, spinning to the right and yanking Robinson across a dirt-and-gravel berm, about two feet high, that ran like a parapet around the base of the ridge, the edge of the road.

Again, the gun muzzles swung right. About thirty yards up the slope ahead — "at two o'clock," Caulder remembers — the first three members of the team saw a man step from behind the trunk of a thick hemlock. He was clean-shaven — not bearded; wearing a plain denim shirt — not checkered blue flannel; and a state police Stetson. Pfeifer sighted on the man, but hesitated — there might be other cops in the woods besides Brooks and Batchelder. Caulder hesitated as well.

Robinson was the first to see the man's black rifle, to see that it was trained on them. "He's got a gun!" Robinson cried. "State police — let me see your hands!"

Rob Haase had come up behind Caulder and was astonished to see a thread of fire, what looked like the path of a tracer bullet, drawn from the slope to his foot. The bullet was still burning as it struck the ground in front of Haase and ricocheted, creasing the toe of his boot and spoiling his aim as he fired his shotgun. Haase's toe felt as if someone had dropped a fifty-pound weight on it and set it ablaze.

The second round hit Caulder, flabbergasted by the crashing thunder of gun reports in this narrow valley. It seemed to the trooper that he'd been hit above the knee. The M16 flew from his hands, pinwheeling into Black Creek, and he felt his left foot curl up like a snail in his boot as his leg went crazy. It kicked up in a fast twitch that somehow knocked his ankle against his rib cage.

Caulder felt not so much pain as a burning sensation. His mind went to work as he danced on one leg: Fuck, I'm shot. That thought ran several times before the next arrived: Hey, stupid, get down or you'll get shot again.

What seemed to unfold in slow motion for Caulder was eyeblink swift to John Pfeifer. He had fired a dozen rounds in the direction of that hemlock when he heard a yell, saw Caulder lying facedown on the road, then crawling hand over hand toward the berm.

Other members of the team were there already, hunkered down and firing in narrow sight lines, or blindly, through the mesh of trees. Albright's borrowed shotgun had jammed after three rounds, and he took out his sidearm, emptying a clip.

Robinson had turned Major loose, but it looked to the rest like the dog was still leashed. Major was trained to attack in the direction of gunfire, but since gunfire came from everywhere, the animal was baffled. Robinson fired several times with his sidearm as he pulled Major by the collar down to the berm. There he had to lie on top of the dog to keep him contained.

Pfeifer knelt over Caulder and fired up the slope while the wounded man sought cover. Then Pfeifer was behind the berm too, asking Caulder where he was hit.

"I think my leg's shot off," Caulder said. He could feel blood pulsing in a freshet along his thigh, and Pfeifer saw Caulder's camouflage pants turn red. Pfeifer put down his M16 and shouted into his portable radio, his handi-walkie: "Shots fired, trooper down, need to get him out of here."

Ben Batchelder answered from the other side of the ridge and said he would get help. Amos Colby was already headed that way, splashing his way down Black Creek. Meanwhile bursts of tracer fire from up the hill rocketed into the berm and tore holes through the air.

Caulder twisted to one side and yanked his .45 Smith & Wesson out of its holster. Pfeifer had a hand on Caulder's leg, feeling for a place to apply pressure to stanch the bleeding, and as he did so, he felt something touch his shoulder. His arm contorted crazily, like Caulder's leg had done, and all the way down at the end of the berm, Rob Haase heard the moan that escaped from Pfeifer.

Caulder knew that if his leg's femoral artery had been cut, he had less than a minute to live. With storm drains roaring in both ears, he started counting. He heard Pfeifer tell Batchelder on the handi-walkie that he'd been hit too, saw Albright and Haase firing up the hill as if they were at the end of a tunnel. He turned to see Pfeifer lying on his back in the road next to him. Was he in shock? Caulder asked Pfeifer to say his name, and he did so, but with pink foam bubbling at his lips. Pfeifer's bullet had spun through a lung.

Caulder ticked off the seconds, exceeded a minute — and found himself still alive and conscious. Pfeifer had discarded his handi-walkie and was struggling with one good arm to get his sidearm, a .40 Beretta, out of its holster. Then the two men lay side-by-side, pistols clutched to their chests, with the same thought in their minds — sooner or later, the gunman would come down the hill or along this road to finish them off.

The three others behind the berm felt nearly as helpless. They knew it would be a simple matter for Drega to flank them, for him to slip away from that tree, angle down through the brush to the end of the clearing, and fire unimpeded down the length of the road. But so far the shots were still coming from two o'clock uphill.

Pfeifer heard someone calling him on the handi-walkie, but he couldn't answer, couldn't speak. His left side had gone numb, and he could taste the blood in his mouth, feel more of it coming up his throat. He knew his lungs were filling like sponges, that he had only so much time before he drowned in blood. But no one could reach him where he lay in the road without also being an easy target. During lulls in the shooting, Pfeifer knew the gunman could hear him coughing, could hear the static hiss of his walkie.

He wondered how long it had been since he'd been hit. Five minutes? Pfeifer stared at the heavens through crows' nests of tree limbs.

He turned his head to the right and was amazed to find that Caulder had vanished. Pfeifer decided he must have passed out and woken up after Caulder's rescue.

He wondered how long ago that was and if Caulder had been alive when they took him. He wondered if death could be something so intangible as this — a mere touch on the shoulder, like the brush of a wing, and then just a sneaky lapse in awareness.

Chuck West, forty, knew Les Lord when Yogi Bear was still the young police chief in Pittsburg. West, a Pennsylvania native, had just gotten out of the air force. He had been stationed at a base in New Hampshire's Seacoast Region and wanted to stay in New Hampshire. He got into the state police, Troop F, and soon the convivial Lord invited him to share one of Bev's home-cooked meals. Later West, Lord, and two other guys took a motorcycle trip to Martha's Vineyard. Lord, so sure at the controls of a car or snow machine, was just learning to ride a motorcycle, and West remembered how he steered white-knuckled through the traffic on Route 1 near Boston.

By 1997 West was a detective, a member of Troop F's Drug Task Force. That day he was undercover, in plainclothes and driving an unmarked Mercury Cougar, when he flew up from Twin Mountain with Steve Hersom. West had been at the command post with Chuck Jellison when Steve Brooks arrived to tell him that Lord was gone, and who else had died as well: the good-natured judge who signed some of his search warrants, the newspaperman to whom it was safe to speak frankly, and Scottie. West stared and shook his head, and poor Brooks had to say all of it again. Meanwhile Jellison looked at these two men in plainclothes, and at West's unmarked

Cougar, and told them to pair up — they might be able to approach the fugitive unawares, like Breton and Marini had.

West and Brooks joined the search up and down 102 and were returning to the CP when they saw several vehicles turning into the road that led to Brunswick Springs. West figured they were all checking out a reported sighting, imagined this would be another in a string of false leads, but he followed them in, just in case.

They arrived as the entry team, with all those Border Patrol guys, was forming. Brooks was grabbed for that team as well, paired with Ben Batchelder and sent off down the right-hand spur. West, wearing a state police raid jacket and with his .45 Smith & Wesson in hand, walked up Black Creek some distance in the wake of the entry team.

Then the shooting broke out. He sprinted up to the bend in time to see Caulder fall, to see the rest take cover at the berm, and Pfeifer take a hit. Like Pfeifer, West had a handi-walkie on his belt, but he couldn't raise anybody on it. He ran back to the bridge, to the phalanx of vehicles parked on its far side. On the Cougar's radio, he was able to reach the CP and shout that at least two officers were down, the rest in bad trouble.

Then it was back to the firefight. West came up to the bend and saw that Jeff Caulder had turned on his belly and was hauling himself down the road by his elbows. A trail of blood colored the dirt behind him.

Caulder yelled twice, then once more, for West to get the hell down, but to no effect. Instead the detective ran into the line of fire, grabbed Caulder by the carrying strap on the neck of his ballistics vest, and began dragging him up the road like a steamer trunk. Caulder was no easy load — a fit two hundred pounds and wearing another fifty pounds of gear and armor. It was slow going, terrifically so.

They cleared the bend, which got them out of immediate danger. Then came the long stretch back to the bridge. West was doing a number of things at once: still trying to raise someone on the handi-walkie, moving Caulder up the road, asking him where he was hit, and promising — with obvious lack of conviction — that he was going to be all right.

Caulder, for his part, no longer feared that he'd bleed to death, and he still felt more of a burning sensation than real pain in the leg. "Take it easy, Chuck," he said. "I know I'm gonna make it."

They saw Steve Brooks running down the road to meet them, along with Batchelder and another Border Patrol agent, Marty Hewson. Behind them came a pair of white-faced EMTs, one of whom was Penny Henry, carrying a stretcher-like backboard.

"One of your guys is still in there, and he's hit bad," Caulder told Brooks. "He's spitting up pink foam."

The backboard proved awkward and tipsy, especially as gunfire thundered through the woods. Finally Caulder cursed and told West to help him stand. "You can't walk," West said.

"Bullshit. I've got one good leg. Just get me up."

Supported at both shoulders, Caulder gritted his teeth and hopped, still trailing blood, the remaining twenty-five yards to the bridge. The ambulance was another twenty yards beyond that. It had been unable to get closer with all the cruisers parked near the bridge, but lawmen came running to help — Gerry Marcou, Sam Sprague, Todd Bogardus, several others. Standing sentry at the ambulance was Dean Hook. At the CP, Jellison had ordered his men to clean the ammunition out of Hook's deer rifle, but since then the constable had taken the liberty of reloading.

Caulder was laid on the backboard again, a man at each corner. One of those was Todd Bogardus, who had his shotgun on a sling over his shoulder. As Bogardus lifted his corner, the gun slipped and nearly clubbed Caulder in the eye. When this happened a second time, the trooper took action. "Hey, give me the fucking gun," he said.

"You want the shotgun?"

"Yeah, just give it to me, okay?"

Caulder was carried that way out of the woods and up a rise in the dirt road to the ambulance. Reporters had arrived by then, and an Associated Press photographer captured a shot of Caulder as he was hustled into the back of a Colebrook ambulance. The photo showed Caulder rolled on his side and his right hand clutching that shotgun, its barrel erect as the flag over Iwo Jima.

The next day newspapers all over the country would run that photo, often with captions about the spirit of the wounded trooper who refused to relinquish his weapon, even as he was taken from the field. "Yeah, except it wasn't my weapon," Caulder said later. "And all I was doing was trying not to get cold-cocked."

In the emergency room of the Weeks Memorial Hospital in Lancaster, doctors found that Caulder had not been hit in the thigh, as he thought, though he did have an exit wound there. Instead, once they cut off his blood-soaked underwear, they found he had been shot in the scrotum.

Kevin Jordan and John Wimsatt were still nosing around Maidstone when they heard over the radio that shots had been fired, officers were down. They sped past the hayfield where they had talked to those farmers and saw that the next turnoff had to be the place: cruisers parked along the guardrail, cops spaced out as sentries in case the gunman forded the brook and broke out of the woods. Frank Prue was there, and so was Mike Doucette, who asked Jordan if he had a ballistics vest on. Jordan said no. Doucette pulled the steel back panel out of his own vest for Jordan to stuff inside his shirt.

They arrived moments after Jeff Caulder had been whisked away to Lancaster. The woods were quiet, and had been for fifteen minutes or so. When Jordan and Wimsatt got to the bridge, they found West and several others throwing together a plan for rescuing Pfeifer.

They talked. It was thought a good possibility that Drega was on the run again, but no one was going to bet his life on it. Jordan and Wimsatt, along with two Vermont troopers in plainclothes, were assigned to a back-side detail that would climb the ridge, as the Hooks had done, and come over the top behind Drega's position. West, Brooks, Batchelder, Marty Hewson, Sam Sprague, and Amos Colby would go in after Pfeifer.

Jordan's group set out first, advancing warily to that fork in the road and then turning right to the back of the ridge. In the woods they fanned out to intervals of thirty yards and climbed in a staggered sequence — one man moving while the other three provided cover.

This was the twenty-seven-year-old Wimsatt's first shooting incident, and not only did he lack a vest, he felt like an easy target in his light Fish & Game river driver T-shirt and the sort of blue jeans Drega was described as wearing. When he wasn't moving, Wimsatt grabbed handfuls of dirt and scoured them into his clothes. He was a skilled hunter, like Jordan, and he felt glad at least to be in the woods. If he had to be in a gunfight, Wimsatt thought, let it be here.

On their way to the ridge crest, they learned there were already other cops on the hill. Wimsatt heard someone shout, "State police, freeze!" — and a reply to the effect that they were both state police. We're in a nest of hunters, Wimsatt thought, with no one wearing orange. By the time they reached the crest, where there was still no glimpse of the cruiser through the slope's tangles of spruce and hemlock blowdown, a New Hampshire State Police helicopter was working back and forth overhead, as was a chopper from WMUR in Manchester.

Jordan's blood was hammering in his ears. It was hard enough to hear as it was, without the clamor of these choppers. And now it was impossible to pick up the movements of other people in the woods. Jordan had Wimsatt within sight to his left. Enraged, Jordan signaled him to find cover and stay put. They'd have to be like deer hunters in blinds, waiting to see what came to them.

Jordan crouched behind a thick white pine. He still couldn't see the cruiser. Nor could he see Pfeifer or the men still pinned behind the berm, though somehow — despite the choppers — he could hear Pfeifer's moans. The sound made Jordan blink back tears. It also pricked another sort of rage, making him wonder why Drega — if he was still on the slope — didn't just finish Pfeifer off. The bastard must be using him for bait, he thought.

If so, Drega was about to have his way. Jordan could glimpse a short stretch of the tote road along the creek, and there it was: Amos Colby's county sheriff's Jeep Cherokee, its tailgate thrown open, slowly backing down that road.

Jordan didn't think it was much of a plan. Surely there was a SWAT team on the way, but Pfeifer might not last that long. Neither Jordan nor anyone else could think of anything better. Colby in particular had had his doubts, but here he was just the same. Jordan watched the Jeep's slow progress and whispered a prayer, please God, that Amos wouldn't panic.

Somebody said they heard on the radio that Drega had been seen fording the Connecticut. The woods were still quiet. It was also possible that

Drega had finally turned his gun on himself, as he should have done in the first place. Sam Sprague hoped that Drega was dead, but he'd settle for him being gone.

The son of an art dealer (his father) and a mother who did proofreading for the *New York Times*, Sprague had siblings who were all in education or medicine. He thought law enforcement might be more interesting, though, and he answered an ad in the newspaper for a job with the Enfield, New Hampshire, Police Department. He was a cop in Enfield and Claremont for eight years, rising through the ranks, but he also liked to hunt and fish, and envied the more regular work schedule of a conservation officer. He was hired by Fish & Game in 1995, at age thirty, in the same month as Wayne Saunders. Earlier that day he had questioned his "interesting work" theory while washing shit out of a bear trap at the agency's Twin Mountain fish hatchery. No doubts about that now.

The plan for getting Pfeifer was to go in with something like a tank platoon — that is to say, Amos Colby's beloved Jeep, followed by a number of men in vests and carrying big guns. Colby was at the wheel of the Jeep, and he'd been warned once already about going too fast as he backed down this road. Of course he wasn't driving a tank, and an AR-15 could drill through that driver-side door like it was so much cardboard.

So Colby could be forgiven for wanting to be quick about it. But the men crouching and moving behind the Jeep — West with a shotgun shooting rifled slugs, Steve Brooks with an M14 out of Ben Batchelder's trunk, and Sprague with a .257 deer rifle — didn't want to get left behind. Border Patrol agent Marty Hewson was at the rear fender with an M16. Moving parallel to the road and a short distance up in the woods was Bogey — Todd Bogardus — with the shotgun that had threatened Jeff Caulder.

Once they reached the bend that opened into the clearing where the cruiser was parked, Sprague saw the men pinned to the berm — Robinson with a hand on Major and then Albright and Haase, all pressed to the ground like marines on a hostile beach. Pfeifer lay on his side in the road, an easy target, his Beretta held with both hands to his chest as if in prayer. He was alive — Sprague could hear him cough and spit blood.

They didn't stop at the bend — they just kept going. West didn't signal Colby to halt until the tailgate of the Jeep was nearly on top of Pfeifer.

Once he did so, rapping on a window, Colby put the Jeep into park and rolled out of it, down to the road and against the berm, with his sidearm drawn.

"Okay," said West, leaning his shotgun against the rear bumper and stepping from behind the cover of the Jeep. "Let's pick him up and put him in the truck."

Brooks followed, taking hold of Pfeifer by the vest and managing with some difficulty to pry the Beretta out of his hands, while West took his feet. Pfeifer was only semiconscious and too heavy for the two of them. Sprague tipped his rifle against the Jeep and came around to help. He took Pfeifer's feet, and West grabbed at his belt.

Sprague would remember that first shot feeling like a hard cuff on his right ear, and so loud that Drega seemed just a few feet away. Sprague knew the sound of rifle fire on a shooting range, the pinging whine a bullet makes as it flies to a target somewhere else, but he found the roar of a round headed straight your way to be wholly different. Pfeifer, in his haze, felt himself dropped to the road with a bloody, rib-rattling thud.

Sprague didn't know if he'd been hit when he fell with the others around Pfeifer. In a tangle of limbs and weapons — West had his shotgun, but Sprague's rifle was on the far side of the Jeep — they scrambled to the berm, dragging the agonized Pfeifer by his boots after them.

Somehow the second shot, Sprague thought, was even louder and closer than the first.

Kevin Jordan had no doubt he was about to die. He was behind a tree and planted into the ground, but a hailstorm of ordinance — shotgun slugs, rifle and pistol bullets — shrilled through the leaves overhead, slicing off branches and shivering into tree trunks. It was inevitable, he thought, that something would come in low enough and smart enough to find him. He trembled in equipoise between being and nothingness, and his fright swallowed him whole like a whale.

The barrage progressed in fits and starts — and then it was over. Jordan couldn't begin to count how many shots had been fired or guess how long the shooting had lasted. But it had concluded with two simultaneous reports, the crack of an assault rifle and the artillery blast of a shotgun. A moment later, Jordan heard Colby's Jeep rumbling back up the tote road and finally a few more bursts of rifle fire.

Then a species of silence settled into the woods that — outside the *whump-whump* of the choppers in the sky — seemed to have its own pulsing timbre, as if it were ringing in decibels beyond human hearing.

That odd silence settled over Jordan and his sheltering pine like a quilt. He waited. Five minutes? Ten? Maybe more? When at last he lifted his head high enough to see some piece of the clearing at the bottom of the ridge, he glimpsed a gray squirrel moving placidly, in a squirrel's idle fits and starts, across the grass.

John Pfeifer was conscious enough to feel — and remember — the scalding hot shells that rained on his face as they ejected from the chamber of Steve Brooks's M14. Pfeifer groped for his Beretta, but it had disappeared. From bad to worse, he thought.

By then Chuck West had an idea of where Drega might be. He had glimpsed two muzzle flashes out of the corner of his eye, and while others laid suppression fire up the slope, he shifted a step or two to the left of where he had dropped behind the berm — he didn't want to pop up in the same place where Drega might have seen him. Then he eased his shotgun over the berm and sighted toward that spot.

He saw someone behind the thickest trunk in that part of the slope, a tree with sight lines to the whole breadth of the clearing. Whoever it was had on a blue denim shirt and was holding something black in his hands. West watched him slip just a bit and scramble for footing.

Steve Brooks had seen him too. He remembered shooting woodchucks on his parents' dairy farm in Colebrook. The woodchucks weren't as smart as Chuck West — the trick for Brooks was to just wait a minute, and sooner or later the varmint would pop out again in the same spot it had before.

During a lull in the shooting, Brooks heard West yelling up the slope for Drega to surrender, that he was surrounded. Something came back in reply. "And at that time, I remembered some of the words Drega said," Brooks recounted later during his debriefing. "I mean, some of them were understandable, but I don't know now — I can't remember what he did say. And I do remember that, seeing Drega, I raised my rifle."

The gunman had stepped out from behind the hemlock again, in that same place, the AR-15 trained in their direction. "It appeared to me Drega was yelling something to us, but I was unable to distinguish what he was saying," West would write in his report. "It was evident that he was not going to surrender. With the totality of the circumstances, I felt I was justified in using deadly force."

Brooks aimed at the blue shirt above the ballistics vest and shot four times in quick succession. West drew a bead on the gunman's center mass and fired one slug. The two men dropped at once behind the berm, and then Brooks had second thoughts. Someone had just shouted from the woods above for them to watch what the hell they were doing, and Brooks remembered seeing a trooper's Stetson on the guy he had fired at. West was sure they had the right man, but Brooks remembers him yelling up the slope, "Who's wearing a blue shirt?"

No one answered. The seconds ticked off, and West looked down at Pfeifer suffering at his feet. He grabbed him by the vest and said, "Let's get this guy out of here."

Sam Sprague, who had emptied his .40 Beretta, was still incredulous that he was alive and unhurt. Could he be that lucky again? He thought about leaving home that morning, and his casual, complacent farewell to his wife and two little boys. That was unforgivable. With winter in his blood, he went again to help with Pfeifer, as did Brooks.

Marty Hewson was in back of the Jeep, covering the men at the tailgate. This time Pfeifer was lifted and thrown head first, like a golf bag, into the back. Amos Colby, whose hair had been blown back by the second bullet Drega fired, climbed once more into the driver's seat. Sprague snatched his deer rifle off the Jeep's fender and dove into the creek.

The Jeep lurched into drive, and Robinson leaped from the berm with Major, Albright following. Rob Haase had his hand on the tailgate, shielding Pfeifer with his body as he ran limping behind it. Hewson fired several times in the direction of that hemlock as they retreated. Colby went slowly enough for everybody to keep up, but fast enough to get the hell out of there. The road was rough, humped with old blowdowns, and Pfeifer groaned with every jolt.

West and Brooks remained a moment, ready to fire if they had to. Once the Jeep cleared the bend, they saw men moving through the trees at other places on the slope. Covering each other, they gathered discarded weapons — Caulder's M16, Pfeifer's M16 and Beretta — and headed back to the bridge.

Cops had sifted into the woods from all directions, once Drega opened fire. Among the first was Chuck Jellison, who led six other men into the trees across the road from the CP. He asked Paul Fink to take the point position as they advanced.

"Our small group got on line fast and moved slowly forward, looking from side to side, trying to see movement — anything to alert us to the bad guy's position," Fink would write in his report. "Behind me I could hear Lt. Jellison, in low tones, telling everyone to take it easy and spread out on line while at the same trying to get a handle on the situation. He was just great, and if he told me to walk across the water, I wouldn't have hesitated a millisecond."

Border Patrol agent Dave Perry had reported to the CP after abandoning the search at Maidstone and was a member of that group. Perry had heard two officers were down, but no one could say which ones. Perry knew John Pfeifer was in the middle of it, though. Perry remembered sending Pfeifer to the presumed safety of the CP because he himself had wanted a chance to confront Drega and avenge Scottie. It's funny — no, it's terrible, he thought — how things work out sometimes.

Steve Hersom — the New Hampshire trooper who had met Chuck West at the Dennis Pond turnoff and then had thrown a scare into Paul Fink — had gone in earlier with a Vermont trooper, John Sinclair. They had entered from that same general direction, approaching the cruiser from the opposite side of Black Creek. They got there in time for the second exchange. Hersom had also picked out the guy in the blue denim shirt and had drawn a bead on him with his shotgun, but then he heard somebody yell that there were cops on the ridge, and he wasn't certain enough to shoot.

When the Jeep took off, Hersom jumped the creek and ran briefly behind it alongside Rob Haase. Hersom looked down at Haase's bloody boot and said, "Man, you gotta take care of that." Then he and Sinclair turned back to the clearing — either to reengage with Drega or to finally secure the cruiser.

They took a step beyond the bend and heard Kevin Jordan whistle from near the top of the ridge. Then they saw him waving.

"Approximately twenty feet further, the bank on the east side of the road curved to the east," Sinclair would write in his report. "As the other side of the bank became visible, Trooper Hersom said, 'Man down on the bank.' There was a trooper's Stetson lying on the bottom of the bank. The subject appeared to have rolled down the bank and lodged against a tree approximately 15–20 feet from the bottom of the bank. The subject was lying on his back with his head facing in a northerly direction. I observed a black automatic-type weapon on the bank approximately 5–10 feet above the subject."

Hersom was afraid this was a friendly-fire victim. With Sinclair and Jordan covering him from opposite directions, he climbed the berm and went up the slope saying, "It's okay — you're going to be all right."

Then Hersom saw that this guy was not going to be all right. Sam Sprague was still in the creek bed with his deer rifle. "Steve gets up there and says, 'He's 10-2. He's 10-2,'" Sprague said during his debriefing. "I was just kneeling at the side of the road with my rifle pointed at the woods. Steve, I saw him reaching, and he grabbed some ID out of the guy. He was trying to read something, and he said, 'Carl Drega.' He said, 'That's him. That's the guy.' So Steve starts yelling, 'We got him. He's dead. He's dead!'"

15
"THIS IS WHAT WE DO"

JOHN HARRIGAN STOOD IN THE NEWSROOM of the *News and Sentinel* with the crowded pasteboards reared up behind him. "This is what we do."

It was somewhere around 4:30 p.m. Charlie Jordan and Leith Jones were in the darkroom watching — hardly able to breathe as they did so — the prints of Charlie's black-and-white photos rise like fever dreams out of their chemical baths.

Kenn Stransky had been posted to the front door to answer the phones and keep the out-of-town reporters from bursting in. Chandra Coviello had fled straight home after escaping from Ducret's. Claire Lynch said she had gotten a phone call from the missing Jana Riley, who had run out of her shoes on her way to Ducret's. Jana was safe with some friends at a shop on Main Street, Claire said, but she wasn't coming back. And Susan Zizza had left for the hospital.

The rest, for whatever reason, had not left, and were still here — now ranged around John in chairs at the press table or in front of the desks that lined the room: Claire, shivering as she recalled the forebodings that had haunted her that morning; compositor Jeannette Ellingwood, an exuberant woman in her seventies who had no truck with forebodings, who had been blindsided like the rest; the gentle typesetter Vivien Towle, who was being held up, almost literally, by her boyfriend Monty Montplaiser, an off-duty U.S. Customs officer; and the courtly bookkeeper Gil Short, who had no bookkeeping to do but who couldn't find it in himself to walk out the door just then.

No one sat in the empty chair before Dennis's desk. "We've lost him," John had said a moment before. He had learned as much in a phone call to Julie Riffon, the nurse who had driven Susan Zizza to Dennis and Polly's house, where Susan had elected to stay for the time being. Kenn Stransky also knew as much and by then had whispered the news to Claire and Gil. The announcement struck the rest like one more lash of a whip.

John sighed and groped for the right words in getting around to what he really wanted to say. Eventually he found phrases to the effect that state troopers and municipal cops, emergency room doctors and EMTs all had something in common with journalists — they had to be there, sometimes, at the worst moments in people's lives. And sometimes those suffering people — especially in a small town — were colleagues, near neighbors, family members: "People you know, people you love."

A muttered curse — or was it a moan? — came from the darkroom. Claire couldn't tell if it was Leith or Charlie. John looked down at the floor, rubbed his eyes. "But, you know, they keep doing their jobs," he said. "They're dying inside, but they keep at it. And today it's been our turn for something like that. And reporting — yeah, this is what we do."

Thoughts were scratching around like mice in John's head. He knew that every daily in the Northeast had someone out on Bridge Street, or on their way there. He knew that down at the *Coös County Democrat*, Gene Ehlert, with his bigger staff, was dispatching reporters to the IGA, to Bloomfield, to Drega's house, to wherever else the story had gone — as John would want him to. In an industry where the reporting done by weekly newspapers was often discounted, even held in contempt, at least one of John's weeklies would have a good accounting of a story that involved the gunshot murder of a weekly's editor. This paper, though, the one robbed of that editor, was uniquely positioned, an industry analyst might say, to tell the story. Or was it just the grief that John wanted to scream aloud?

Claire remembered the man who was always exasperated when a big story broke on Tuesday afternoon, on press day. Well, there are big stories, and then there are nuclear bombs. Jeannette was biting her lower lip, trying to keep from breaking into pieces in her seat.

"I don't know — it's like a meteor dropped on us from outer space," John said. "But some of us are still standing, crawling out of the crater — to tell the story, to say what happened and write down who these people, these friends of ours, were. Well, okay — that's all I've got. What do you think?"

"You know how to do pasteup?" Jeannette Ellingwood was speaking to Charlie Jordan as if she had just learned he could speak Aramaic.

"I do," Charlie said. "So where exactly are you in the process here?"

Jeannette and most of the other staffers didn't know Charlie. They had assumed he was one of the old Uglies who happened to pass by and have a camera handy. Now he'd been deputized as the newspaper's acting editor while John locked himself away to write the feature story and a new editorial.

"Just give me an hour," John had told him. "When you tear up the front page, leave a couple of Claire's stories there, about a third of the page — I don't want the whole front page to be about this. And you can rip all the sports stories. We'll need that space for jump pages for the feature."

Jeannette took Charlie through the finished content in the newsroom, the stories printed in two-inch columns and cut into long strips by Jeannette's scissors or X-Acto knife, then run through the roller of the hot-wax machine, then pressed with a burnishing roller onto the pasteboards. Now it would be Charlie's task to cut all this into pieces and puzzle the stories and graphics onto sticky art boards, each of which would be one page of the newspaper. Twenty-four art boards made a complete issue, what was called a mechanical. That and photo negatives taken by Leith Jones of each board would go this very night to John's Coös Junction Press in Lancaster, where the image of each page would be etched into an aluminum roller and printed.

Charlie saw that the original content of the issue had been nearing completion: features, the editorial, letters to the editor, the "Locals," obituaries, sports. He noticed the headline piece among the features, that story by Dennis about the town manager's resignation. Big news until this afternoon, Charlie thought. He'd keep it, but he'd have to move it back to page 3 or 5. Page 4 would be staked out as usual for John's new editorial and readers' letters.

Also among the features was Dennis's piece about the 45th parallel sign: "It's nice to be in the middle of things, and Clarksville is once again taking note of its place in the center of the northern hemisphere. Last week Charlie and Donna Jordan erected an original 45th parallel sign on Route 145 near the old Clarksville School."

Charlie and Donna had lived in that school building for years, had made a good house out of it. Charlie remembered the day Dennis knocked on its door in 1975. Dennis had just written a profile of J. C. Kenneth Poore, a ninety-year-old hill farmer who had also done some newspaper work. Poore was of the opinion that any young writer should go meet Charlie, who was publishing pieces in *Yankee Magazine* then. Two decades later, Dennis had loved the feel-good quirkiness of this 45th parallel story. Now Charlie had to finish it for him.

The Colebrook police log, assembled by Claire, had a sweet poignancy to it: a car off the road on Vermont 102 after it swerved for a deer, for example, or the theft of a picnic table from the Route 3 rest area. That was what we had to worry about yesterday.

Charlie saw in the obituaries that a joint memorial service for Dr. Herbert Gifford and Dr. Marjorie Parsons — Doc Gifford and Parsie — was planned for Saturday afternoon in the Colebrook Village Cemetery. Most likely the family would want to postpone that. Charlie would have to check. Many of the ads in the newspaper had to do with sales, offers, or events connected to the Moose Festival next week. What the hell was the town going to do about that?

And what about the photos to accompany John's lead story? Leith was still in the darkroom, hanging wet prints on clothesline strung from the ceiling. Charlie would have to talk to John about which ones to use. That would be a tough call.

Claire had run out the door to learn what else had happened. Jeannette and Vivien — with pitch-in help from Leith, Gil, and Monty — were proofing, printing, and waxing whatever hadn't made it to the pasteboards yet. Charlie went back to where the features were posted, to what would have been the front page. He stood where people had run for their lives two hours before and went to work, pulling columns of text off the boards.

Kenn Stransky never saw the *Sentinel*'s newsroom that night because the three separate telephone lines at Jana Riley's desk were lit up constantly. "When reporters called, I tried to keep my statements down to thirty seconds," he said later. "I told them as much as I knew was true from what people at the *Sentinel* had told me, what Claire was finding out on her trips back and forth between us and town hall and the police department, and what was coming over the scanner."

One call came from a TV station in Texas. The voice on the line said, "Hold on just a minute while I get somebody to talk to you."

"Sorry, I don't have even a minute," Kenn said. "If you want any information, it's now or never."

Kenn wasn't surprised that the calls were coming from all over the country, given that in this event "all three points of the triangle," he said, were represented in terms of people civil societies most need to protect: cops, judges, and journalists. Of course a lot of the calls were local. Many thought the *Sentinel* editor who'd been killed was John Harrigan. Some wanted to talk to John, but that wasn't possible.

John was in and out of his office, but not taking calls. Twice he went to see Bunny and Irene at Earl and Pam's house, and both times he paused to talk to the reporters outside the building, all of whom were barred from entering while John's staff was at work. Otherwise the reporters made do with Kenn's periodic updates. John went back to the newsroom once to see how production was going and disappeared once into the darkroom with Charlie Jordan. But his instructions to Kenn were explicit — no calls unless there was one from his daughter Karen.

That meant even the *Union Leader*, the state's biggest daily. "The publisher down there called," Kenn said. "He was not polite, and he demanded to speak to John. I said, 'You're obviously not his daughter' and hung up on him. He called right back, reamed me out, and I hung up again."

The *Union Leader* was granted favors, though. There were those photos that Charlie Jordan had agreed to share. Then the *Union Leader*'s North Country correspondent, and only she, was allowed into the building to take some shots of Charlie doing pasteup, to ask a few questions.

She didn't see John, though, and neither did Attorney General Philip McLaughlin when he visited at six o'clock with Mike Ramsdell, Dick Flynn, Sergeant John Pickering of the Major Crime Unit, and Colebrook's Chief Sielicki. They came in through the rear door, lingered for five minutes, and left through the back again. They paused in the parking lot where Vickie still lay. Kenn didn't see them until they were on their way across Bridge Street to Town Hall.

For the most part, John's improvised staff was disturbed only by the lingering presence of Vickie beneath that blanket. "It was sad — and unsettling," Kenn said. "We're all saying that they've got to do something with that body, but somebody told me that there were a lot of crime scenes, a lot of bodies, and that it was just going to take time before the crime lab people could get here from Concord and take care of all the stuff like that. We tried not to think about it, but that was hard too."

Kenn had to correct many callers in regard to the body count, at least as far as he knew — their numbers tended to be higher, sometimes a lot higher. And yes, the alleged perpetrator was still at large.

Calls came from householders around the region, from people who said they were watching this on TV, and Kenn realized that things were different from when he moved to the North Country from New York in 1993, when on a clear day he might pull in one network channel on his aerial antenna, when he had to ask his parents in Kansas to tape and mail him episodes of *Melrose Place*. "Now, via CNN and WMUR and all these satellite dishes," Kenn said, "this terror was being beamed into every home out there, or a good number of them."

Kenn had been a corporate executive in New York, the national director of sales and marketing for a multinational food manufacturer. Then he quit that at the age of thirty-seven when he inherited a farmhouse in Norton, Vermont. One day a couple of ragged hunters, lost for days, came stumbling out of the woods fringing the house. Kenn called the *News and Sentinel*, and Dennis suggested he write the story himself.

So he became a reporter, and especially a courthouse reporter in Essex County. A court reporter often writes about matters that some people — relatives of the accused, for example — don't like to see in the newspaper. When Kenn received threats in the aftermath of one or two of his stories he had, on Vickie's advice, gone undercover, adopting a pen name and an unlisted phone number. When he got home late that August evening, though, he had messages on his answering machine, albeit sympathetic ones, from some people who shouldn't have known his number.

"So I knew someone had been giving that number out, and of course I'd been on TV that night under my real name as the face of that story, and so was recognized wherever I went," Kenn said. "Everybody knew me, offered good wishes, and that was wonderful, but it continued, and I wanted to put this behind me. So for several reasons, it was time to get out."

Eventually he would shift into adult education, helping people earn their GED diplomas. That night, though, while he was still a reporter, he wept with other reporters. "I was outside at one point, talking to the press, and I saw an AP reporter from Concord with tears running down her face, and that's when I lost it as well," he says. "It was one of those weird moments, when suddenly it smacks you in the head that we're all in this together. It happened again the next morning. I was being interviewed by Fredricka Whitfield of CNN — I'd watched her for years on TV in New York — and she was crying, and again I felt this, I don't know, blood-brother connection to other people in the media, and through Fredricka to people all over the country."

In the clearing at Brunswick Springs, Sam Sprague, Steve Brooks, and Dave Perry joined Steve Hersom and Kevin Jordan as they stood around the body.

They stared at the ruins of a man who looked like he had shot himself in the face. The jaw was curled in — "like he was sucking his lip and making a fish face," Sprague said — and the skin had already assumed its death pallor. There wasn't so much blood around the facial wound, but a lot of blood and what must have been brain matter lay in a spattered streak up the hill, sat pooled behind the head. The eyes were closed, keeping their secrets.

Perry saw that the dead man's black ballistics vest had come partly undone. What seemed a bloodless hole in the center of the chest was actually a peculiar, thumb-sized indentation.

Brooks noticed the blood spattered on the brim of Scottie's hat, the scope mounted on the AR-15 lying in a bed of moss just up the hill. He considered how a scope was actually a disadvantage in close woods like these, making every sapling look like a redwood, and was glad his M14 wasn't scope-mounted. He also saw that Drega had cut down the barrel of his rifle, and that was why it had looked like he was shooting tracers — there was still powder burning on his rounds as they exited the gun's muzzle.

Sprague and Jordan began a conversation about what should be done with the body. "I'm not picking the bastard up," Jordan spat. "Leave him here for coyote bait."

It didn't matter. Into the clearing trooped the first several members of a New Hampshire swat team, in their helmets and face shields and bulging body armor. This was like the army arriving after the National Guard had already settled things, but the army was in charge. When Sprague stooped to collect an empty ammunition clip from his own sidearm, he was scolded into letting it lie — "This is a crime scene, buddy." Jordan, who had picked up Scottie's Stetson to give to Christine, had to put the hat back on the ground.

They went back up the tote road, where other men were gathered around the vehicles near the bridge. Jordan lit up a cigarette, and Sprague stopped to ask for one. "You don't smoke," Jordan said.

"Do those things settle you down?" Sprague asked.

"Well, they do until they kill you."

"Gimme one."

Jordan's hands shook so much that it took several matches to get Sprague's cigarette lit. Then Sprague could barely maneuver it into his mouth between deep, sucking drafts and peals of coughing.

Chuck West had gone back for a brief look at the body and had then returned to the bridge, to his unmarked Cougar. In his statement later, Steve Brooks would praise West for "conspicuous calm and inspiring self-possession under fire." West knew Jellison would want his shotgun, and he had sent someone else to deliver it. Now, alone by the Cougar, he had to hold onto its roof with both hands as he felt terror careening like a wrecking ball around his gut.

John Harrigan and Charlie Jordan had wrestled with this before when they worked together at the *Democrat*: how to choose photographs — of a motor vehicle accident, say — that honestly told a shocking story without being in and of themselves shocking. It was always hard, but never so hard as this.

In the green, ashen light of the darkroom, John — who had already rejected a dozen images — stared at a photo of Dennis, whose face was obscured, strapped into a gurney and being wheeled by several people to the curb of Bridge Street as a pair of EMTs bent over him. In the background were the hanging sign for the *News and Sentinel*, a parked car on the street, Collins's camera shop on the corner of Main, and a motorcyclist heading unperturbed for the intersection. The life-or-death episode in the foreground seemed to unfold against a museum diorama. "Well, okay, we'll use this one," John said.

"You think it's okay?" Charlie asked.

"I don't know. I don't know — I think so."

"So just one photo on the front page?"

John shook his head. "I don't know about that either. That would suggest Dennis was the only victim — or the more important victim."

But the photos of Vickie were more problematic. Charlie had waited until she was covered, but even so . . . "Maybe this one?" Charlie said.

In black and white, the camo-pattern tarp that Dave Robidas had laid over Vickie looked like leopard skin. Paul Nugent stood over the body and looked back at Robidas and John Brunault, both of whom stood stunned, fifteen or twenty feet distant. The pool of blood that trailed toward Brunault seemed to reflect his face and shoulders.

John was straining at the seams as he looked at this, and Charlie was suffering as well. "They need to see what happened," Charlie said eventually. "They need to see what it looked like, at least in some way. It's part of the story."

"Yeah — I suppose."

"And, you know, the story in these photos, either one of them, isn't people dying — it's people helping, or trying to help. Doing their best."

John sucked in a long, empty breath. "Okay — we'll use this one. Yeah, okay."

They went on to picking out photos to send to the *Union Leader*, but they chose to share none of Vickie with the *Union Leader* or any other press organization. That part of the story was just for Colebrook.

Late that afternoon, John Harrigan nearly got arrested — along with everybody else in the Sentinel Building.

State police corporal Scott Champagne, in his mid-thirties with hair to his shoulders and wearing a T-shirt and old blue jeans, was in an unmarked car and doing undercover narcotics work in Littleton — specifically, trailing a suspected pot dealer, with Chuck West nearby for backup. Then Champagne got a call on his cell phone from Howie Weber at Troop F. Weber told him the names of the people murdered and ordered him to Colebrook to secure crime scenes at both the IGA supermarket and the News and Sentinel.

Champagne argued for permission to help with the manhunt, but Weber stood firm. Champagne arrived on Bridge Street as Norm Brown and some others were stringing tape around the area. He went on to the IGA, where Tom Yorke was interviewing witnesses and Dan Couture was keeping a log. So that scene was already secure. Still fuming about this backwater assignment, Champagne returned to the Sentinel.

With his badge and ID on a chain around his neck, he began taking photos of the scene — and stopped short when Brown showed him five bullet casings scattered like cigarette butts near the back door of the building. "So shots were fired right here," Champagne said.

"That's right," Brown replied.

"How many gunmen?"

"I'm pretty sure there was just the one."

"Were there any shots fired inside the building?"

"I don't think so."

"Are you sure?"

"Well — "

At precisely that moment, John burst through the door, skipped over the casings, and rushed to fetch something — he can't remember what — from a vehicle in the parking lot. He hastened back into the building past an open-mouthed Champagne. "Who was that?"

"That's John Harrigan. He owns the newspaper — and the building."

"So there are people in there?"

"Yes, there are."

"And what the hell are they doing?"

"Putting out a newspaper, it looks like."

"In the middle of a crime scene? Where this lawyer had her office? No, I don't think so."

"Well, you'd better have a word with Mr. Harrigan."

"Have you gone through there yet? Checked it out?"

"Talk to John."

Suddenly Leith Jones was at the back door, and Champagne nearly took a bite out of him. Then Champagne's conversation with John went off the rails within its first few words. "You've got your job, and you're doing it," John said. "And we've got our job, and we're doing it, no matter what you say. There is no way in hell we're leaving."

Champagne emphasized the importance of protecting a crime scene, the uselessness in court of mishandled or contaminated evidence. "Crime scene?" John cried. "This is a dead scene — four people are dead. The crime's been done. Why aren't you out chasing this guy?"

That touched a nerve. "I can shut you down, Mr. Harrigan."

"You do that, and you'll have to live with the consequences — if you can figure out how to stop me, or anybody else who wants to stay. You want to try that?"

That was exactly what Champagne wanted to try. But he took a step back and considered — the whole town in chaos, one or more perpetrators still at large. He conferred out of earshot with Brown, who said he was nearly certain that no shots had been fired in the building. "But I can take a look around," Brown promised, "talk to people while they work."

In his report, Champagne would ascribe John's "poor attitude" to "the shock of the circumstances that were unfolding." He added that "there was no time or available resources that permitted this writer to argue with or arrest these people." Instead he went back to John and proposed a deal — everyone could stay in the building so long as no one went out the back door, where the shell casings lay, or into the parking lot.

John agreed — grudgingly, still angry. The problem with the front door was all those other reporters gathered on the other side. Half an hour later, when Monty and Vivien said they needed something from Vivien's car, John sent them out the back.

That was just as Champagne was explaining his handling of the situation to a skeptical Sergeant Guy Kimball of the state police. Kimball marched into the building and assured John that the newspaper would indeed be shut down, and he arrested, with another instance of traffic through that door.

At 5:39 p.m., with an okay from the Major Crime Unit's John Pickering, Guy Kimball lifted the tarp that had been thrown over Les Lord's cruiser at the IGA.

Kimball had gone from the Sentinel Building to the supermarket and had met Pickering in the parking lot. Lord was still in that cruiser, and its motor was still running. Kimball reached breathlessly across the body of the driver and turned the ignition switch off.

With that, the cruiser lurched forward as Lord's foot slipped off the brake pedal. Kimball lunged to throw the transmission into park, holding the body away from him with his right elbow. Then the vehicle was still. In a place where the mutter of its engine had become white noise, the sudden hush was palpable. It was as if Lord's soul had fled.

At seven, in Hardwick, Vermont, Gerry Upton was outside and seated in his car, in the driveway, listening to the car radio as the color started to drain from the sky, as the surrounding trees faded to black. Above the voices on the radio and a chorus of crickets from the pond in back, he heard footsteps. He looked up to see his next-door neighbor, a friend who had done some jobs together with him and Carl, coming down the driveway. "Did you hear about Carl?" he asked.

"Yeah," Upton said. "I did."

Margaret appeared at their home's front door. She had been watching TV. "Who are they talking about?" she called. "Do you suppose it's Carl?"

"Yes, it's Carl," Upton said. "They just killed him."

"Oh, God help us. Did they have to?"

Earl Bunnell, Jr., and his wife, Pam, were doing for Earl's parents what Kenn Stransky was doing for the *Sentinel* staff: shielding them from the press — even the *New York Times*. "The *Times* had a girl there who was especially nice," Bunny said. "But we said no, we'd rather not do any interviews. We didn't want to be treated like the only ones who had lost someone. Others were grieving too."

Friends were let in, other grievers, people nearly as enmeshed in loss as the Bunnells. Electrical lineman Woody Crawford was typical. He had counted Vickie as both his friend and his lawyer, and her brother, Earl — who was still Pearly to Woody — was his daughter's godfather. Lord's wife, Bev, was his cousin, and he had painted Scott and Christine Phillips's house. When Dennis and Polly had decided they wanted to be on the electrical grid, it was Woody who had done the work on that.

The Reverend Peter Dyer — a chubby, amiable man who suited up convincingly as Santa Claus each holiday season — came from the Congregational church, along with his wife, Rosalie. Like Earl, Bunny and Irene had been prevented from going to Vickie, but as the evening wore on, they grew upset that Vickie had yet to be moved. Lawyer David King heard Bunny cry, "Can't they at least get her off the pavement?"

At 7:10, nearly an hour after the gunfire had ceased at Brunswick Springs, the Vermont State Police issued a press release: "It has been confirmed that the suspect in this incident, Carl Drega, has been located and apprehended. The suspect has suffered a gunshot wound. Three more police officers were injured during this incident. . . . It is unknown at this time as to the seriousness of their injuries."

A young state trooper, Eric Johnson, new to Troop F, had been posted to Pam's house to stay with Bunny and Irene until they went home. He was more candid about the status of the suspect. "They got the son of a bitch," he whispered into Bunny's ear. "They killed him."

Bunny nodded and bowed his head, weeping. He didn't know why. He guessed later that it was because they had killed the only man who could tell him why his daughter — or anyone else — was dead.

John Harrigan couldn't remember who got through to him on the telephone in his office. John took a reporter's notes on the events and circumstances. Then he went out to tell his staff.

"There wasn't anything like applause or jubilation," Kenn Stransky said. "It was just another fact to add to the story — and an opportunity to exhale, since in the back of our minds we'd been afraid all along that he'd be back."

16
PATIENT
IN AFFLICTION

WITH THE DEATH OF CARL DREGA, John Harrigan's headline story in the *News and Sentinel* had a beginning — albeit a mystifying one; all this from a traffic stop? — a middle, and an end. John was a first-draft writer anyway, and it was one of those leads that nearly writes itself: "It was a crime of unbelievable proportions, that left at least five people dead, a newspaper and a police fraternity in shock, and a community stunned to its core."

The editorial was tougher. Here John eschewed mentioning the "deranged gunman" by name — indeed, John would vow to never utter Carl Drega's name again — and he punctuated the fate of each victim with question marks: "Dennis Joos, this paper's co-editor, a newspaperman's newspaperman who loved rural and small-town life, gunned down as he tried to stop a madman? Vickie Bunnell, a small-town lawyer in the classic sense of the term who kept her dog in her office and saved the lives of everyone else in the building by shouting out a warning with her last words, lying dead in the parking lot? Scott Phillips, one of our all-time favorite troopers, cowlick and all, taken from his wife and kids and the town that he loved, and loved him? Les Lord, a great guy with a landmark laugh who was about the most likeable guy around, shot down in cold blood?"

Each question mark was a spike of incredulity. "Yes, it happened here. Yes, these wonderful people are gone. It is a nightmare from which there is no waking up. God love these people as their families and their town did — and God help us all deal with what has happened, and remember these fine and cherished faces, and their smiles."

The column ended with an account of what was happening as John wrote the piece, as his staff — "Some had narrowly escaped the volley that killed Vickie Bunnell," he wrote, without hyperbole — put it all together. "We left the photos and stories and bylines that Dennis did this week in the paper," John continued. "It was, after all, his last work, and he put his best into everything that he did. We'll do a better job with the loss and what this has all meant in next week's paper. Right now it's just too much, and getting this paper out is all we can manage."

In the newsroom, Charlie Jordan pasted in a headline in a font size much larger than the *Sentinel's* usual: "Four Gunned Down in Colebrook; Editor, Lawyer, Two Officers Dead." His photos of Dennis in the gurney and Vickie beneath her blanket rested above brief articles by Claire Lynch about the vandalism at the post office and the runaways from Camp E-Toh-Anee. There was also a Leith Jones photo from the West Stewartstown Old Home Day parade: two young boys on a float with their arms around a docile black calf.

John hadn't quite finished his editorial when his children Karen and Mike arrived at eight thirty. They had to tap on John's office window, since the front door was locked and the back door taped off. Kenn Stransky let them in, and soon Karen settled into helping Kenn on the phone lines.

She found that some people were still calling to ask if her father was dead. Then Karen couldn't help getting angry at a reporter calling from the *Philadelphia Inquirer.* "What are you doing at the newspaper now?" the woman asked. "Are people standing around in groups, hugging and crying?"

"No, we're not, and you need to think about how you phrase your questions," Karen snapped. "We're busy getting the paper out."

Lieutenant Rick Estes of New Hampshire Fish & Game was proud of Eric Stohl's men and how they had conducted themselves that day, but none of the men felt proud — least of all Kevin Jordan. At the top of the foul-up list he recited to Estes was letting Wayne Saunders drive off alone. "I screwed up. I left him," he said.

"Well, you didn't leave him," Estes replied. "Everything you did, Kevin, was right. It turned out okay. Unfortunately, yes, some guys lost their lives here. That's the nature of this business."

They sat alone at 8:30 p.m. with a tape recorder between them at Fish & Game's Region 1 office in Lancaster. Estes himself was not at all reconciled to these deaths — but he had to be, and somehow he had to bring Jordan around to that point as well. Jordan, for his part, was not to be persuaded that any part of what he did was right, or enough. He didn't mention the Ruger assault rifle he wasn't qualified to carry. He had never used it, but just the same, at Brunswick Springs he had had to hand it over to Eric Stohl, who accepted the weapon with raised eyebrows and no comment.

Then Stohl — an old-school kind of guy, with nothing touchy-feely about him — astonished Jordan by giving him a hug and insisting on chauffeuring him and John Wimsatt to this debriefing session. They became part of something that still seemed eerie to Jordan: a funereal, bumper-to-bumper parade of law enforcement vehicles of every stripe and size, along with an ambulance or two, plodding north on 102. Some of those drivers were blinking through tears, especially since word had gone around that John Pfeifer had died.

"There's nothing we can do about those guys who died," Estes said. "There were a couple of guys whose number was up, and there was just no way around it, and this guy wasn't fooling around. This wasn't somebody running scared."

"Nope."

"This was a guy who wanted to hurt somebody."

"Yeah, and he wanted to get killed."

"Probably he did." Estes paused, stubbing out his cigarette in an ashtray on the table between them. "And I don't want to be the pathetic guy here, but I'm going to tell you something — somewhere, somebody's going to take his side in this. Somebody's going to say, 'Oh, poor Carl, and all those bad police officers, hundreds of them, shooting at him.' And he's going to become a Robin Hood. But Kevin, he's no Robin Hood. He was a nut with a gun, and he was wrong. You guys did the right thing."

Jordan nodded. "Yeah."

"You know in your heart."

Jordan looked into his heart and saw how much he had had in common — at least at that time — with Carl Drega. "I set out to kill this guy," he said. "But luckily, none of us had to do it. I don't think any of us did it. I think he did it on his own."

"Well, it damned sure wasn't you, because you never fired a shot."

Jordan was glad of that, at the same time ashamed of it. "No, I never fired, so — "

"And we're all just a phone call away. I don't care if it's me or Eric, all you have to do is call, and I'll go meet you anyplace you want and we'll sit down. We'll talk, we'll drink, we'll smoke, we'll do anything you want to do."

"I'll be okay. I got a good wife."

That good wife had known only that a New Hampshire game officer, name withheld, had been shot in Bloomfield. At home that night Louise wrapped her arms around her husband and wept.

At the same time that Kevin Jordan was meeting with Rick Estes, Patrolman Dan Couture was at the Colebrook Police Department providing his official account of the day. The lights around Monument Lot were bright as flares. Vickie still lay in the parking lot, and Bridge Street — with its throng of camera-wielding strangers from away — looked like Times Square on New Year's Eve. Still in his shorts and T-shirt, Couture had breasted his way through the crowd unmolested.

His statement was taken by an officer up from Concord, Sergeant Dave Crawford of the Major Crime Unit. "I inquired how far away Patrolman Couture was when the cruiser drove by him, and Patrolman Couture said about sixty feet," Crawford wrote. "I asked if Patrolman Couture had a clear shot at the cruiser, and he said for a short time he did."

A lot had happened since then, and more people had died. Couture, even more so than Jordan, was unreconciled to those deaths. Crawford was sympathetic, but it was sympathy from someone Couture would never see again.

"It should be noted," Crawford added to his conclusion to the statement, "that Patrolman Couture was very emotionally upset by the sequence of events, and I encouraged him not to blame himself and to seek counseling."

From the crime scene report of Sergeant Guy Kimball: "At 2100 hours on August 19, 1997, the body of Vickie BUNNELL (dob 7-9-52) was removed from the scene by Robert Moore and Neil Couture of the Newman Funeral

Home, 136 Main Street, Colebrook, New Hampshire, for transportation to the Concord Hospital, 250 Pleasant Street, Concord, New Hampshire."

That was after Jana Riley — kicking and screaming, as it were — had come back to the Sentinel Building to provide her own witness statement. Jana had run straight through Ducret's, out the front door, and into a hair salon, where her cries and exhortations were greeted as the ravings of a mad woman. Friends had picked her up there and taken her by car to their own business on Main, which happened to be another hair salon. Jana's car was among those impounded in the parking lot, and eventually her boyfriend had to give her a ride to her mother's house, stopping first at the Sentinel Building. Determined never to enter there again, Jana sent the boyfriend in to find her purse. The front door was locked, however, and Charlie Jordan had to hand the purse out to him.

She came back that evening only at the firm insistence of the state police. She spoke to a detective she didn't know about events she still didn't understand while the newsroom buzzed around her. John Harrigan stopped to put a hand on her shoulder, but Jana would have none of it. "I quit, John — I quit," she said. "I can't come in here again."

By then John had given his lead story and editorial to Vivien Towle for typesetting and then had gone outside — yes, through the back door — to be with Vickie one last time.

It was past eleven o'clock. Charlie Jordan was on foot and worried that someone might take a potshot at him. He moved as quietly as possible, but the dogs knew he was there.

It wasn't until nearly eleven when the newspaper was finally done, when the complete mechanicals were put in a box for Monty Montplaiser, who had volunteered to drive them down to Lancaster, where John Harrigan had pressmen standing by. Monty also promised to deliver photos to the *Democrat* and to a plane standing by in Whitefield for the *Union Leader*.

There was nothing ceremonial or celebratory about the moment — nor was there any sense of relief, really, given that now people had to go home and be alone with their thoughts. They sifted out the front door in ones or twos, with the lights still on at the town hall and big lights like quasars flooding the parking lot, where a single trooper from below the notches stood sentry, having relieved Scott Champagne of that duty only moments before. No one had anything to say to the few lingering reporters that hadn't already been said. Those whose cars were still confined to the parking lot got rides.

Charlie's mother's Plymouth Duster was all by itself in the darkness behind Hicks Hardware. Donna and Tommy had gotten a ride home that afternoon. The night had turned cold, and Charlie hadn't brought a jacket. The Duster started reluctantly, but nothing odd about that. Charlie turned out of the parking lot onto Pleasant Street and then north on Main. He switched on the radio and found it full of reports on the shootings.

Charlie was opposite J. C. Kenneth Poore's old farm, about two miles from the 45th parallel and home, when the Duster simply stopped running and coasted to a silent stop in front of the house and barn abandoned since the old man's death some fifteen years before. The car couldn't be coaxed into starting again, and Charlie had this clammy feeling that Poore, or his ghost, was in the passenger seat beside him. "Are you having a bad day, Charlie?" Poore asked him. "Can it get any worse?"

It could, Charlie thought, as he trudged up Route 145. There weren't a lot of houses on that stretch of road, but each had its lights on and a dog to raise the alarm. Behind each locked and bolted front door, Charlie imagined, was a family listening to the news and keeping a loaded gun at hand. Someone could easily choose to fire before being fired upon.

It was a clear night, and the stars wheeled overhead around a three-quarters moon. When at last he reached his own place, the old Clarksville schoolhouse, whose front door they rarely locked, Charlie wasn't surprised to find it locked tonight.

He knocked — a knock without the usual precedent of headlights or engine noise. Donna's voice was webbed in fear when she said from the other side, "Who is it?"

At midnight, the fifth of bourbon on Bunny's kitchen table between him and John Harrigan was more empty than full. And yet neither of them was feeling the effects of the alcohol — which was too bad, John thought.

After Monty had left with the mechanicals, the Harrigans had all gone home to the house on South Hill, John and Karen in the Lincoln, Mike in his car. But John wasn't ready to sit at home just yet. He went back out to his '88 Ford pickup, stashed a bottle of Jim Beam's behind the seat, and drove up to West Stewartstown, to where Dennis and Polly lived — or where Dennis had lived.

Susan Zizza had gotten a ride home by then. But Sue Wright, who owned the printing business Dennis had worked at for a while, was there. Polly said their son, Aaron, an engineer, was on his way home, that he had been doing surveying work for an oil company in Alaska. He was just about to leave for a lengthy job in the bush somewhere when he had been found by Alaska state police. "That was lucky," John said.

John had forgotten how beautiful this house was, what good carpenters and stone masons the Jooses had become, and to what wholesome uses they had put their local spruce, cedar, and granite. He said as much, which got him around to saying what he had come to say — "I'm so sorry, Polly. I'm sorry he's gone."

Polly yielded a smile and shook her head. "He's not gone," she said, glancing around at the plank floor, the cathedral ceiling, the little indoor pool, the fulsome hearth and chimney. "He's all around me here."

When John left Polly and Sue, he drove to Bunny and Irene's house in Canaan, on the other side of the river, with its American flag in the front yard hanging limp against the moon and the inky bulk of Monadnock to the west. Irene bade goodnight to John and went to bed. Bunny had nodded his assent when John broke out the bourbon. "Might as well," he said.

In a couple more hours, John would drive back to the Sentinel Building. He wanted to make sure everybody had left, and Trooper Brett Beausoleil, in his crime scene log, would note John entering through the front door. The rooms were empty, and John listened to the sound of his own footsteps shuffling among the empty pasteup boards and vacant desks. He looked into Vickie's office, and maybe he only imagined a trace of her scent, her perfume and its tinctures of grass and sky. The lights were still on, and John would choose to leave them that way.

"HARRIGAN's daughter also arrived on foot," Beausoleil would write in his log, "and spoke briefly to her father prior to both leaving." Karen was worried, was looking for John, had parked some distance from the building because of other vehicles still lining Bridge and Main. John can't remember what he and Karen talked about. "I think I might have asked her if the back door was locked," he said. "Or maybe about my idea to throw the front door open the next morning, let the media in."

For now, John was at rest at Bunny's kitchen table, in the house where Vickie had grown up. Bunny said that he believed — believed all the more so now — that there was something eternal in every human being. He remembered a verse from Romans: "Be joyful in hope, patient in affliction, faithful in prayer." But he spoke from the bottom of that chasm into which Job was flung.

John's body and soul were bleeding into each other. He wondered what might have been different. He wondered where you have to go, what number you call, what incantation you chant, to sell your soul for a second chance at life — even if you couldn't change a thing. Just to be there again. "We get to thinking we're going to live forever," he said. "Don't we?"

If John had gone past the wood-burning stove, out the kitchen, and around the corner, he could have climbed the stairs to Vickie's old bedroom. Irene had left it just as it was when Vickie moved out: her old clothes in the closet and dresser, her college texts in the bookshelves, her diplomas on the wall, along with her DAR Citizenship Award and a photo of her and her French horn in the Plymouth State orchestra.

Tucked into one corner was her first keyboard instrument, a General Electric Youth Electric Organ. The device was mostly plastic, dusty and unplugged, but resting on its console was an American songbook thrown open to this page:

On top of Old Smokey, all covered in snow,
I lost my true lover, come a-courting too slow . . .

PART
THREE

17
THE
ARMOR
OF GOD

FROM THE REPORT *of Sergeant Edward J. Ledo of the Vermont State Police:* "On Tuesday 08-19-97, at approximately 1630 hours, this officer was assigned to provide security at the Drega death scene. Upon arrival at the scene I met with Det./Sgt. Tim Chagnon, who advised that security at the crime scene was needed due to the approaching darkness."

Ledo walked with another Vermont trooper, Sean Selby, down the road along Black Creek until, at the clearing, he met the trailer-truck bulk of the Vermont Mobile Crime Lab. Beyond that, a number of detectives were taking notes, marking shell casings, examining the trees and ground litter. They showed Ledo and Selby the body, still lying faceup on the hillside with the Colt AR-15 nearby, and pointed out the New Hampshire trooper's Stetson at the bottom of the slope.

Eventually Ledo and Selby were left alone in the blackening woods. Two other troopers guarded the road entrance on Route 102. At eleven o'clock, a pair of headlights came knifing down the tote road. These belonged to a hearse from the Sayles Funeral Home in St. Johnsbury. The hearse worked its way carefully around the lab truck, its tires digging into the berm where the K-9 detail had taken cover. Then Ledo and Selby helped put the body into a bag, which they secured with evidence tape and pushed into the back of the hearse. The vehicle's receding taillights glowed like will-o'-the-wisps in the woods.

At the funeral home, attendants would find that Carl Drega had not committed suicide, as it had appeared to Kevin Jordan and some others.

Instead he had been hit simultaneously by two different projectiles: an M14 bullet that had cut a tunnel through his jaw and out the back of his head and a shotgun slug that had struck the center of his bulletproof vest with enough concussive power to stop his heart. The body also displayed a bullet wound in the right shoulder, and there had been three other solid hits to Drega's vest.

The Vermont State Police had Drega's wallet, which was found to contain, among other items, identification cards answering to both his birth years, 1930 and 1935; a State of Connecticut birth certificate with the year of birth scratched out; a valid New Hampshire pistol/revolver license, which allowed him to carry a concealed weapon; the business cards of several lawyers and a Bushmaster Firearms sales representative; an expired registration certificate for his '74 Dodge pickup; Rita Drega's Social Security card; and a dog-eared wallet photo of Rita.

Mrs. Drega had been pretty, and indeed looked Native American with her high cheekbones, broad white smile, and coppery skin tone. The photo had been taken with a flash at some social occasion, perhaps. She wore what looked like a zebra-print dress with a cravat-like bow at the neck. Relax, everything will be fine, she seemed to say.

Ledo and Selby checked the scene at random intervals each hour throughout the night. The discarded Stetson, tipped between its crown and brim, looked like a beached seashell in the flicking beam of a flashlight. The hemlocks murmured like ship masts in a light breeze, and the stars were buoy lights winking between their crowns.

On Tuesday night — well, Wednesday morning — the Pappas family's Italian restaurant in Brookline, Massachusetts, closed as it usually did at 1:00 a.m. An hour later, Mark Pappas and several friends were aboard a twenty-six-foot powerboat heading out of Scituate Harbor and into Massachusetts Bay. Pappas intended to have a few beers and get a little sleep before they all baited hooks for striped bass at 4:00 a.m.

"So somebody switched on the TV and said, 'Hey, it's working,' which was exciting for us, because there weren't a lot of things working on that boat," he recalled. "We fiddled with the knobs and got three channels out of Boston. We left it on — I don't know, NBC *Nightly News*? — and there was something going on up in New Hampshire. I was watching the screen, but not paying much attention. Suddenly this guy's face came up, a driver's license headshot. I sat bolt upright and told everybody to shut up. 'Turn it up!' I yelled, and I'm grabbing the shoulder of the guy next to me. 'That's the guy I sold my rifle to!'"

"The guy that shot all those people?" somebody said. "You sold him a gun?"

"At a gun show last winter — I remember that guy."

"What are you selling to that fucking idiot for?"

"Hey, excuse me, how do I know what he's going to do? It was legal — a legal sale, right? — and he seemed okay, seemed friendly. He looked like somebody's grandfather, for Christ's sake."

"I gotta tell you, he didn't look so friendly."

"Well, he looked different there, but — "

"So maybe that's not the guy."

"No, that's him — I remember. I remember those eyebrows. That was the guy. Oh, shit."

The group fell silent amid the slap of the waves, the ionized glow of the TV, the inky void outside the cabin windows. "So you sold him that Colt semi, right?" somebody else said.

"Yeah." Pappas felt like he'd been wrestled down and shot with a syringe full of something he didn't know about. Its effects were complicated. Fear was one of them. Helplessness too. Confusion. Guilt? Should he feel guilty?

"You think that was your gun he used?"

"I don't know." He shivered and shook his head. Guys like this, he thought, they usually have a lot of guns. "Probably not." But he couldn't banish all those feelings.

Pappas was due back at the restaurant the next evening, and he didn't get any sleep that night. At dawn they caught stripers and a small shark, until a school of bluefish moved in.

Early Thursday morning an FBI agent would appear on Pappas's doorstep to claim the bill of sale for the rifle Drega had used.

Susan Zizza would say later that it looked like the Martians had landed, with all the TV studio trucks — and their arrays of antennae, radar dishes, and transmission towers — parked up and down Bridge and Main on Wednesday morning. John Harrigan was the first to thread his way through them at 5:30 a.m.

Then came Jana Riley, who hadn't quit the newspaper business after all. "Well, I couldn't leave John even more short-handed," she explained. As was usual on a Wednesday morning, Jeannette Ellingwood arrived to help Jana sort and bundle for delivery the five thousand copies of the *News and Sentinel* that a trucker from Lancaster had left inside the front door. Chandra Coviello was absent, but Karen and Mike Harrigan pitched in, in her place.

At 8:00 a.m., other staffers arrived, as usual. Charlie Jordan, still working on a volunteer basis, got a ride in with Donna in the family's other car, and then Donna stayed to help as well. Charlie surveyed with a perfectionist's eye the new issue of the *Sentinel*, with its black headline and stark photos, and was shamed by the several mistakes in layout he had made, out of either haste or unfamiliarity with the *Sentinel*'s practices: the wrong headings for the "Locals" columns, some crooked headings elsewhere, some off-kilter font sizes. Nonetheless, he took a copy outside, where he stood in front of the reporters already starting to assemble, many from big East Coast dailies, and raised the issue over his head. Cheers broke out. Camera shutters clicked.

Of course, with its front-page split between homicide and an Old Home Day parade, this was a newspaper unlike any of those dailies, which was exactly the point to John: mass murder, God help us, but don't forget the Kiwanis Club's Layperson of the Year award (Stephanie Lyons, a business education teacher at Canaan High, church volunteer, Sunday school teacher, and officer in the Order of the Eastern Star), or the teenage volunteers who spent a week cleaning up the Kenneth Poore farm, or the restoration of the first settlers' gravestones in Canaan. Don't forget the stories Fred Harrigan might have passed on: the camp runaways, the vandalism at the post office. All these pieces, sun and cloud, combined into a weather system that made the issue's lead story all the more bald and perplexing, like a moon astronomers couldn't explain.

John didn't expect to see Susan Zizza, especially since editors usually took a day of rest after press day. He called her early that morning, though, just to make sure she was all right, and she insisted that she was, that she'd be in later. But she didn't sound all right.

By 8:15, John had everybody in the building gathered once more around the center table in the newsroom. Bouquets of flowers crowded Dennis's desk — Vickie's as well, dwarfing like sequoias the little arrangement Bunny had laid there the previous afternoon.

John said he had made a promise yesterday to all the news people outside the building. "I told them today would be, well, we'll call it 'Media Day,'" he said. "I promised they could come inside and ask questions, but only to those of you who are willing and able. I'll try to handle as much of that as I can by myself. If a reporter approaches you, though, I encourage you to help — if you can. If you can't or don't want to, no problem. Just say so, and if any of them hassle you about it, let me know."

More than a few weren't so sure about this, would prefer just to work, to not be pressed for decisions one way or the other in regard to talking about it. But it was too late for John to go back on his promise. "We'll make it work," he said.

Rumors that John Pfeifer had died would prove unfounded, though his life hung in the balance at a hospital in Burlington, Vermont. Rumors on this day that Wayne Saunders had died were also unfounded, these springing from the fact that Saunders's head had been covered when he was loaded off the medevac helicopter at the Dartmouth-Hitchcock Hospital in Lebanon. "They put that hood on me so reporters couldn't tell who it was," Saunders explained. "Some cop was there and he thought I had died en route."

Saunders remembered hearing from Steve Breton that Scottie and Les had been shot by the same guy who had shot him. At the Colebrook hospital he had asked several times about how they were doing — nobody seemed to hear. Then he spent the night floating in and out of consciousness. He woke in the morning possessed by a full-body ache and the feeling that his chest and left arm had been mauled by a bear.

He would learn that he had been in surgery not only for the repair of vascular damage in that arm but also for the removal of his Fish & Game badge — driven through cloth and into flesh as though by a stamp press —

from his sternum. The first of Drega's bullets, surgeons found, had miraculously struck that aluminum wafer at just the right angle. Just as in the cowboy movies, the badge had deflected the bullet away from the CO's heart, then up into his shoulder.

In the morning he was tangled in tubes and his head was wreathed in fog, but he felt aware enough to click on the TV above his hospital bed, catch up on the news. It took only a few minutes for him to feel like he had been kicked in the chest again, for tears to run unstanched down his cheeks.

By 7:30 a.m., every copy of the *News and Sentinel* had been cleaned out of the building and grabbed off the newsstands. John had to call down to the Coös Junction Press to rush a second printing.

At the same time he conducted what amounted to a running, all-day news conference, from one end of the building to the other, as more flowers and then donated trays of food came in through the door. In his answers to all the questions, he began to find themes that he would return to as the questions were repeated, repeated again. So how is Colebrook different today than it was just yesterday? "The Shangri-La factor," he said. "It's been lost. It seemed like something like this couldn't happen here."

John remembered all the reporters — though not nearly as many as now — who had come to Colebrook in 1984, after Christopher Wilder had been killed, and it struck him that no one then had been asked to explain that event in terms of what sort of town Colebrook was, other than its being a border town patrolled by a tough cop named Jellison. That had been a random event — of all the towns along the Canadian border, or the Mexican, for that matter, Wilder happened to head for this one. John proposed much the same view of this incident when reporters asked him to explain what had just happened, to offer some rationale for why it happened here. It made no difference whether the killer was a fugitive from Florida, he said, or a North Country native, or someone in between. "This guy was just a piece of space junk who happened to get us," he told the *New York Times*. "It was our turn."

Elsewhere in the building, the city reporters moved as though inside a church, speaking in whispers and approaching John's staffers circumspectly. Nonetheless, people were edgy as they started work on next Wednesday's issue. Karen Harrigan had been filmed that morning as she helped bundle newspapers. She had felt odd about that and decided not to take interview requests. Claire Lynch had dressed up in a sleek dress and high heels for the day, but she ended up fleeing the building, glad of the excuse to pass out sidewalk flyers announcing Scott's and Les's calling hours. There, however, a film crew found her and prevailed upon her to walk up the town hall steps for them. They held a microphone down low to catch the clicking of her heels as she flushed in embarrassment.

Around midmorning, Karen took a call from a woman in Portsmouth, down in the Seacoast Region, at the other end of the state. "Yes — I ordered a classified ad for this week's issue," the woman said with brittle politeness. "And I paid with a credit card, but the ad's not in there. I can't find it."

"Ma'am, did you read any of that issue?" Karen said. "Or have you watched any news on TV?"

"No, I went straight to the classifieds, but — "

"Uh-huh. We've had a little incident here."

"Oh — really? What . . ." Karen heard a newspaper rustling in the background. "Oh, my."

"Yeah — we'll credit your account."

A few moments later, Jana Riley took a call from someone hoping to be reassured that Fred and Esther Harrigan were all right. Jana explained that no, actually they weren't, and provided the years of their deaths.

In the afternoon, as rain began to fall, Jana admitted to herself that there was another reason she needed to come to work today — her resolve not to let someone like this Carl Drega change her life or who she was. But as the afternoon wore on, she felt herself getting wound up tight, a little bit anxious. She didn't like it that she had never seen the killer's corpse, that she had to take it on faith that Drega had died in the woods last night. She didn't know any more than the rest of the world why all hell had broken loose yesterday. She wondered if Vickie was just unlucky, if she or Jeannette or anyone else might have just as easily been a target, and if the story about Drega's death might be one of those facts that newspapers get wrong sometimes, if instead he might still be on the prowl. In years to come, she would wake at night crazed by the same nightmare — being chased by a man in camouflage pants and wielding a rifle, but with no face, just a yawning fleshy whiteness.

That day she reached a breaking point when another strange reporter asked her, yet again, how she and her colleagues were feeling today. "Well, how do you expect us to feel?" she snapped. She stomped into John's office, ready to quit again, until John promised she'd be left alone.

At the end of the day, in a drizzling rain, Jana and others were allowed to reclaim their vehicles from the parking lot. But Jana felt faint when she found spatters of dried blood, it must be Dennis's, on her car's hood and right fender.

She wheeled out of the lot with her wipers snapping and her hands almost jumping off the wheel. At home she fetched soap and water and a stiff brush and ran out again into the rain.

Veteran state troopers John McMaster and Jack Meaney were among those summoned Wednesday morning to search the Drega property, where it looked like Drega had tried to burn the barn as well as the house.

In 1972 McMaster and Meaney were founding members of the state police's first bomb squad, a unit formed on the fly when anti–Vietnam War activists planted explosives in Manchester's police and fire stations. On that day, McMaster had held a bomb in his bare hands while a trooper with military ordinance experience set about dismantling it. A young, square-jawed Chuck Jellison was also a member of that squad.

On Wednesday, McMaster was the sergeant in command of the search detail. He stood with Meaney before the barn's middle bay door and pointed out the sort of burn mark that results from a quick splash of a flammable liquid and a tossed match. A five-gallon plastic gas can, half full, rested nearby. If he wanted to burn his barn, Meaney thought, it was a half-assed effort. It looked more to him like Drega was trying to lure someone through that particular door and not the others.

They entered through one of the other bay doors and climbed stairs to the building's second level. There they saw a shiny Kubota lawn tractor, workbenches, and, on a table near an outside door, a pile of fireworks — snaking coils of rope fuse salutes — and a bucket of granulated, or "prilled," ammonium nitrate. A good chemical fertilizer, ammonium nitrate was also a prime ingredient, combined with diesel fuel, of the bomb Timothy McVeigh had used in Oklahoma City two years before.

Meaney found three books scattered on the cowling of the Kubota: "one on homemade survival techniques and devices," he would write in his report, "one on homemade c-4 explosives, and one on homemade grenade launchers." In the first book, *Ragnar's Action Encyclopedia of Practical Knowledge and Proven Techniques*, Meaney found a bookmark providing quick reference to a chapter on booby trapping stairs with explosives. Meaney saw that McMaster was halfway up a flight of stairs to the barn's top level. "John, you better get your ass down from there," Meaney said — loudly.

Twenty minutes later, McMaster was at the Colebrook Police Department and on the phone with state attorney general Mike Ramsdell. "No, we're not losing any more men to this bastard," Ramsdell said. "The barn's a public hazard. That's what it looks like to me. So finish what he started. Just burn it — and we'll see what's left."

That afternoon, Dan Ouimette was called to the property by agents from the federal Bureau of Alcohol, Tobacco, and Firearms. Ouimette knew he was lucky, that his life had been saved by the job he had in Vermont when Drega pulled into his empty shop on Tuesday. The ATF wanted to know about any tunnels or hidden trenches on the grounds, and Ouimette said he wasn't aware of any. Later he stood in the rain in front of the barn with McMaster and Meaney. The sergeant said the barn would be burned that night, rain or no rain.

"That's a nice Kubota he's got in there," Meaney said. "It's a shame."

The ATF agents also thought it was a shame. Booby traps or not, they wanted to comb the barn for evidence of links between Drega and organized groups, militia or otherwise. But Ramsdell wouldn't budge.

Ouimette looked up at the barn, which had towered like a pyramid over the cabin, and admired its unblemished siding, its proud palladium window, its square-cornered workmanship. It occurred to him that Carl would no more have been taken alive than he would have used a mismeasured board.

The rain stopped early that evening. At 10:00 p.m., the barn was set afire via remote ignition. "Within a few minutes the building was fully involved," Meaney wrote. The flames rose to a hundred feet, and then higher. They licked at the clouds and cast a jack-o'-lantern glow up and down the river.

"That's the last of his woodpile," said state fire marshall Donald Bliss. A few minutes more, and the first in a series of explosions was heard.

Gerry Upton and his Case 450 bulldozer had just been hired by the Town of Hardwick to help repair a washed-out road. Upton told the FBI agent on the phone that he had to be at work at seven on Thursday morning. "Okay, we'll be there at five," the agent said.

"So you want to talk for two hours?"

"It may not take that long, but we have a number of questions about Mr. Drega, sir — thank you."

There were two men — Special Agents John Hersh and Daniel Rachek, wearing the sort of sharp suits and crisp ties that aren't seen much around Hardwick — at Gerry and Margaret's door the next morning. The Uptons and the agents sat in the living room while the rising sun gilded the pond outside the back windows. Hersh's synopsis of the interview would cover eleven typed pages, single-spaced, starting with Gerry Upton's life history and then his twenty years of friendship with Carl Drega.

Upton said that a New Hampshire Fish & Game officer had given Carl "a hard time over a river improvement project" that he and Carl worked on together, that Carl filed a lawsuit against the officer, and then Carl got "ticked off" at the judge in the case, whom the agents and the Uptons presumed — incorrectly — to have been Vickie Bunnell. Upton mentioned bailing Carl out of jail once after he had "touched off a round of ammunition in the ground or the air" that had frightened a tax assessor. "UPTON then described DREGA," Hersh wrote, "as the type of individual who did not like authority."

Upton remembered an autumn visit to Carl's house in Columbia the year before. In the solarium he noticed a thick book "dealing with survival tactics." This was probably *Ragnar's Action Encyclopedia*, the book that Jack Meaney had found on the tractor. It provided instructions on, among other things, protecting your privacy and property, changing your identity, stocking and defending a retreat, building weapons and explosives, and avoiding "the costly mistakes of others when standing up to big government and nosy do-gooders." Also in the solarium, Upton remembered, was "a pamphlet detailing a militia-type activity." Upton said that Carl had been present while he browsed through these items but that Carl never spoke to him about them or about anything related to their subject matter. Nor did Carl ever voice any intent to harm another person.

Upton had last seen Carl at Christmas, had last spoken to him five weeks ago when Carl needed that nuclear plant job reference. No, there were no tunnels or bunkers on his property, just a root cellar extending from his barn into a hillside. Both Margaret and Gerry described their incredulity when they heard the news on Tuesday and their unsuccessful flight to the Hardwick police station.

Upton shared photos of him and Carl working on the barn they had built together elsewhere in Hardwick. He mentioned their plan to canoe the Allagash River. "At this point in the interview," Hersh wrote, "it was noted that UPTON became upset emotionally as he related the fact that he would not be able to take that canoe trip with his good friend, CARL DREGA."

Two hours flew by, and they were still talking. At 7:20 a.m. Upton said, "I'm sorry, but I'm already late — I've got to get to that job."

On the road, Upton was in such a hurry that — towing the Case 450 behind him — he passed a truck on a straightaway. Hersh and Rachek, meanwhile, reviewed their notes and decided that things still didn't add up between Gerry Upton's gentle, considerate friend and this killer in Colebrook. They pursued Upton to his job site.

"Brief contact with UPTON was had at the construction site," Hersh wrote, "where he reiterated the fact that he could not think of further information which would have been in his possession concerning DREGA which had not already been discussed with the FBI."

Susan Zizza came in at 10:30 a.m. on Wednesday. She entered through the front door, had to stop and steady herself when the first thing she saw on the counter in front of Jana's desk was a stack of Charlie's photos from the day before. Then she walked back to the newsroom, sat at her desk, found herself subject to interview requests, and went home.

On Thursday she arrived before eight. She parked in the rear lot, where none of the city reporters — back on lockout status — recognized her. As she went in through the back, she had to shield her eyes from that spot where Vickie had fallen. She said hello to ad designer Chandra Coviello, who had also returned to work that day — Wow, she looks even worse than I feel, Susan thought — and continued past Chandra's desk to John's office. The publisher's door was open, and John was there with a producer and cameraman from New Hampshire Public Television.

If Dennis had been here, Susan would be meeting with him that morning to plan the next issue's news stories and make assignments. Instead that meeting would take place with John, Susan learned, with New Hampshire Public Television filming it for a documentary they had in the works. Something inside Susan rebelled — not just at the camera but at the publisher as part of the editorial process. She remembered John and Dennis disagreeing once on a story of some kind, and John wouldn't back down until Dennis said, "You want to be editor? You can have the job."

With Dennis gone, Susan felt that the stories and assignments should be all up to her. But then again, she had been absent, and John had had to pick up the slack. So she submitted to that meeting, filmed around the table in the newsroom. She and John talked about filling in the holes in the story published yesterday — interviewing witnesses and surveying the killer's history, trying to make sense of it all, this for a more comprehensive account to appear next week. But they were short on labor. Susan wondered about Karen, and John said she had an okay from the *Union Leader* to stay for a week. So could she do some reporting? John hesitated. Susan pressed and John agreed to ask her.

Then there were the obituaries for next week's issue. John insisted on writing Vickie's. For an illustration he would use a favorite photo taken by Susan, one of Vickie in a sweater at her desk. The books of Fred Harrigan's old law library fill the shelves behind her, and a contented Tallak — already adopted by friends of Vickie's — rests her forepaws on Vickie's lap while she scratches the dog's neck. It's not the usual sort of photo for a lawyer and judge, but Vickie liked it. Her smile is direct and inviting. Maybe you want to talk to her about a property deed. Better yet, you might just want to play cribbage.

Susan would make the assignments on the other obituaries and stories. There would be no obituary for Carl Drega, but Karen, if she were willing, would go down to the charred ruins of Drega's house and barn to see what the police might have found there.

Susan had arrived this morning determined to hit the ground running, to show John that she could do this. She repeated to herself certain passages from Psalms that had helped her get up in the morning. There was Psalm 30:5, King James: "Weeping may endure for a night, but joy cometh in the morning." And Psalm 125:5–6, New World: "Those sowing seeds with tears will reap even with a joyful cry. The one that without fail goes forth, even weeping, carrying along a bagful of seed, will without fail come in with a joyful cry, carrying along his sheaves."

So far, so good, though this was a sowing harder than she thought it would be. She was better off than Chandra, though — thirty years old, but seemingly younger than that. Susan looked down the corridor to see the girl weeping into the blotter on her desk.

Chandra lived right there on Bridge Street, a few houses down from the police station. After lunch, Susan said, "Chandra, come on — I'm going to walk you home."

There Susan used Chandra's telephone to call the girl's mother, who lived in Stewartstown. Chandra's not coming back any time soon, Susan thought, and in fact she would never return to the *Sentinel* — which left the newspaper without an ad designer. Later that afternoon, Susan went to see Bill Bromage in his office at the First Colebrook Bank. She said, "Bill, I need someone who can do ad design, just for a few days at least."

"When?" he asked.

"Well, right now. This afternoon."

They both knew that one of Bill's tellers, Cindy Faucher, used to design ads for the *Sentinel* before she went to work for Bromage. Chandra, in fact, had been hired to take her place. "Well, let's go talk to Cindy," Bill said.

A few moments later, Cindy was racing to keep up with Susan as they crossed Main Street and ducked past the satellite trucks into the front door of the newspaper building. Only in a small town, Susan thought.

That week the population of that small town nearly tripled. About 4,200 people — policemen, customs agents, conservation officers, firefighters, government officials, reporters, relatives, and friends — came for the Friday calling hours and Saturday funeral ceremonies for Scott Phillips and Les Lord. Men in uniform arrived from twenty-one states, as far as Nevada and Alaska, and two Canadian provinces. At the Northern Comfort Motel, officers were packed four or five to a room. Others were on couches in private homes, in sleeping bags on classroom floors.

Norm Brown of the county jail persuaded the National Guard to install three hundred cots in the Pittsburg school gym. Helen Lord, Les's mother, worked in the kitchen at that school and was busy at all hours feeding her tenants. Frank Prue and Gerry Marcou were in Pittsburg frequently that week, checking in with Helen, Bev, and Les's sisters, helping to shield them from the media, to "keep the wolves from the door," Prue said. Next month Frank, no longer the Park Ranger without Yogi Bear to play off of, would be granted his request to take over Lord's patrol and would spend the next two years, until his retirement in 1999, keeping a park ranger's guardian eye on the Lords.

Calling hours on Friday for both Phillips and Lord were held in the Colebrook Elementary School gym. The Balsams, the big hotel at Dixville Notch, donated food for the wakes, which was served by volunteers from the Catholic Women's Club and the Colebrook Garden Club. Coffee was kept hot in maple syrup buckets and evaporators. Balsams manager Steve Barba had ordered seven thousand rolls to be delivered with other items via refrigerator truck through Franconia Notch, but when the truck was unloaded early that morning, the rolls were found to be absent. No matter — Barba and Sergeant Howie Weber called all the bakeries and grocers in town, including the IGA, and in the nick of time a sort of miracle of the loaves was achieved.

The gym was a riot of flowers, a hush-spoken hubbub of mourners circulating past the caskets. These included John Harrigan and his staff, all wearing the black armbands they would also wear to Vickie's wake tomorrow. Trooper Steve Hersom, who had been first to the body at Brunswick Springs, noticed that Scott was wearing gloves. He wondered aloud about that, and someone reminded him that Phillips had been shot several times in the hands — hands raised trying to protect himself as Drega loomed over him. Hersom felt ashamed for not having been there to protect Scott himself. He saw Christine Phillips but was too ashamed to approach her, speak to her. He joined a group of troopers clustered around Chuck Jellison — Rob Haase, Chuck West, some others. "You could see it in his eyes," Hersom said about Jellison. "The wind had gone out of his sails. It was time to retire."

Rain was in the forecast for Saturday, but the day dawned cloudy and dry and stayed that way. The parade formed on Bridge Street, and its files of uniformed men — their dress blouses a North Country quilt of brass-buttoned blue, green, red, and gray — stretched from Vermont to the corner of Main. Mixed into that quilt were Governor Jean Shaheen and her husband, Bill. At its rear, Trooper Tom Yorke led two groups of pallbearers, a pair of riderless horses — empty boots reversed in their stirrups, Stetsons laid backward on their saddles — and the hearses.

It took half an hour for that assembly to move itself onto Main, turning south past silent, crowded sidewalks, hands over hearts as the color guards passed, and then a right turn on Colby, back to the elementary school. Court clerk Jan Corliss remembers the thunderous percussion of that many boots on pavement and the skirling strains of the bagpipes above, echoing off storefronts hung with black bunting: "Will Ye No' Come Back Again," "Amazing Grace." Karen Harrigan was darting about the sidewalks taking photos, not for the News and Sentinel, but rather New Hampshire Trooper magazine. She regretted taking the assignment, wanting instead to simply stand and mourn. "And now I just can't handle bagpipes," she said. "I fall all apart."

Seated near the front during the service in the school were two of the wounded officers. Jeff Caulder, using a wooden cane and wearing a suit, not his uniform, entered with his wife, Stacy. Wayne Saunders had put on his dress red blouse, but had left it partly unbuttoned to accommodate a left arm in bandages and a sling, the sleeve hanging empty. Meanwhile, at the hospital in Burlington, John Pfeifer had lapsed into a coma.

The gym filled up like a room at the Northern Comfort, and many had to be content with listening to the loudspeakers outside. An uneasy murmur rippled through the throng when the Reverend Albert Bellefeville of St. Brendan's Catholic Church in Colebrook said, "And we must not forget Mr. Drega. The world can be a lonely place if you have no family, no love."

Claire Lynch would write Les Lord's obituary. Susan would pick that photo taken by Charlie Jordan as an advertisement for the Upper Connecticut Valley Hospital. It was taken, Susan thinks, on the very day the Department of Safety was gobbled up by the state police. Maybe so, but Les's grin, as he stands in his DOS uniform behind the open door of his cruiser, seems too warm and authentic for that particular day.

Scott Phillips's obituary, written by Karen Harrigan, would include a photo taken by Dennis. It was an image that could have been used as a recruiting poster for the state police, Scott looks so trim and male-model perfect, so sunlit Mr. Wonderful, in his short-sleeved summer uniform, smiling and raising an unblemished hand in greeting. Dennis took the photo at the scene of a minor traffic accident, and a line of yellow tape bisects the image at Scott's hips. Scott waves from the other side, from a place where we can't go.

Susan Zizza wrote Dennis's obituary, and he likely would have hated the photo she chose, a headshot she took of him once in tousled hair and reading glasses, a tie and an outdoor jacket, a wry half grin as he confronts the camera lens. Dennis despised those glasses, Susan knew, but that Mona Lisa smile so nicely captured all at once his irony, humor, toughness, compassion. It occurred to Susan that on Monday she had been talking to Dennis about how to handle the layout on the obituary page. As quickly as that he had disappeared into it himself.

On the morning of the police funerals, there was a private ceremony at the Jenkins and Newman Funeral Home in Colebrook. Aaron Joos was still home from Alaska. He was there with Polly and a few other family members from away.

The Reverend Bud Hulse of St. Stephen's Episcopal, a veteran of many funeral services, presided. The onetime communications officer, sixty-eight, had never "cracked," as he said, at any of those others, never himself broken down into tears, but it happened this time when Hulse came to these lines from John 15:13: "Greater love hath no man than this, that a man lay down his life for his friends."

There was no respite. The graveside ceremonies for the fallen troopers — Scott was interred at St. Brendan's Cemetery, near the turn to Fish Pond Road into Bungy Loop; Les at the Indian Stream Cemetery south of Pittsburg, where the rebellious Republic once stood — were succeeded that

Saturday afternoon by calling hours for Vickie at the Jenkins Home on Main Street.

The line out the door seemed to stretch to eternity, and lawyer David King thought it might be almost that long before he and his wife would get inside. In September, David would be appointed by the state's Supreme Court to close out Vickie's practice. For years to come, sitting in his chambers in Lancaster as Coös County's probate judge, King would get a clenching sensation in the heart whenever he came across a will with Vickie's signature on it. Then he would sit and wonder what she would have been doing by then, if she were alive. That day, stuck in a long line, the Kings noticed that at least they were ahead of Governor Shaheen and her husband. They would stay that way too. When someone from the funeral home offered to conduct the governor immediately inside, she said no thanks, she'd wait in line.

The calling hours extended long past schedule, into Saturday night and very early Sunday morning. Bunny and Irene, Earl and Pam, shook all the hands that come through. One woman, at some time near midnight, asked Bunny how he was managing to hold up this long. Bunny replied — hoarsely — that he drew a little more strength from each hand that was extended, each familiar face that appeared.

On Sunday morning, at the Monadnock Congregational Church on Main, there was again an absurd overflow, a thousand inside and three hundred out the front and into the street, where loudspeakers were hung. It had rained Saturday night, but the rain had dwindled to a stop before dawn, and across the river, above and beyond the belfry and steeple, the green whaleback of Monadnock was wreathed in gossamer wisps of fog.

During the prelude, tunes from *The Sound of Music* floated from the organ to the stamped tin ceiling inside the church, a ceiling that Bunny had helped paint some years before. Put on the armor of God, exhorted the Reverend Peter Dyer, whose sermon was taken from the reading he had chosen from Ephesians 6: "For we wrestle not against flesh and blood, but against principalities, against powers, against the rulers of the darkness of this world, against spiritual wickedness in high places. Wherefore take unto you the whole armor of God, that ye may be able to withstand in the evil day, and having done all, to stand."

John Harrigan's eulogy, the second of the service — "When first I walked with this great woman . . ." — described the hike they took together in early spring, into the woods on Blue Mountain, when John swung on a birch from one side of a swollen stream to another and coaxed Vickie into doing the same. Having done all, Vickie stood, triumphant, on that other side. In a middle pew, Karen Harrigan thought that Vickie had always deferred too much to John, that on that day, for example, she should have told him, "Screw you — go find me a log to cross on." But Karen couldn't help it — the story caught her, swung her aloft, and she grieved for how beautiful the white and yellow birches are in the spring woods on Blue Mountain, how hungry we are for love, how we yearn to lay aside our armor and put trust in one another.

During the offertory, Beno and Karen Lamontagne were much surprised to see the commander of the state police rise from his pew, struggle his way to the aisle, and hasten out the front door of the church. That was Colonel John Barthelme, whom Les had once taken on an on-duty, out-of-jurisdiction joyride across the border into Maine. "Holy cow," Beno whispered to Karen. "And he did that right in front of the governor."

Governor Shaheen took a turn with members of the family in ringing the steeple bell at the close of the service, as people filed out. Then she and her husband joined a long caravan to the Village Cemetery. The cemetery sprawled across a wide bluff between Route 3, the Connecticut River, and Monadnock on one side, the woods, meadows, and old farmhouses of South Hill on the other. Immediately to the north, with its parking lot unusually sparse of cars and trucks — as had been the case all week, actually — lay LaPerle's IGA supermarket. The cemetery was crosshatched by single-lane gravel roads, dotted with stands of birch and cedar, mountain laurel and lilac.

There were two Bunnell family plots. The second, the newer, was set apart in open space on the northeast quadrant, on the edge of the cemetery and not far from the spot where Roland Martin, his grandson, and one other were taking a break from mowing grass only five days ago. Then Roland heard shots from the IGA. And then he was drawing the shades on Scott's eyes, which had been spared at least the sight of his friend's cruiser with blood seeping out the seam of its passenger door.

So was complete a circle in time and space. And another: John Harrigan sat behind the wheel of the Lincoln Town Car and remembered the first time he thought Vickie was beautiful, the day some twenty-five years ago when he swung his truck into this very cemetery to say hello to Roland Martin, and she was home from school and working with Roland that summer. Clad in a dirty T-shirt, she rose grinning out of the grave she was digging, and John sucked in his breath. He had seen pictures of a lovely Irene Bunnell when she had been Vickie's age. She looks just like her mother, he thought. In the car that day, he thought of her popping out of the grave, as young and pretty as she was then, when he thought he had a million years at his disposal, but still not enough time to look at her.

In an hour or so Karen Harrigan would be among throngs of well-wishers at the Bunnells' house in Canaan. Bunny would direct parking and then the seating of people in the tent out back. Irene would manage the many women helping her to serve food. Both would be wild with grief, both eager to make sure everyone was comfortable and attended to. Karen would see Bunny sprinting up the steps that led from the driveway into the mudroom and kitchen, and Irene hurrying out and down the steps in the opposite direction — and she would see them halt and take each other's hand for one unhurried, one eternal instant, before continuing their errands.

Now, however, the gravel lanes were filling up, space by space, as people pocketed their keys, or just left them in the car, and struck out on foot. Vickie's friend Rob Roy — who had flown Eric Stohl over that stretch of the Connecticut in Columbia where Carl Drega lived and who had meant to go flying with Vickie on Tuesday — had just taken off in his plane from Gifford Field, the little airport named in honor of the doctor whose memorial service that day had been postponed.

Roy would stay under the clouds as he flew over the church and on up the river. He'd loop down to a hundred feet or so, dip each wing as he passed over the crowd encircling the gravesite, and then climb, rising over their heads and above the mountain, over powers and principalities, as if strands of gossamer were all that held us to earth.

TIME
IS
THE
FIRE

IT DIDN'T TAKE LONG for Beno and Karen Lamontagne — and everyone else in town — to learn why Colonel Barthelmes had to hurry out of the Congregational church during the service on Sunday.

Among the officers present in Colebrook for the police funerals the day before was Jeremy Charron, twenty-four, a rookie municipal cop from Epsom, a little town in central New Hampshire. The president of his senior class at Hillsborough-Deering High School, Charron had served four years in the U.S. Marines before joining the Epsom police.

After the funerals, Charron had gone home to work the overnight shift. At 5:00 a.m. Sunday, he was called to check a suspicious vehicle in Epsom's Webster Park, a popular swimming hole on the Suncook River. The Nissan Sentra contained two young men, both asleep. Charron tapped on the window, asked the driver if he had been drinking, requested that he get out of the car. Gordon Perry, twenty-two, climbed out with a handgun hidden behind his back and fatally shot Charron in the face.

Perry was on parole from the New Hampshire State Prison for being an accomplice to robbery. Companion Kevin Paul, eighteen, had been in the Hillsborough County House of Correction for assault and was also on parole. They fled the park and within a mile abandoned the Nissan and stole a Ford pickup.

Then they sped north up I-93, along the Connecticut River. In the foothills of the White Mountains, they robbed a convenience store of a few hundred dollars. In Franconia Notch, with police in pursuit, they stopped for an exchange of gunfire. Then the pickup crossed the highway's median strip and continued north in the southbound lane, sending oncoming vehicles skidding off the road.

Colonel Barthelme, sitting in a pew in the middle of the church, heard via his pager that yet another officer had been murdered. And once the fugitives came out this side of the Notch, Lieutenant Chuck Jellison found himself in command of another manhunt for a cop killer. He set up this command post in Littleton, in the Elks Club Building, and the media entourage covering the Bunnell funeral moved there en masse for this next event.

Still heading north, in between Bethlehem and Littleton, the fugitives steered the Ford across the highway median again, but this time the truck spun out of control and into a stand of trees. Paul was quickly captured and disarmed. Perry managed to disappear into the brush.

Officers formed lines, shoulder to shoulder, and made long sweeps up the median. It took three hours. Norm Brown was the acting chief of police in Bethlehem that day and a member of that detail. He wasn't as nervous as he should have been — he thought he was looking for a mere robbery suspect.

"I looked down, and there's this guy's feet right in front of me," Brown said. "So I reached down to grab him and cuff him, and I see all these guns drawn and stuck in his face. I said, 'Guys, do we need this much firepower?'"

"A Week of Terror" read the front-page headline in the *Union Leader* on Monday the twenty-fifth. John Harrigan was relieved at least that the murderers didn't get far enough north for him to have to cover the incident in the *News and Sentinel*.

Karen Harrigan's article in the August 27 issue of the *Sentinel* was headlined "Bunker of an Angry Man." "State police and fire marshals allowed the press to view Carl Drega's property in Columbia last Thursday, where the remains of his barn were still smoking from a fire the night before," she wrote. "The media group was led to where a gruesome display was laid out on the ground, items of destruction found in Drega's bunker behind the burned-out barn."

By then the dailies and television stations had found members of the Drega family, as had the FBI. In East Haven, Connecticut, Drega's sister Sophia Linnane told FBI agents that "her brother was harassed by the town from the first day he moved to Columbia. She is very angry at the town officials and feels they take part of the blame for what happened. A lot of good people were lost." Drega's eldest sister, Jane Drega, told reporters that her brother was certainly not deranged: "He was harassed by the police, by the officials, and what-have-you," she said. Then she stopped answering the door and the phone with such steely resolve that even the FBI gave up trying to contact her.

Early reports of underground bunkers and booby-trapped tunnels on the Drega property proved wrong, but not those of a great arsenal. One of Karen's photos showed ranks of media ranged behind a rain-jacketed John McMaster on Thursday and, in front of them, placed in neat rows on a tarpaulin, all the ordinance found behind a false wall in the barn's ten-by-twenty-foot root cellar. This included plastic jackets for 86 six-inch pipe bombs, each capable of dismembering a car or, if put in a building, being lethal to a range of a hundred yards; twenty pounds of gunpowder; assorted fuses and homemade blasting caps; eleven gallons of nitromethane, a fuel used in the manufacture of C-4 plastic explosives; the sixty-one gallons of diesel fuel — which becomes explosive when mixed with the ammonium nitrate Jack Meaney had found — purchased at the Blue Mountain Variety store Tuesday morning; twelve pounds of just such a potent mix; a hundred rounds for an M79 grenade launcher; steel boxes containing thousands of rounds of ammunition — .223, .30-30, 12-gauge; a couple of military surplus steel helmets; a second AR-15 rifle (not the gun Mark Pappas had once owned); and one pair each of high-caliber rifles and shotguns.

The explosions heard the night before, McMaster said, were probably from gunpowder and ammunition, along with — possibly, we'll never know — a booby trap or two. McMaster mentioned that this was all weaponry that could be legally obtained, and probably was. "This was a bomb factory, but what its purpose or reason was, we don't know," he said. "I've never seen anything like this. It's obvious he was a very angry man."

People offered theories about what it was for. Maybe a bomb on Main Street in Colebrook when the streets and sidewalks were crowded for the Moose Festival, which ended up being canceled that year. Or else a bomb to breach the dam on First Connecticut Lake in Pittsburg, unleashing something like a tsunami through Pittsburg, Stewartstown, Canaan, Colebrook, and Columbia. But nothing like a plan, or the clues to such, could be found in the ruins of the barn or cabin.

Another of Karen's photographs revealed that part of the barn's foundation where, years before, the builder had meticulously blocked his name into the concrete. Only a portion of the last name was legible above bent sheets of aluminum roofing and carbonized wisps of tarpaper. The rest had been shot away, obliterated, by volleys of .223 rifle fire.

Among the big-city reporters who came to Colebrook that week was John's sister Susan Harrigan — then a financial reporter for *Newsday* and a resident of Manhattan. Susan appeared sometimes in John's newspaper columns as Hanoi Jane, a name he gave her for the antiwar, left-leaning politics of her youth. She had grown up with Vickie, and she came not as a reporter, actually, but as a mourner. She stayed through Vickie's funeral and went back to Manhattan that night.

Before she had even arrived in Colebrook, though, she had written an article for *Newsday* that was picked up by the *Los Angeles Times–Washington Post* News Service and reprinted on Wednesday in dailies throughout the nation. In it she described Colebrook as a place where people bragged about never locking their houses or cars. And until last Tuesday, she wrote, "violence always had to travel far to get to Colebrook. Christopher Wilder was from Florida, and Harry K. Thaw, the killer of Stanford White, nabbed in Colebrook near the turn of the century, was a genuine big-city crazy person. Although Colebrook did not exactly consider Drega one of their own, he was no flatlander."

Susan Harrigan was one of their own, but she had fled to the flatlands. "I had to kick Colebrook pretty hard to get away," she continued. "Small towns, as people who come from them know, can be suffocating — especially if your parents have a pretty high profile. I'd always resented the attention my parents lavished not only on the people in the gray building, but the residents of the whole town. Adolescent as I was, I thought they should spend more time with their family. But as I tried unsuccessfully to sleep Tuesday night, with images of Vickie and Dennis covered with blood flashing through my head, I understood something for the first time. This was family. It was special. And I was lucky to have had it."

On Thursday, Susan herself was corralled by an outside reporter for an interview. When asked about the impact of the killings, she took an angle that John, a little more than four years later — on September 11, 2001 — would find eerily prescient. "Four people out of a town this small?" she said. "Well, you can just run the numbers. That's like — what? — five thousand people dying in Manhattan on one day. That's your impact."

In late August, Beno Lamontagne drove out to the Joos place in West Stewartstown. He steered past Dennis's "No Hunting" sign, the one that said he didn't want to get shot, and then into the driveway. Polly's gardens had gone to seed, and when Beno saw Polly in a bathrobe, with her hands tight to the railing of the front porch, he thought about his wife, Karen, who lately had been crying herself to sleep. If Karen were a house, the windows would be broken, the paint peeling, Beno considered; with Polly, the roof had fallen in. "I understand Dennis was in your store," Polly said.

"He was," Beno replied. "He finally bought that antenna booster. Did Aaron install it for you yet?"

Polly shook her head. "I don't even know where it is. And Aaron's not here right now."

Dennis's pickup was parked near a shed, and Beno found the booster, still in its packaging, lying on the passenger seat of the truck. "Let me just get this installed for you, then."

Polly looked at her old friend like he was a bear come out of the woods and into her blueberries. "I'll pay you," she said finally.

"No, you won't — taken care of."

A few days before, Sergeant Howie Weber had come around with a woman from the Attorney General's Victim's Advocate office. The woman wanted to leave a packet of articles with Polly about the resources available to her for grief counseling and legal help. Howie was also an old friend — Polly had been the speech therapist for one of his sons. "She's a great lady," Howie said. "But she didn't have a lot to say, didn't want to talk with us."

Twenty minutes later, safely down from the slick shale roof Dennis had fallen from, Beno drove out thinking that if Dennis had been here to enjoy that reception, he'd have wished he'd bought the booster three years ago.

He hoped Polly would like it, but he would never find out, and in fact would never see her again. Polly had already begun to close her doors to the friends and acquaintances of that former life.

When once, years later, John Harrigan called to say he had a package that someone had asked him to deliver to her, Polly told him just to leave it on the front steps. Her friend Sue Miller, who stayed with her on the night of the shootings, would see her only once or twice after that.

Polly would die a recluse at the age of sixty-two, with her son, Aaron, and his wife at her side, in the house she and Dennis had built for living the good life, a few days after Christmas in 2010. "She was always a very private person," Susan Zizza says. "I think she just lived the balance of her life the way she was happiest."

The 45th parallel had indeed become the center of the Northern Hemisphere. The letters and emails arrived first in a torrent from all around New England and then, swelling to a flood, from all over the country and from several continents. Three complete pages of the August 27 *News and Sentinel* were devoted to "Letters to the Editor," an amount of column space that would be sustained through the next five weeks, with many going unpublished for lack of space.

The letters expressed shock, sympathy, a communal grief — and recall a time in America when gun rampages were unusual. Some stretched out into analysis. In the August 27 issue, Jack Authelet, a Massachusetts newspaperman, wrote about a knowledge now peculiar to many in Colebrook: "At times like this I am reminded that inside each of us is an enormous, unanswered question: How would we react in a life-threatening situation for which there was no warning, no preparation, no opportunity to plan a response or to consider the consequences? Would we boldly face the danger or turn away to live a coward's life? For most of us, the question will remain unanswered. We will not, in our lifetimes, face the greatest of human challenges."

Others drew on characterization and anecdote. "I think back 34 years and wonder if this writer of 'strange stories' is the same Dennis Joos who wrote strange stories in a room down the hall in a small Franciscan educational enclave in Callicoon, New York State," remembered Bill Halpin of Camden, Maine, in the September 24 issue. If so, "the Dennis I knew would tilt his head, half-smile, and begin to compose a strange story about a new kind of holy person, a new version of the catcher in the rye, where the 'called' learn how to divert bad guys and gals from their misguided behaviors. I bet there'd be a poor, happy and whimsical anti-hero with a glint in his eye. May we be merciful and compassionate with each other in memory of Dennis Joos."

By the end of September, Susan Zizza still felt all unraveled, was still harrowed by headaches. She began to wonder if the letters, as compassionate and well intentioned as they were, might have something to do with that.

Later that month, John Harrigan — once his daughter Karen had, reluctantly, gone back to Newmarket and her beat with the *Union Leader* — asked Charlie Jordan to come aboard on a full-time basis; in effect, to replace Dennis. Susan was spiraling into the gloom that would send her on a leave of absence for several weeks, and she preferred not to continue as coeditor. Instead she became associate editor, an assistant to Charlie, and she supported Charlie's suggestion that they cut back on the space apportioned to letters. John wrote in his October 1 editorial that the newspaper henceforth would print only letters "celebrating the rich lives" of the victims, as opposed to mourning their deaths.

Some letters satisfying this criterion came from people who knew none of the victims. Ekeanyanwyn Chukwudi of Owerri, Nigeria, wrote in the October 18 issue that he was "shocked to my marrow" to read in *Time* magazine about the murders and that he had witnessed murder himself. "You people are fortunate to have a good system which ensured the prompt stopping of the carnage Carl Drega unleashed on the people, unlike over here where lawlessness, poverty, a weak legal system, and general insecurity prevail," he continued. "I love you all in America, your values, democracy, human rights, and all that the Stars and Stripes stand for. God bless America."

Not all the messages offered comfort or blessings — as Rick Estes had predicted. Some from the local area John simply discarded. In late August, a reporter from Vermont's *Burlington Free Press*, a daily, looked to see what was being posted on the Internet and in certain chat rooms.

In those forums, for example — and regarding John Pfeifer, still fighting for his life in a Burlington hospital — a resident of Nashua, New Hampshire, wrote that the Border Patrol agent should be "thrown into the dumpster with the rest of the garbage." A man in Cincinnati pronounced that "they [the troopers] got what they deserved. Pulling a guy over for rust in a pickup is an abuse of power. Drega held them accountable." A Memphis correspondent called the theft of Phillips's cruiser merely "asset forfeiture of a vehicle used in the commission of a crime against him. He should have burned it on the spot."

Ed Brown, forty-two, of Plainfield, New Hampshire, consented to an interview with the Vermont reporter. In 2007 Brown would orchestrate a nine-month standoff with police over his and his wife's refusal to pay income tax and would ultimately receive a thirty-seven-year prison sentence. But in 1997 he was leader of a group he called the Constitutional Defense Militia, and he asserted that Phillips and Lord had only themselves to blame: "He [Drega] enacted Article 10 of the Constitution — the right to revolution in the State of New Hampshire." Such actions might be unethical but not illegal, Brown said, adding, "Enemy officers are fair game wherever they are and whatever they're doing, so I don't mind it when I read in a paper that a couple of cops got killed."

Vin Suprynowicz, forty-seven, an assistant editor at the *Las Vegas Review-Journal*, a daily newspaper, shot out an eight-page single-spaced press release on September 21 that was picked up in a few media outlets and would be shared for years on the Internet. Drega was a martyr, claimed Suprynowicz. "Carl Drega tried to fight them, for years, on their own terms and in their own courts," he wrote. "We know how far that got him. What I do know is that this is why the tyrants are moving so quickly to take away our guns. Because they know in their hearts that if they continue the way they've been going, boxing Americans into smaller and smaller corners, leaving us no freedom to decide how to raise and school and discipline our kids, no freedom to purchase (or do without) the medical care we want on the open market, no freedom to withdraw $2,500 from our own bank accounts (let alone move it out of the country) without federal permission, no freedom even to arrange the dirt and trees on our own property to please ourselves — if they keep going down this road, there are going to be a lot more Carl Dregas, hundreds of them, thousands of them, fed up and not taking it any more, a lot more pools of blood drawing flies in municipal parking lots, a lot more self-righteous government weasels who were 'only doing their jobs' twitching their death-dances in the warm afternoon sun, and soon."

In 2002 Suprynowicz would publish — through Mountain Media, his own publishing company — a book, *The Ballad of Carl Drega: Essays on the Freedom Movement, 1994 to 2001*. There an account of the Colebrook shootings leads off a collection of pieces celebrating Drega and others "who have given their lives in this War On Freedom." The book's cover illustration depicts Sam Adams, in Boston's North Church, proffering a rifle to a group of men gathered around him. All are dressed in Revolution era garb, but Adams's rifle is a modern (and oversized) AR-15.

In the fall of that same year, in Nashua, Suprynowicz would be the guest of honor, the featured speaker, at the thirtieth annual convention of the New Hampshire Libertarian Party. "I am horrified that anyone would attempt to find excuses for the actions of Carl Drega," said Governor Jeanne Shaheen, when asked for a comment by the *Concord Monitor*. "Carl Drega was not oppressed — he was unwilling to follow the law. Carl Drega was not a modern-day patriot — he was a murderer."

The *News and Sentinel* would ignore the event, but John Harrigan would be asked for comment as well. "And they would shoot a woman in the back," he said to the *New Hampshire Sunday News*, adding, "I have a real short fuse when people call and try to pick apart what happened here, in this beautiful place in God's country, and try to apply it to their own damned, zealous agenda. I'm so angry that people from away would think that he's some kind of symbol, some kind of role model. He doesn't even deserve the ink to spell his name."

This was all excruciating for John, not least because he describes himself as libertarian, even beyond libertarian — "close to being an anarchist," he would say. He wears the dirt of the Indian Stream Republic beneath his fingernails, is himself a living hybrid of New England's "communal libertarianism," per Jason Sorens, and the frontier license of the American West. But in "communal" John allies himself, at bottom, with people — not agendas.

Phippsburg is a little town, about the size of Colebrook, hidden like a periwinkle on the coast of Maine — on the west bank of the Kennebec River, to be exact, just about at its mouth. Once you leave Route 1, you drop like a plumb line due south into one of those stalactites of land that bite into the Gulf of Maine. The scent of the river is laced with salt, and you think from the ranks of staghorn sumac and pitch pine lining the road that you're farther south than you are, that you've suddenly driven to Cape Cod, if only the Cape were still as forested as this.

This is the town where former Colebrook patrolman Dan Couture lives now. These days he's a patrol sergeant in Bath, a town back up on Route 1 and almost four times the size of Colebrook. In 1999 Couture took a trip to Portland, Maine, to visit the girlfriend who would become his wife. There he noticed ads in the newspapers for municipal cops. "In Bath they had a nineteen-man department," he recalls. "I walked in, said I'm a New Hampshire cop, and they talked my ear off. Then they offered me a job, and from day one I was making three dollars more an hour than I was in Colebrook — where all the guys in our department were eligible for food stamps."

"A cop gets paid less than a school janitor," Dick Marini once observed. "Where else do you take bigger risks for less pay? I can't think of anywhere."

By that time, Colebrook police had already gone several years without raises. Couture had joined a department of four full-timers, if you include Chief Mike Sielicki, at a time when the rank and file — which is to say, Steve Breton and one other guy, and also some part-timers — were trying to unionize for better pay. Sielicki was not standing in the way, which kept morale high in his department but also helped to make for strained relations between the chief and Colebrook selectmen. Certainly Sielicki must have felt that in this political/budgetary climate, he and his men couldn't afford any bad news.

Then came August 19, 1997, and that moment when a limping, inexperienced young cop in civvies and with a sidearm in his shorts, saw someone who had just shot at him and Steve Breton drive by in a stolen cruiser. The kid wondered for only an instant if he should risk a shot on this public road at an obvious bad guy, though not someone he knew then to have succeeded in hurting anybody. He remembered his training at Police Academy — you can't call a bullet back — and kept his handgun in his pocket. Later he choked back tears as he told his story to a state cop from Concord.

Then, once the funerals were over, people wondered who was to blame. Why wasn't this stopped before it began? Why wasn't Carl Drega punished more severely for refusing to leave the Columbia town hall, for firing a gun over the heads of Vickie and tax assessor Louis Jolin? Why wasn't he jailed for his threats against Vickie?

"Is our legal system so lax that a nut like him is allowed to run the streets and do as he pleases?" said one of Drega's neighbors to the *Maine Sunday Telegram*. "I think the community deserves an explanation of why we didn't know what was going on there. Had all those bombs gone off at one time, it could have wiped out my house and everyone around here."

For his part, bank president Bill Bromage suggested that the news industry itself was part of the problem. "If the town had arrested Drega last week or a year ago when he was threatening people in authority like Bunnell," he told the *Los Angeles Times*, "you people in the media would be up here pounding on us for locking up some guy just because he looked weird, or for taking away his rights because he was a strange dude."

Nonetheless, the newspapers and TV reports were full of statements by people near and far who thought authorities should have done something earlier. Libertarian John Harrigan would have none of it. "The North Country is proud of its eccentrics, and nothing's going to change that," he told *Life* magazine. "We give them the space they need to get the snakes out of their heads, and most of them do. This guy won't change the way we treat our crazies."

Some in Colebrook and neighboring towns wondered just who it was that appointed John Harrigan as spokesman and psychiatrist for the whole region, even if it was his old gray building that had been one of the crime scenes. Others were glad there was somebody willing to accommodate so many of the reporters who kept coming back, like wolves to a cached carcass, to take the pulse of Colebrook. At least it meant that other people were left in peace.

Meanwhile, talk in the restaurants and bars — and newspapers — soon got around to what might have been done differently once the shooting started. And given the tensions that already existed between the town and the police department, given then the toe-to-toe battle fought at Brunswick Springs, with (so far) no loss of life, it was hard for a lot of people not to view the parking lot of LaPerle's IGA as the site of an ignominious defeat. One day in the kitchen of his home in Phippsburg, Dan Couture folded his hands around his coffee mug, offered the thinnest of smiles, and said, "Oh, sure, the infamous dumpster."

This was the version of that episode that went from ear to ear around Colebrook in the days following: a couple of the town's finest cowering behind a dumpster while state police were being slaughtered a hundred yards away. Then one of the cops had a clear shot at a man on his way to murder several more people, but the cop didn't have the nerve to take it. "All we heard was how great the state police were that day — and the Border Patrol, Fish & Game — and how the local police sucked," Couture said. "The worst thing was that there were other guys in those agencies who bought into that." Couture was grateful at least that they did not include his buddy Wayne Saunders.

Nor did everybody in town buy into that. "The only complaint I ever had about the Colebrook police," said Julie Roy, who had seen the first shots fired at the IGA, "was about getting stopped for a little hole in my exhaust, or a crack in the windshield, while that orange pickup was being driven all around town just a little faster than it was falling apart."

She went on. "One of the things I do is tend bar, and I listened to it for years, to what people were saying. I wouldn't let them know I was there at the IGA — I didn't want to get into it. But I have to commend those cops. The smartest thing they did that day was not to fire a shot. A lot more people could have died."

Couture says that Sielicki was great, that he stood up for him and Breton, but of course the chief was disqualified from the debate on conflict-of-interest grounds. Rumors circulated during the following weeks that Sielicki had been suspended, that Breton and/or Couture had been fired, that they and several other officers were resigning.

The September 4 issue of the *News and Sentinel* took the unusual step of reprinting an article from the *New Hampshire Sunday News*, one that dispelled those rumors. It contained a statement from Jules Kennett, who was both a town selectman and a part-time patrolman. Without naming Steve Breton, Kennett pointed out that this was a cop who had arrived at a crime scene unaware of the situation and who fell immediately under rifle fire. "I don't know about you, but if I'm getting shot at, I'm going to take cover," Kennett said. "If this was a dead Colebrook officer, would that have made things better? I think he responded properly. I'm glad he's still with us."

That issue also contained an editorial by Susan Zizza. "There is no rewind button," it read in part. "The horrible events of Tuesday, August 19, cannot be played over again or rewritten. This man brought irrevocable change and damage into the lives of all of us in the North Country. But we do have some control over how far the damage will extend. We can continue to let him harm and hurt us from the grave by letting him pull apart our community, divide us with recriminations before the facts are all in, or we can save our breath for words of comfort, our energy for strengthening each other to get through this time of trial. . . . Let's rejoice that others are still alive, that we can see their familiar faces on our streets and grasp their hands in friendship. Let this man's hate and bitterness die with him. Let it stop here, with us."

But the recriminations against local police never did quite stop. Couture kept waiting for them to die off, but they wouldn't, such were people's anger and grief. Nor was there counseling available to Couture or his peers of the sort offered to officers of other agencies. In the end, he left Colebrook not because of the money but because of the heartache and blame — as did Steve Breton.

Within two years, every other member of that department, full or part time, including Mike Sielicki, had left as well. Steve Breton is in Rhode Island, working as a sales executive in the food industry and coaching Nicholas's youth soccer team. Mike Sielicki is the well-regarded chief of a twelve-man department in Rindge, New Hampshire. In the end, the rumors about resignations would prove true. "But you can see it was a fantastic department," Couture said. "Every one of those guys has gone on to success elsewhere."

Couture himself regards moving to Maine as the best thing he ever did. "There are always other cops around, you never have to go into situations alone, and you're respected — it's nice to be part of that."

A long way back on rewind lies that other thing he might have done. In the Hollywood version of August 19, he would have spun on his one good heel, swung his 9 mm Ruger in an arc like a man shooting skeet, opened up just enough of a lead ahead of the perpetrator, and taken him out with one clean shot to the head. In that version, Phillips's cruiser would have come to rest harmlessly in a ditch. Scott and Les would have been avenged that quickly. Vickie and Dennis would still be alive. Couture could have lived out his days in Colebrook a hero.

"Sure, I would've taken that chance if I'd known what else was about to happen," he said. "So I wasn't a hero that day, and I'd trade everything in the world if I could have been, and prevented those deaths. The guys who were heroes — their information was different. They knew what was going on, what had already happened. Me? I made a decision. It had unfortunate consequences, as it turned out, but on the basis of what I knew then, I can at least say it wasn't the wrong decision. I think things happen for a reason. I used to relive those events, that moment, every single day in my head. I'm not like that anymore. I'm all through with it. I can sleep."

Except for Carl Drega, all the men who went into the woods at Brunswick Springs came back — even John Pfeifer. He remembers tottering on the edge of consciousness at the hospital in Lancaster and hearing the radiologist say, "Oh, shit, he's got a bullet in the heart." Then he lapsed into a long sleep, and it was only later he learned that the doctor was looking at an x-ray taken before they had torn off his ballistics vest. After cutting a swath through Pfeifer's lung, the bullet had lodged in the back of the vest and so fooled the radiologist.

The men came back, but they were different. Even Major, the Vermont K-9 that had saved six lives by barking out a warning just in advance of the trap snapping shut, was different. On the night of August 19, the German shepherd forced his way into bed with handler Russ Robinson and his wife. "Russ said the dog had never done anything like that before," Steve Brooks recalled.

Three days later, Kevin Jordan did something he had never done before. A neighbor fired a shot at a woodchuck in his garden, and in a panic Kevin dove for cover under his kitchen counter.

Then Jordan was among several — Brooks, Rob Haase, some others — who at various times felt compelled to revisit the site. They found Vermont detectives still scouring the litter and hanging color-coded tags on tree trunks and branches — red, blue, yellow, green, white — to distinguish the impacts of bullets of various calibers, shotgun slugs. Brooks was amazed by how big the place seemed, how radically the tunnel vision of a man under fire had shrunk its margins. Jordan was stunned by the surreal fun-house look of all those colored tags. He also went to see Wayne Saunders's strafed cruiser and took at least a step toward forgiving himself for not riding with Wayne when he saw a bullet hole punched square through the passenger-seat headrest.

Fellow CO Sam Sprague took a few days off following the shoot-out. He threw his uniform in a pile on the floor and finally took it to a dry cleaner. When he picked it up a week later, he found a note fixed to the shirt: "Sorry, unable to fix the tear in the epaulet." Only then, with his knees going watery beneath him, did he realize that the epaulet had been sheared by a bullet.

State trooper Jeff Caulder, on the other hand, couldn't help enjoying the startle response — the quick intake of breath, the whispered "Oh" — he elicited from Governor Shaheen when she visited his bedside and asked where he was hit. He attended the funerals with a packet of gauze in place of the lost testicle and was back on his feet without a cane within three weeks. He was puzzled, though, when Chuck Jellison told him that he wasn't wanted back at work until he had gotten a deer that fall.

Among family and friends, Caulder is famous for needing only one shot each season to bag a deer. "But that fall I missed three bucks," he said. "I wondered what the hell was going on."

Finally he realized that he was rushing his shots, pulling the trigger as soon as he had a patch of brown in his scope, as if he needed to fire before the deer fired back. Once that fourth buck was dressed out and in his freezer, Jellison welcomed him back.

When Caulder returned to Brunswick Springs the next spring, he found the colored tags shredded but still fluttering in the trees. He also found a snapping turtle laboring across the tote road, probably a female who had just laid eggs. Very carefully he helped it across and left it near the creek. "That was enough," he said. "I don't need to go there again."

On August 19, 1998, Jeff Fair — erstwhile member of John Harrigan's Gang of Uglies, a wildlife biologist who had moved to Alaska in 1995 and who had watched reports on the shootings on a TV in an Anchorage hotel room — got lost up around First Connecticut Lake. It wasn't that he didn't remember the roads around there. Rather the directions he had been given to the lodge where John had holed up under an assumed name weren't working out. And since John had sworn him to secrecy about this whole event, Fair was reluctant to ask directions — if he could even find anybody to ask.

Finally he came to a turnoff in the woods marked by a hand-lettered sign on a stake. The sign was enigmatic, reading, "¢-nel." This took a moment, but Fair puzzled it out. "Sentinel," he said to himself, and turned down that road.

John was content to spend that day and night, on the first anniversary of what had come to be known as "the Colebrook incident," with a select few friends, invitation-only and keep your mouth shut. Fair had come back East anyway to do some fieldwork on loons for the State of Maine. John was delighted that this old buddy would be able to join him at the lodge. The trick was not to have any reporters.

Even John Harrigan, great champion of the media and its right to know, had grown tired of it all. At his own newspaper, the one in Colebrook, things had improved from bad to tolerable. Charlie Jordan was updating and professionalizing the look and content of the *Sentinel*. Susan Zizza was back at work and feeling a little better. Karen Harrigan had quit at the *Union Leader*, moved back to her hometown, and joined the staff as a full-time reporter. Her husband, Russ, had caught on as a chef at the Balsams.

But absenteeism remained a problem, and in all the other newspapers the story wouldn't die. From the *New York Times* in October: "It had been scarcely six weeks since Earl and Irene Bunnell's only daughter, Vickie Bunnell, a 45-year-old lawyer and part-time judge, was gunned down, one of four leading townspeople murdered by a local recluse nursing a twisted grudge over his property rights. And yet here the Bunnells were at LaPerle's IGA supermarket the other afternoon, buying a chicken to roast for the family of Harold Sheltry, 75, who had died the day before after a sudden illness. The Bunnells' son, Earl, Jr., serves in the Colebrook volunteer fire department with Mr. Sheltry's son Brad.

"'Other people have their sorrows too,' said Mr. Bunnell, a 72-year-old retired postal clerk, clasping his wife's hand as they wheeled their cart past the poultry section at the IGA."

Bunny and Irene had kept on doing their shopping at the IGA during the fall, and their appearances there played no small part in luring other people back to the supermarket. Of course reporter Sara Rimer had caught them at a moment — buying food to comfort another family — that was perfectly expressive of who they were.

Still, in phrases like "a 45-year-old lawyer" or "a 72-year-old retired postal clerk," Rimer was doing the necessary work of introducing people to strangers, and that was just the problem. In short-form journalism, her characters could be nothing other than reduced and flattened, shorn of all that Vickie was, for example, besides being a "45-year-old lawyer" and murder victim. The truths of who people are — the breadth of their identities, the ways their lives fold into the lives of others — become shrunken and compressed. Multiply that through many newspaper stories, through many spot descriptions, and a composite portrait of Colebrook emerges that not only collapses short of reality but is weirdly skewed by the gravity of one day in its history.

People who live in Colebrook and are journalists themselves are perhaps bothered most by this. In 2010 Karen Harrigan Ladd — after her divorce and remarriage — would write an editorial in the *News and Sentinel* that mentions this: "I once stood in a Manchester hotel lobby, feeling as if I'd been punched in the stomach, after a clerk cavalierly threw out, 'Oh, Colebrook — isn't that where all those people got shot?'"

After the *New York Times* update, there were stories in the dailies about the heartache of Thanksgiving in Colebrook, the sorrow of Christmas in Colebrook, and then the solemnity of Memorial Day, when a black granite slab, etched with ghostly portraits of the four victims, was dedicated on Monument Lot near the spot where Dennis had been shot. The microphones and cameras were sure to be back in force on this first anniversary, and John, unable to talk about it anymore, had gone to ground on a lake he used to fish with Vickie, and still fished with Bunny from time to time.

He chose a silence and anonymity that probably wouldn't have been available to him if he were a Pulitzer Prize winner, as he nearly was. Last February, John had been astonished when an Associated Press reporter called asking for a comment about his nomination for a 1998 Pulitzer in journalism, in the category of Breaking News Reporting. His staff at the *Sentinel* was no less surprised, and pleased — recognition like this, for a small-town weekly—though some couldn't help wondering why the whole newspaper and its staff had not been nominated, as was the case with all the competition in that category. Why had just the publisher been singled out?

Susan Zizza, in her shame, had a theory. She wondered if it was because the newspaper staff, before they returned to work, had run away, had turned "to live a coward's life" as Drega approached; if it was because only Dennis, who had fought and died, and John, who had been absent, were felt to be clean of that stain.

That wouldn't have been it, certainly. John couldn't explain it himself, but he understood the nomination's injustice. "If I won, I was going to make it right at the podium," he said. "I was going to emphasize that it was a team effort, that everybody pitched in, that I was accepting only on behalf of the whole newspaper."

But it didn't make any difference. In April, the Pulitzer was awarded to the *Los Angeles Times* for its coverage of a botched bank robbery and police shoot-out in North Hollywood. "Congratulations," John told his staff the next morning. "You lost to a newspaper with a hundred people in the news room.'"

At the lodge, once he'd found it, Jeff Fair met John Lanier and several other former Uglies. John Harrigan was there with a woman he'd been dating, a pretty and warmhearted soul who had already guessed, Fair thought, that John was looking for a way to end the relationship. There was a big table, plenty of food, lots to drink.

John was his usual hail-fellow self, a little tipsy, and pleased that security had held thus far. At the same time there was something opaque and distant in his manner. Lanier took note, shot a worried glance to Fair. That afternoon, John started a blaze in the lodge's fireplace, or tried to, but the smoke from the smoldering flame kept stalling at the flue and puffing into the room. "I'll fix it," John said, but nothing he did seemed to help.

Fair took over, saying, "Jesus, John, this is the first time in your life you don't know how to light a fire."

With a slight adjustment in architecture, the fire was burning cleanly. Fair is a widely published nature writer as well, as good at literature as he is woodcraft, and he was reminded of a line of poetry from Delmore Schwartz: "Time is the fire in which we burn."

FOND
BLUE
HOPE

TEN YEARS GO BY, and Monadnock Mountain is bitten away a few fractions of an inch. In 2008, August 19 once again falls on a Tuesday, which begins with a Kiwanis Club meeting at the Wilderness Restaurant, where a chair is left vacant for Vickie Bunnell, where John Harrigan chips in a Happy Dollar in honor of his first grandson, by way of his son, Mike, now married and working as an editor at a publishing house in New York City. The Moose Festival was canceled in 1997. It's been held every year since, and this year it begins on Friday the twenty-second, as it would have that long ago.

Friday is another day of spun gold in the North Country: sunny, clear, low 80s. The clouds above the cliffs in Franconia Notch, as travelers drive up I-93, are like spilled milk. Mr. Moose himself—someone in a moose suit with horns as wide as an SUV—waves from the shoulder of the Scott Phillips Highway section of Route 3 as it dips into downtown Colebrook (the Les Lord Highway runs up to Pittsburg).

Main Street has been blocked off to traffic from Parsons Street down to Bridge. The boulevard is filled instead with booths and tables devoted to handmade baskets, custom T-shirts, homemade soy candles, goat's milk soaps and lotions, several varieties of fudge, a half dozen church raffles and bake sales, much more. People in shorts and sandals crowd the road and move in murmuring, high-spending clusters from cash box to cash box.

John Harrigan owns a cherry red 1947 Willys Jeep that he brings out of the barn for working on his fence lines or else for parades and auto shows like the one scheduled for later this afternoon. Today the Jeep is parked across from the entrance to Bridge Street, in front of the old Walker House, now First-Run Home Entertainment. Each fender of the Jeep is spiked with a crisp American flag, and the vehicle sparkles in the sun like something you might put a nickel into for a ride. John is on the sidewalk, chatting with some friends. Despite the heat, he sports a winter hat with earflaps and a floppy rack of moose horns.

Someone asks if Bunny and Irene are around. "You must have walked right past them," John says. "They're up there on a sidewalk somewhere selling tickets for the Kiwanis raffle. I went to see them a few days ago — on the nineteenth, you know, just to give them a hug — but they were gone. I guess Bunny had a doctor's appointment in Littleton."

Bunny is eighty-two and feeling his age. Since a heart bypass in 1996, he's had a colectomy and been diagnosed with diabetes. "I can't be a Play-girl model anymore," he'll lament, blaming the needle bruises across his midsection from the insulin injections. Last May he was hospitalized with another heart attack. But John's friend is referring to that anniversary of the nineteenth when he asks how they're both doing.

"Pretty well," John says. "I think it gets a little better for them each year."

"How about you?"

"Not me. It's still fresh."

That previous October, Bunny went with a friend out to Clarksville Pond for an afternoon's fishing. It was the last day of the season. Around Cole-brook, gardens were being put to bed, firewood split and stacked. Flocks of crows had stripped the kernels out of the last of the summer's standing corn, and John Harrigan was hosting his annual cider-pressing party at the South Hill farmhouse.

The pond is up in the hills of Stewartstown, and there Bunny rented a rowboat — it had grown hard for him to get in and out of a canoe — from Rudy Shatney's daughter Kathleen. Kathleen and her husband now run Rudy's Cabins and Campground, the business her father started on that pond after World War II.

"Rudy was quite a fellow — a commando during the war, one of those folks who went up the cliffs at Normandy ahead of everybody else," Bunny said, once he had settled himself into the bow of the rowboat. "Earned two Purple Hearts and a Silver Star. Then he married Joan, his English war bride, came back here, and became the greatest woodsman I ever saw. One time I was fishing here and called out for a net. Rudy brought it out to me humping a canoe. You ever see anyone do that? He was jumping up and down on the gunnels, and got that canoe moving like a speedboat. One of their two girls was the son Rudy never had — she was quite a deer guide herself."

That would have been Jeannette Shatney, who could hump a canoe as well as her father could and who was also the first girl John Harrigan loved. During the summers that he lived with the Shatneys, he and Jeannette hunted and fished together as he would later do with Vickie. While still in her teens, she became the second woman in state history to qualify as a registered deer guide. But then she was dead at twenty, shot and killed while guiding a hunter who was a friend of Rudy's.

"The fellow mistook her arm-brush of a fir tree for the push of a deer," Bunny said. "That was the start of Rudy's downfall. He was never the same after that."

The two men rowed out into a stiff breeze, the water riffled like corrugated tin. The clouds were a threadbare gray, with gauzy patches of light. "Might not catch our limit today," Bunny said. "Trout don't like to feed on a choppy surface. The wind stirs the silt up too, and the fish stay down."

Out on the lake, they tried Hornbergs — downy, tufted compounds of feather and fur that work well as both dry and wet flies, floating a long moment on the surface, then sinking beneath for trolling. Bunny cast in classic four-count rhythm, the tip of the pole arcing neatly between ten o'clock and two. His line and its leader scrawled voluptuous curves against the clouds, the fly settling into a distant patch of water like a dandelion seed.

Once the Hornberg sank, Bunny let it troll for a while. He mentioned that it was actually here, and not Fish Pond, where his father Sliver had first taught him to fly-fish. Then he said he was thinking of putting the cabin on Fish Pond up for sale. "Ma and I have never spent a night there since Vickie died," he said. "Save ourselves the taxes. Brother doesn't need it. He and Pam have their own camp on Bungy Loop."

The rowboat drifted into a part of the lake away from the cabins where the shoreline was an unbroken parapet of bare limbs and dry, rustling leaves. Above that, the sky was slowly draining itself of light. "Look at that," Bunny said. "Isn't that beautiful? It looks like a dinosaur could raise its head right over those trees."

Bunny thrills to any pond, stretch of river, or corridor of woods that looks this wild, and of course so did Vickie. Now a great swath of the North Country is protected in her name. In 2000, three years after the Champion International lumber company put the Bungy-Cranberry Bog area up for sale — 18,540 acres of woods in Stratford and Columbia, where John and Vickie used to hunt and hike — the property was bought by the Nature Conservancy, with fund-raising help from John and other friends, and christened the Vickie Bunnell Preserve. The tallest mountain in that tract, 3,700-foot Blue Mountain, was renamed Bunnell Mountain in 2003. Susan Zizza took a photo at the 2001 dedication of the preserve: Bunny and Irene, Earl, Jr., and Pam, arranged around the rough-hewn sign marking it. The smiles are all genuine. You'd think Vickie was there, lurking modestly off-camera.

"She was supposed to go flying that afternoon, you know, with Rob — Rob Roy," Bunny said out of the blue, stripping his line in preparation for another cast. "He had no idea she had almost earned her pilot's license herself. She was saving that for a surprise. But Rob got held up, and — and she was at the office instead."

Bunny had mentioned this before. His mind keeps circling back to this and other circumstances of the day, small events that might have made a big difference had they gone another way. He doesn't include among these Scott Phillips's traffic stop of Carl Drega. "No, no matter — something would have set him off," he said. "I don't know if I ever even saw the man. I wouldn't have known him on the street."

Bunny sent the fly on a tailing arc toward a nesting box raised above the water for wood ducks. The fly dropped right beneath the box, and Bunny said, "He was one of those SOBs it's awful hard to love."

Bunny and Irene have held up so well, really, and have loved so well that some suspect they move in a state of grace beyond the corrosion of grief. Their closest friends know better. Once, at the kitchen table in South Canaan, with one such friend, amid bowls of homemade beef-and-barley soup, Bunny opened a scrapbook he had made of all the newspaper clippings. There was no telling if it was one particular clipping or an accumulation of them. Suddenly he turned his head, then choked and broke open like a cask, leaning over the table and pouring tears onto the clippings. Irene said nothing, just bowed her head and allowed him his turn. Hers would come around again soon enough.

But neither Bunny nor Irene is like Rudy Shatney. They refuse to lock horns with the grief. Sometimes they lower their heads and butt against it for a while, but then they slip loose and get back to the living. In his eighties, Bunny has reached the age of being solicited for summary statements. "It's been fun," he'll always say, looking back over the decades. "A lot more good days than bad."

After an hour without a nibble on the Hornbergs, Bunny switched to a wooly worm, a good imitation of a bite-sized caterpillar, and a wet fly as well, heavy enough to sink right away. On his third cast, Bunny felt a little something and set his hook. The fish rose like a glowing ember out of the gray water, and then Bunny had it in his hands and was working the hook free of its lip. "Pretty little fellow," he said.

The rainbow, with its flicked-paintbrush spatterings of pink and rose, was indeed small, probably a little more than three pounds. But it was legal, and big enough for breakfast the next morning.

An hour later, with nothing more than that in his basket, Bunny said, "Well, that'll have to do for this season." They drove home with the sun shining beneath the cloud cover. Every leaf was like a lamp, lit from within, until they came into the shade of Monadnock. It had been one of the good days.

At the Moose Festival, on a grassy field opposite Howard's Restaurant and the South Hill Road intersection, the Kiwanis Club has set up tents and is selling meals of barbecued chicken and all the fixings, as well as watermelon, which John Harrigan is helping to slice and serve.

A man in a Patriots baseball cap comes up to greet John, grinning and extending his right hand. John hesitates, but the man grabs John's gloved hand and pumps it anyway. "I don't mind a little watermelon juice," he says.

After he leaves, John whispers, "The guy didn't understand — that sort of defeats the purpose of the gloves."

This calls to mind another handshake. John says that several weeks after the shootings, someone hosted a party far out of Colebrook — in the town of Franconia, way down around the Notch — for anybody who was there that day and needed to blow off some steam. A number of the law enforcement people came, and John made a beeline for Steve Brooks.

"I told him, 'I want to shake the hand of the man who killed that bastard,'" John said. "And Steve looked at me just like he'd been pole-axed. That was still confidential information then, about him and Chuck West. But somebody told me, I can't remember who. And Steve was a little, let's say, nonplussed to hear that his cover had been blown to a newspaper guy. Of course we never printed that."

Kevin Jordan — in the summer of 2008, Lieutenant Jordan, in charge of Fish & Game's District 5, in southwest New Hampshire — suspected Carl Drega may have meant to come here after setting his house on fire.

He stood with a friend in a meadow spangled with the last of the asters and black-eyed Susans and bordering Route 102 in Vermont. From there they could look across the Connecticut River into a property that had been for sale for some years, with no takers yet. A couple of sheds still stood, leaning now, and a few dry, black timbers from where the cabin and barn once stood.

"He would have had an easy time of it from here," Jordan said. "That AR-15 is good for 300 yards, and I guess we're about 150. And it's a very flat-shooting weapon, accurate at long distances. From here he could have picked firefighters off at his leisure. If you ask me, that's the reason he torched his house. But then Wayne got on his tail, and then we went Code 3, lights and sirens everywhere. He had to change plans."

No one will ever know if Drega planned that ambush in Brunswick Springs or if it was something he improvised. Of course Jordan never fired a shot, but he was there in the woods with little knowledge of where the killer lurked, was certain he would die when friendly fire screamed overhead. Later he was among many given medals for their service that day. Deservedly so, one thinks, but some had a different opinion — Les Lord's pal Gerry Marcou, for example, who left the state police in 2001 when they wanted him to quit highway work altogether and go full time on patrol. Now he's the sheriff of Coös County.

"Dennis Joos, now he's a hero, though he shouldn't have done what he did," Marcou said. "A cop, if you get shot and killed, yeah, there ought to be a plaque. Yes, we should remember. But that doesn't make you a hero. When you put on the uniform, it's your job to take a bullet. Cops and firemen, you should never hear about us. Put me in charge of the hero awards — there wouldn't be many."

Jordan wouldn't quibble. His teenage son, Kevin, Jr., always wondered why his dad's medals weren't on display somewhere, why instead they were hidden away in a drawer. Then the boy went into the army, served a tour of duty in Iraq, and earned a unit citation and medal for courage under fire. Jordan remembers waiting for him to get off the bus when he came home and how much he looked forward to seeing that hardware pinned to his son's chest. After they had hugged, these two warriors, the father asked the son, "Where's your medal?" The younger Kevin smiled, saying he understood now about medals.

He understood the shameful things your body does in the midst of a firefight and the fright you don't think proper to a hero. Then there are the dreams and flashbacks and the way the dead accuse you — or at least you think they do — of not having done enough.

A dispirited Steve Hersom, who would have been Scott's backup that day but for a traffic accident elsewhere, left the state police for work as a security officer at Plymouth State College. "I visit both graves once each year, Scottie's and Les's, and I leave stuff — patches, name tags, flowers, a flag, maybe a hat," he said. "And I apologize, even though I know it's stupid. Sometimes the stuff is gone the next year, sometimes not."

Back then, it took a week for John Pfeifer to come out of his coma. Eventually he returned to work and has since risen through the ranks of the Border Patrol. He went back to Texas, where he was deputy chief of the Rio Grande Sector, and would return to Vermont in 2010 to take charge of the Swanton Sector, from Maine to Ogdensburg, New York. But first, when he woke from that sleep, he found himself under assault from infection and with radial nerve damage in his left arm. Subsequently he contracted diabetes, which still afflicts him. "I was a thirty-three-year-old healthy male with no chronic illnesses," he said. "I worked out, I ran, and there's no history of diabetes in my family. But I lost thirty to forty pounds after I got out of the hospital, and suddenly my blood sugar is off the map. You can't tell me it's not connected."

But he's alive, and he knows why. When Steve Brooks retired from the Border Patrol in the summer of 2007, a letter from Pfeifer was read aloud on the occasion. "Not a day goes by that I don't remember August 19, 1997," Pfeifer wrote from Texas. "We heard that an officer was down, and we all responded. When I went down myself, and was calling out, I knew help would come. You were among those who came, and for that I'm forever grateful."

Wayne Saunders might have left Fish & Game, or at least the North Country, had not Kevin Jordan helped out in altering Saunders's patrol so that it didn't include Colebrook. It was a year before Saunders could resume full-time duty, after months of physical therapy and then more surgery to clean out remaining bullet fragments. When he did start work, he wore his ballistics vest all day and carried eight thousand rounds of ammunition in his cruiser. Once, during a domestic violence call, he was told that Drega didn't do a good enough job on him. "I didn't want to ruin my career slugging a guy for something like that," Saunders said.

He kept his temper, and in 2002 he married a local girl, a waitress he knew previously from the Green Mountain Rest Stop, near the IGA. They moved into an out-of-the-way log cabin near a sparkling river in Stark. In 2013 — by which time Kevin Jordan had risen to the rank of major, second in command of state Fish & Game — Saunders was named the lieutenant in charge of District 1. He was still angry that he'd never had a chance to return fire at his assailant, still remembered to approach each day as if it were his last. But the ballistics vest? "No, I don't wear it all the time anymore," Saunders laughed. "It started getting tight around the waist."

From that meadow by the Connecticut, Jordan took his companion down Route 102 to the tote road into Brunswick Springs. There a pine log laid across the entry to the stretch along Black Creek had become redundant. Mother Nature had dropped thick trunks of pine and hemlock, studded with spears of broken-off branches, every ten or twenty yards along the road. Tire traffic was impossible, and the men saw no sign of foot traffic as they clambered over each barrier.

The ridges closed in on both sides of the road, and they felt some part of that ancestral unease that had troubled John Pfeifer. Then the woods gave way, and the road flared into that grassy clearing, a parklike space still clean and inviting, still grand for a picnic perhaps. The surrounding conifers rose like pillars in a cathedral. The bull hemlock that Drega once hid behind had been riddled with ordinance, but its bark was smooth and whole again.

Jordan betrayed no emotion as he went to where he had found the body on the hillside. "Me, I'm still mad he wore Scottie's hat," he said. In the leaf litter and still fixed to some branches, he found a few colored scraps of the ribbons used afterward to mark the bullet impacts.

Jordan mentioned that Jeff Caulder was doing well. When Caulder eats at Howard's or the Wilderness Restaurant, he meets townspeople who know who he is and remember that he was there. He's the father of two daughters, the second conceived after he was carried out on a stretcher with a testicle shot off. This allows him to laugh at the gifts of spare aluminum nuts he still receives from his buddies or the custom T-shirt his wife once gave him: three glum squirrels on a tree limb, looking down, captioned, "It's all fun until someone loses a nut."

Once Chuck Jellison let him come back to work, Caulder's first SWAT team call was to a hostage incident in Raymond — a teenager with an AK-47 threatening to kill his father. Caulder made the arrest in an armed, face-to-face, finger-twitching standoff. "I firmly believe I'm a shit magnet," he said.

By August 1997, Chuck Jellison had already announced he would retire in a few months, but then stayed on the job for more than a year beyond that. "That was for our sake, for Troop F," Steve Hersom said. "He still ran things like he always did, and joked around with us, but it was never the same. Troop F had the youngest personnel in the state police when he took charge, and we'd all grown up with him. He was the best commanding officer I ever served with, and I would've traded places with Scott Phillips if it meant not hurting Chuck. When he finally did retire, that family-style cohesion we had kind of fell apart."

The journey back to the gap-boarded bridge and then back to 102, where a tractor-trailer rumbled past, was like coming out of a rabbit hole. The men drove south, past Dean Hook's neat corn-stubble fields and back into New Hampshire at Guildhall. They went north on Route 3 to the little Northumberland Cemetery, just across the road from the house where Jordan and his family lived, where Wayne Saunders had stopped to chat that afternoon. Jordan parked in the cemetery's northwest corner, near a row of white pines that stood in a palisade overlooking the Connecticut River.

No one else was there. Jordan pointed to a raised stone just off the hardtop that circled through the graves: "Rita Belliveau Drega 1920–1972." Hidden in the shadow behind that stone, flat to the ground and directly adjacent, was a small brass plate: "Carl Drega June 19, 1935–August 19, 1997."

"You'd never find this, unless you knew where to look for it," Jordan said. "I had just completed my counseling sessions when I heard he was buried here, of all places. But I guess Rita was from here originally." He looked down at the plate. "It's bizarre, hiding a grave like that — even this guy's."

He glanced up at the flick of a blue jay in a yellow birch. The lines of his face seemed to tighten. "For the first few days and weeks, everything was about Drega," he said. "You didn't hear much about the people who died, who obeyed the laws and paid taxes, and for the survivors, that's a killer. Then you had these people — some people — who sympathized with Drega. They never knew the whole story."

He added that he's tried, but he's never been able to forgive Carl Drega. "I attend church, and I know I'm supposed to forgive, but I can't — I can't. He took the best we had, didn't he?"

No more than can some others forgive. "The cops know where this grave is. Some of them come in here, one by one, every August nineteenth. I can hear it when a cruiser arrives. It's not to leave flowers."

Jordan turned and inhaled the scent of the Connecticut like a good cologne, admired its cut-glass glint through the trees, saying, "Well, there were only two things this bastard ever loved — Rita and this river. He's got 'em both here."

Charlie Jordan is a musician as well as a newspaperman, and his group Folk Tree is playing at the Moose Festival tonight beneath a tent set up on Main Street. With Charlie on vocals, fiddle, mandolin, and harmonica, the band includes Donna, their son Tommy, and two other musicians, play-ing a mix of folk, bluegrass, and soft-rock classics from the '60s and '70s.

This afternoon he and Tommy are assembling the sound system, shut-tling between the tent and a parked van with their arms full of wires and electronic equipment. A passerby asks if Susan Zizza will be on keyboards with them. "No, Susan hasn't performed with us for a year or so," Charlie says. "She's been writing a book."

Charlie stops to talk for a few minutes. And how is the *Colebrook Chron-icle* doing? "Great," Charlie says. "Good circulation, adequate ad revenues, and since we're free and come out on Friday, we're not in quite such direct competition with the *Sentinel*. We cover the same beats, but we're doing all right."

It's already nine years since Charlie was called into John Harrigan's *News and Sentinel* office and told he was being let go. Leith Jones was instructed that same day to drastically reduce the number of rolls of film he shot each week, and he chose to quit. The next day Susan Zizza decided to leave as well.

Claire Lynch refers to the occasion as Black Sunday. If Charlie was angry then, he's okay with it now. "It was an evolving situation," he said. "Karen wanted to be editor, and it was always a family operation — I understand that. John gave me a song and dance about how he wanted to get back into the news cycle and edit the paper, but it wasn't long before Karen was installed, and he was just publisher again."

John has said simply that Charlie was doing things he didn't understand, couldn't agree with. Newspapers everywhere were coming under pressure from the Internet and digital media; newsmen everywhere were disagree-ing about how to respond to that. Leith was brilliant in the darkroom and frankly didn't want to come out of there. Charlie, with his own affection for the ink stains and chemical baths of traditional journalism, may not have had the heart to demand that Leith use a digital camera.

Instead he and Donna — with Susan Zizza and Leith also on the staff — started their own newspaper. Like Merle Wright's old *Civic*, where Dennis Joos had gotten his start, the *Colebrook Chronicle* is free for the asking, supported entirely by its ad revenues, and is maybe a little more nimble than the *Sentinel* in posting online video as well as text content.

Karen Harrigan became editor of the *News and Sentinel* in 2000, and three years later she and her second husband, Butch Ladd, bought the newspaper from John. By then John had already sold the *Coös County Democrat*. "The big box stores were coming into Littleton and Lancaster, and I knew the *Democrat* couldn't survive without an owner with a lot of money, willing and able to pay for fine writing, or at least it needed to be part of a group," John said. "And I needed to come home — not try to be in two places at once anymore."

John also shut down the Coös Junction Press and sold off its equipment, including its great beating heart — the seventeen-ton, thirty-three-foot Goss Community web press that he and Calvin Crawford had jackhammered out of the concrete of an abandoned press south of the notches some thirty years before. "Somebody bought it, put it on a truck to Miami, and then into a container aboard ship to São Paulo," John said. "From there I heard it was barged up the São Paulo River to God knows where."

Karen has said that her dad really did want to get back into the news cycle in 1999 and that he jumped out of it again earlier than he wanted to. "He didn't want to put me in the same position he had been in with Fred — a young person ready to do the job and a parent standing in the way. But yeah, he missed it. Still does."

Indeed, John can't help but sound wistful describing that web press vanishing into the rain forest. He's glad that the *Democrat* is still in business, but he says the staff has been cut back so sharply that each press day is like a ride over an Amazon waterfall.

Karen's husband, Butch, is the *Sentinel*'s advertising and circulation manager. Together they've put the newspaper on a sound enough footing to maintain a more humane — and practical — level of staffing. As of this Moose Festival, Claire Lynch is still there, as are Vivien Towle and Gil Short. Jana Riley left in 2002 to sell real estate, and Jana's work is what Butch Ladd does now. Jeannette Ellingwood retired and then died in 2007. Plaques advertising the law offices of both Fred Harrigan and Vickie Bunnell remain by the front door. The crater of a bullet impact on the west side of the building is still there as well. John wants it left that way.

Meanwhile John and Charlie have become friendly again. Charlie stoops to move a speaker out of Tommy's path on the sidewalk and says, "I worry that I'm witnessing the end of the last generation of newspapers — at least the sort I'm familiar with. At the same time, around here, it's come down to two different family operations, the Harrigans' and the Jordans'. I guess that was inevitable. But nothing's written in stone. We've worked together before, and might do so again."

One of the other band members comes up the sidewalk carrying bundles of electrical wire. She's singing a Joni Mitchell tune, one that Folk Tree would cover that night, something about how they paved paradise and put up a parking lot.

One day in 1997, a week or two after the shootings, Susan Zizza saw an ad for a tropical juice drink on TV, an ad that included a parrot. Suddenly she remembered — remembered vividly — seeing just such a bird perched on the shoulder of an EMT tending to Dennis. The memory made no sense to her. Her nights were sleepless anyway, but the sort of challenge this posed to her sanity made rest all the more impossible — until a month or so later, when, while shopping at the IGA, she saw a woman walking the aisles with that very bird on her shoulder. Susan stopped to introduce herself to Cherie Leavitt, the RN who, on August 19, had been off duty, out with her bird, and using the ATM at the First Colebrook Bank when she heard gunshots.

That helped. Susan held onto her sanity, if not the cheerfulness and whimsy that once possessed her in the newsroom. Black Sunday, for her, had hastened the inevitable. "I just couldn't take another loss," she said. "And I was ready. I think I needed to go."

Eventually she had to leave newspaper work altogether. "I just wasn't your hard-boiled city editor," she explained. "I'd love to talk to people at the *Wall Street Journal*, for example, after the murder of Daniel Pearl in Afghanistan — how they handled that on the personal level."

She needed something else to think about and found it in the photographs brought to her in 2000 by her neighbor Beverly Uran, whose aunt, North Country painter Glenduen Ladd, had used her revolutionary Kodak Folding Pocket Camera to record images of Colebrook and its people at a time when the advent of the automobile and paved roads was tolling the death knell of nearly all the region's grand hotels — and thereby, paradoxically, restoring much of its former isolation.

For eight years, Susan organized, restored, and reproduced the images.

Then she wrote text and arranged them into the chapters that make up *The Turn of the Twentieth: Early 1900s Northern New England Through the Lens of Photographer Glenduen Ladd*, which had been published just in time for the Moose Festival.

In the book's preface, Susan writes that the photos Beverly Uran came to share were not "the usual images of hardy loggers in spiked boots, rugged farmers behind plows, and roughly clad children in front of one-room schoolhouses." Inside there are in fact a few farmers, plows, and roughly clad kids, but much more by way of fine clothes, big houses, a surprising number of automobiles, and other accoutrements of Colebrook's prosperity at the time. That Kodak Pocket Camera was one of the first to allow the photographing of ordinary people by ordinary people — though Ladd, starting when she was sixteen, wielded her camera with the eye of a budding artist.

You might linger at a photo of Ladd's uncle, George Keysar, in a suit and tie and a dapper straw boater, seated incongruously atop a pile of pulpwood that stretches nearly to the horizon behind him — and later a teenage Harry Ladd, then the photographer's boyfriend (who would become a great uncle to Butch Ladd), in drag with a friend, a winter wind snatching at the boys' Victorian dresses and purses. It's a family album as the genre might have been invented by a good photographer with a sense of fun and an eye for the peculiar, for the parrot on the shoulder.

Some of Ladd's paintings are here as well, mostly landscapes: a crumbling abandoned barn in Columbia, the Dix Dam on the Swift Diamond River in Dixville. The paintings have a soft-focus gauziness that reminds Susan of the 1954 MGM film version of *Brigadoon* and its story, as she writes in her introduction, of "an enchanted town that remained unchanging and invisible to the outside world except for one day every hundred years."

On Sunday, after the Folk Tree concert Saturday night, Susan occupies a booth beneath a tent on the athletic fields at Canaan Memorial High School. She's signing and selling copies of her book, is almost hidden behind two stacks of them on the table at which she sits and her line of customers. Elsewhere on the fields, the Kiwanis Club is selling hot dogs out of a boxcar-sized food truck, a towering Uncle Sam is striding on stilts among festival-goers, the Berlin Jazz Band is playing a Charleston, and a moose-calling contest is in full-throated vigor.

During a moment when Susan has no customers, she remembers a trip to Sea World in San Diego that she once took with her husband's sister and her two children. "We were sitting right by the platform and watching this killer whale leap entirely out of the water in what seemed like a burst of joy," she says. "It was such a gorgeous day, and this was such a beautiful and magnificent animal that it was painful — and I began to cry. I couldn't help thinking how Dennis, Vickie, their families, and Scott and Les too should be sharing this joy as well."

She recalls that Scott's little boy was just three at the time, his daughter one and a half. "All those years they could've been with their father," she says. "They were robbed of those years. Dennis's son has grown up to be a civil engineer. He's a smart young man."

She turns away and puts her hands to her face. "I'm determined to get to the day when I'll shed my last tear over this," she says after a moment. "I probably never will."

She smiles then and composes herself. "I believe in resurrection. But the years that were still owed to those lives on earth can never be given back. Who knows what made that man do what he did? Not God."

The centuries collapse, one superimposed on the other: the well-heeled, if rough at the edges, log-boom town of Glenduen Ladd and Sliver Bunnell at the turn of the twentieth; and the hardscrabble, ghost-haunted town of John Harrigan, Bunny Bunnell, Charlie Jordan, and Susan Zizza at the turn of the twenty-first — visible to the outside world only in eyeblink glimpses at great intervals, the faces and expressions frozen in time, like the portraits on that slab in Monument Lot.

Susan once believed that such a lightning bolt as they endured would give way, at last, to a *Brigadoon* kind of life, perhaps, in which subsequent griefs would be ephemeral and events would flatline into a pleasant, gauzy stasis.

"You think when you go through something like this and live through it — survive — that you'll lead a charmed life afterwards," she says. "But things go on happening — bad things, happy things, sad things. Nothing ever stays the same."

Pick a moment. It doesn't make any difference which, here in the provinces north of New York at the beginning of the twenty-first century. Any will do.

In April, on South Hill farm, John and Nancee Harrigan are waiting for the sheep shearers, who are late. Some thirty head, about a fifth of the Harrigan flock — ewes, a crop of lambs that arrived early this spring, a few wethers (castrated rams) — are penned inside the barn. The sheep are snug inside the wool they wore this winter, and they mill about in shifting, puzzle-piece patterns of black, white, gray, and umber. They bleat and stare with their gemstone eyes at Nancee and her teenage son Micah. The sheep stand content to be petted or scratched. The wool is as light as gossamer, and its lanolin dries like aerosol on Micah's fingers. The tails of the nursing lambs, as they suckle, wag like dogs'.

John decided in the early 1990s that he wanted this to be a working farm again, at least in some respects. He bought a small flock of sheep and began to run into John and Nancee Amey at agricultural fairs and Farm Bureau events. In 1992 John found himself short on ewes, and he arranged with the Ameys to pasture some of their sheep at South Hill farm in exchange for the lambs. Then Nancee's life changed — and her marriage dissolved — when her stepson, Eric, fell from the back of a moving pickup and died. John and Nancee started dating late in 1998, and they married in 2000.

Nancee is pretty, raven-haired, sturdy, and no less hollowed out by grief than John. But John — persuaded by now that people indeed are meant to go through life two by two — has in Nancee, once more, a woman with whom he can hike and hunt birds, or the occasional rabbit, and his wedding present to her was an Italian 20-gauge double-barrel shotgun.

In the barn today, Nancee waits impatiently for two of the few people left in the North Country — a middle-aged man and his twentyish son — who can still take the wool off a sheep as if it were a matter of unzipping a mackintosh. Nancee could shear these animals herself, has done it before, but it would take longer, yield less wool, and leave Nancee bruised, some of the sheep nicked and cut.

Most of the wool will be sold at the red-ink price of fourteen cents per pound. The rest Nancee will spin into yarn and then weave into blankets for sale. There is little by way of a local market for the meat, and the nearest federally sanctioned slaughterhouse is in St. Johnsbury. In one of his "North Country Notebook" columns, John has written that sheep farming this far north, these days, is "an admittedly delusional enterprise." But the sheep do help keep the pastures clear, fields that John himself reclaimed from brush and early succession forest, and so are good friends to that thirty-five-mile view he adores.

While Nancee waits, she attends to another necessary task — she and Micah are castrating the male lambs, which with sheep this young is a bloodless operation. Micah catches a lamb and delivers it squirming to his mother, who sits on the floor and holds the animal's back to her belly, its legs splayed out front and no longer thrashing. Then Nancee takes a coarse rubber band, hardly bigger than a Cheerio, and uses a pair of spreaders to widen it enough to go around the lamb's scrotum. Once in place, the rubber band pinches off blood supply to the testicles, which in several weeks will shrivel and drop off. When Nancee's done, Micah lifts the lamb from her lap and drops it over the fence into the chicken yard outside the barn. The lamb kicks up its heels and runs bleating through a flock of hens.

A laugh rings out from the east end of the house, on the other side of the chicken yard. "I thought it was supposed to be quiet in the country," exclaims Josh Jaros, who has been hired by John to build a greenhouse for Nancee's flowers and vegetables. "Sheep yelling, chickens squawking — I can't hear myself pound nails."

Josh is a young carpenter from Minnesota, a literal sort of flatlander, easygoing and affable, who drifted like a tumbleweed out of the Midwest to the Maine coast, turned and started west again, and has settled, at least for a while, in Colebrook, where he likes it just fine. John has given Josh work and made him a steady fishing partner.

Micah splits this Saturday morning between helping his mother and pitching in with Josh as the minutes slip by and the shearers remain overdue. When the farm's rooster crows on the cusp of noon, Nancee walks stiffly out of the barn. She says she'll fix some sandwiches in twenty minutes if someone will fetch John. "Where is he?" says Josh.

"Across the road," says Nancee. "He's mending fence in one of the pastures over there."

Josh knows the story. Three drunk teenagers on a riding mower tore up some line a few weeks ago. They knocked on John's door, confessed to the damage, and promised to fix it. And they did, but so poorly that now John has to repair their repairs. Josh lays down his hammer, walks under the sugar maples budding into green that line the road, and goes through the gate into the first pasture.

The balance of the Harrigan flock, another 120 head or so in all their unshorn splendor, advance from under a copse of beech trees at Josh's approach. The sheep are escorted by Bella and Lupa, the two great Maremmas that serve as the guardians of the herd against coyotes and the rumor of wolves (Kane having died in 1998). One of the dogs — Josh thinks it's Bella — has developed a taste for mutton herself, and John has chained an old auto tire to her collar to guarantee that the sheep can outrun her. The dog walks in march step with the herd, dragging the tire behind her like a ball and chain, but without complaint or visible discomfort. Josh intervenes when the tire snags on a moss-covered boulder.

The sheep and the dogs trail Josh across the width of the pasture. He leaves them staring after him at the second gate, the one that opens into the farm's farthest pasture. This space is bigger, wider. No sign of John along the fences on either side. The pasture slopes up, rising in a hump like a wind-whipped swell at sea. Josh feels like he's climbing to the sky as he labors up the hill. At its peak a grass-scented westerly breeze snaps at his sleeves and shirttail.

Josh can see almost the whole circumference of the pasture from here — can see Monadnock and the greening cattle-grazed pasturelands of Vermont and Quebec. But still no glimpse of John. Not until he spies the still form of a man down on his back in the grass on the downhill slope ahead of him.

Ten yards? Twenty? Josh covers it in a sprint, halts at the spot, breathing hard. He looks down, then looks up into the sky, still panting. At last, without a word, he falls into the grass himself, on his back against Pleistocene granite and its patina of soil, spread-eagled. He lies there goggle-eyed. The clouds wheel overhead like out-bellying sails, like billowing curtains drawn in fond blue hope against the moon and the stars and the lineaments of eternity.

"This is rough, isn't it?" John says at last.

Josh murmurs his assent.

A few moments later the rattle of an old truck arrives faintly from the west as it winds up South Hill Road. John can hear the truck slow and make a turn just about where his driveway should be.

"That'll be the shearers." John stakes his elbows to the grass, rising upward, but then, sighing, thinks better of it. Instead he falls back, folding his hands across his chest and settling ever more deeply into the whispering breast of the hill.

EPILOGUE

FROM *THE NEWS AND SENTINEL*, WEDNESDAY, APRIL 20, 2011: "Earl 'Bunny' A. Bunnell, Sr., 85, of Canaan, Vermont, died on Thursday, April 14, 2011, in Concord, after a long period of declining health and with his loving family at his side. . . .

"Earl was preceded in death by his daughter, Vickie Bunnell, in 1997."

SOURCES

1 | THE NOONDAY OWL

William H. Gifford, *Colebrook: A Place Up Back of New Hampshire*,
News and Sentinel, Inc., 1993.
John Harrigan, "Newsprint Through the Press, Thoughts Through the
Mind," *News and Sentinel*, October 28, 1999.
John Harrigan untitled North Country Notebook column, *News and
Sentinel*, December 11, 2008.

2 | THE SWEET SMELL OF NEWSPRINT

John Harrigan, "You Never Knew in Changing Times What Was
Coming Down the Road," *News and Sentinel*, May 11, 2010.
Albert Barker, editorial, *Northern Sentinel*, April 26, 1872.
Alma Cummings, *Northern Sentinel*, September 1, 1910.
Details about Merle Wright and the Sentinel fire from Granvyl G.
Hulse, Jr., *The News and Sentinel: The Evolution of a Country Weekly*,
News and Sentinel, Inc., 2011, page 97.
John Harrigan, "A Nation of Cooks Morphs Into a Nation of Watchers,"
News and Sentinel, August 13, 2009.
Carl Drega letter to Fred Harrigan from incident police file volume 5,
page 1663.
John Harrigan, "Now Even 'Motor Drive' Is Antiquated," *News and
Sentinel*, December 19, 2012.

Details about the Duplex web press from Hulse, Jr., *The News and Sentinel*, page 105.

John Harrigan, "A Reader Sends a Reminder About the History of Print," *News and Sentinel*, September 22, 2010.

Fred Harrigan, editorial, *News and Sentinel*, July 20, 1960.

3 | DEATH OR HIGH WATER

Kenneth Parkhurst in the *Union Leader*, August 20, 1997.

5 | THE REST IS BLANK

Jason Sorens, "What Can 20,000 Liberty Activists Accomplish in New Hampshire?" www.freestateproject.org, April 12, 2004.

John Harrigan, "It Appears as Though Life Is Getting Easier for Pedestrians," *Meredith News*, September 28, 2006.

Details about Carl Drega in jail from the *Maine Sunday Telegram*, August 24, 1997.

George E. Tetrault in the *New Hampshire Sunday News*, August 28, 1997.

Details about Carl Drega's cover letter to Jeffrey R. Howard from *Union Leader*, September 28, 1997.

6 | THE REASONS OF THE HEART

Scott Stepanian, *New Hampshire Trooper* magazine, winter/spring 1998.

Details about Scott Phillips in *News and Sentinel*, August 27, 1997.

John Barthelmes, *New Hampshire Trooper* magazine, winter/spring 1998.

13 | NO INKLING OF CAT AND MOUSE

Philip McLaughlin, *New Hampshire Trooper* magazine, winter/spring 1998.

14 | LIKE THE BRUSH OF A WING

Joseph A. Citro, *Green Mountain Ghosts, Ghouls & Unsolved Mysteries*, Mariner Books, 1994.

"New Brunswick Springs House a Total Loss on the Verge of Its Opening," *Coös County Democrat*, May 15, 1930.

17 | THE ARMOR OF GOD

John Harrigan in "A Grieving Little Town Unites, and Moves On," the *New York Times*, October 17, 1997.

18 | TIME IS THE FIRE

John Harrigan in the *New Hampshire Sunday News*, May 5, 2002.

Carl Drega neighbor in the *Maine Sunday Telegram*, August 24, 1997.

Bill Bromage in "N.H. Town Struggles to Live Free After 4 Die in Rampage," the *Los Angeles Times*, August 22, 1997.

John Harrigan in *Life* magazine, August 1998.

"A Grieving Little Town Unites, and Moves On," the *New York Times*, October 17, 1997.

Karen Harrigan Ladd, editorial, *News and Sentinel*, November 10, 2010.